PIGTOWN CHRONICLES
By
Joy Butler

Some of the names in this book have been changed to protect the guilty.

Pigtown Chronicles: Sink or Swim by Joy Butler

Cover design by Joy Butler
Cover photos by Genevieve Pedulla

ISBN: 987-1-7171-1589-8

Second U.S.Edition 2018

Dedication

For way too long I tried to hide from my dream of being a writer. I buried it so far down in me; I didn't remember I even had a dream. I walked around trying to attach myself to others dreams and assist them in what they wanted to achieve. In return, I got my heart broken more than a few times.

I sold drugs to make a living in the hopes that I could make enough money to run away to an island and live quietly. The only problem with that plan was it was stupid and futile. There is no retirement plan in drug dealing. Not one that doesn't include a penitentiary.

My friends have always told me I should write a book about my life. I tried writing that book a few times, always quickly losing interest. The life they were talking about was my life as a child and what I had endured during those years. I'm not interested in writing about those years. So, I didn't write. ANYTHING.

I missed writing; I had always written poetry and short stories all through school. Once I was in my thirties I stopped completely. I don't know why, I guess the world had gotten to me and I drowned it deep down there where a person places the confidence they had as a young doe eyed kid and left it there for the better part of a decade, but I missed it every day of that decade. I saw myself writing a book but the pages were empty because I didn't know what I was going to write about.

One day I was on the phone and the person I was talking to told me about a friend of his who had recently written a book and got it published while the author was in prison. He told me I should write a book of my own. At first I had a slick comment but then the story I wanted to tell literally just popped into my head. That night I started writing Pigtown Chronicles and in 15 weeks I had written my first book. I was a new person. I had completed the first part of my lifelong dream. The second part of that dream is to share it with you.

I want to dedicate this book first and foremost to my Grandmother Elaine and my daughter Jasmine, the alpha and omega of my very existence, the two most important people in my life. My Aunt Nick, for teaching me kindness. My Aunt Lisa for being my moral compass. Next, my brothers, Kenny, Karriem, Warith and Tupac you are the trampoline that catches my falls every time I jump into the world.

Finally, I want to dedicate this book to everyone who has had their dream buried deep within them for whatever reason it has been. This book is tangible proof that YOU can live your dream. This book is my dream and after all that life has thrown at me I still wrote it, not for anyone other than me. Not for any other reason but, this is my dream. If I am the only person to ever read this book I will pass this life with a smile on my face simply because I wrote my book. I did it and I love every word I wrote. I look forward to YOU living your dream. May the heaven smile on the lot of you and see you to your own dreams.

SINK OR SWIM

Contents

Fluorescent

My mother went to prison when I was 17 years old. I was homeless and uneducated. What was I supposed to do?

My mother was going on trial and I had to be in Atlanta because I was her star witness. After that she would send me to New York to live with my "father".

The first day I testified I was scared to death. I was being asked questions I knew I would have to lie about. I knew what the papers were saying about my mother were true. She was a drug dealer. I couldn't admit that because that would surely seal her fate. So, I did what I was supposed to do. I lied. No she doesn't sell drugs. Her Congressman boyfriend pays all of our bills. That's what I had to say. So, I did.

She was convicted of possession with intent to distribute cocaine.

She was sentenced 22 years to serve.

So, off to New York I went. To live with a "father" I didn't know and didn't like. He was living with my two half- brothers, (I love them) in my grandmother's rent controlled project apartment in Harlem. Grrreaaaat.

He's a fanatical Nation of Islam Muslim who can't keep his contradictory bullshit straight. I never saw how Elijah Muhammad convinced all those people to believe his bullshit. I saw through it before I was 9 years old. How are you going to tell your biracial kids that all white people are the devil? My mother's Puerto Rican but, her bloodline is from Spain. Really? Your kids are half devil? Add to that, he once beat me with hangers because he thought I was a lesbian when I was 10. Either way, I don't fuck with him.

When I was a little kid, no one talked to me. I mean I had conversations, but no one taught me anything. My mother was no different from any other single mother out there. She just happened to sell drugs. She was paying bills and making money while keeping a roof over our heads. She slipped up on some parenting things but, who hasn't? She did what she had to do. I'm grateful for it.

I had a hell of a time once my mother went to prison. I was on my own. I had to spend all my time trying to figure out what I was supposed to know about the world, while not letting anyone know I didn't know. I was so green, I was fluorescent.

At first my ignorance manifested in the form of "I know everything". No one seemed to like that very much. So, I had to change that. It then occurred to me, that if I read a lot, when I did speak, no one would know I only finished the 9th grade. So, that's what I did. I became an avid reader. I read everything current. Can't really tell you too much stuff that was taught in school, but I can tell you what's been going on in the world since 1988.

I can't sit here and say that what I'm about to tell you is a unique and profound story. It's not to me because it's the only story I know by heart. My heart.

My name is J.O., Nice to meet you.

South Baltimore

It was Father's Day 2003 and I was living in West Baltimore, Maryland with my Godfather Leonard. I decided to cook dinner for him and my boyfriend Antonio. We had a good time in the two bedroom row house in the middle of what use to be a nice neighborhood of working class families. It now resembled a ghetto. Complete with crack heads, stray cats and rats. The block had just as many dilapidated houses as it did lived in. My Godfather had remodeled his in the early 90's with my help. It had mirrored walls on both sides of the living room, to give the appearance of a bigger room. Row houses only have windows in the front and back of the houses. They're cramped and tend to be dark. We fixed the darkness with chandeliers. His ex-wife called it a white elephant. I think it was the Jacuzzi we put in the bathroom that could seat 6 adults. It could've been the all black marble walls and floors in the bathroom too. Complete with a black toilet, sink and shower all with gold fixtures. Once again we used mirrors to open up the room by placing them on the wall facing the window that overlooked the alley. I'm not really sure at what point it became a white elephant, I just know we had fun tearing that house down and building it back up. We had apricot suede couches and plush carpeting. Everything in the kitchen was bought brand new. That was in the 90's though. Now time has taken its toll and my Godfather wasn't the big time drug dealer he was back then. Without money flowing in, the house was wearing down. The Jacuzzi still works though.

My boyfriend, Antonio, and I had our ups and downs. He's a dead ringer for Lenny Kravitz. He stands 5'9" 155 lbs. He had a big afro at the time. He would get it braided by one of the neighborhood girls he knew down in South Baltimore. He has the type of personality that makes people want to tell him all of their business when they first meet him. He has an honesty about him that gets him in a lot of trouble. He's a loving and dangerous person at the same time. No one's ever loved me as hard as Antonio has. I know he loves me. I have no doubt about it.

I also know that Antonio is a heroin addict. I give him credit, he stayed with me all day in pain, but as the sun was getting closer to setting he made it clear he had to go. He told me he'd be back as soon as he got what he needed. I knew he was lying. Once he was in those streets it was hell getting him out. I'd go days without seeing him sometimes. I'd have to find him again and I knew it.

Sure enough, the next morning he hadn't come back. I got myself together to go across town to the neighborhood he was from and extorted, to keep his habit going. South Baltimore. The neighborhood is known as Pigtown. I'm told it was the first integrated part of Baltimore and back in the day when it was still an industrial city; pigs were walked through the streets on their way to the slaughter houses. That's my depth of knowledge on Baltimore history.

So, the next day I head to Pigtown to look for Antonio and make sure he's okay. I take a hack, which is an illegal cab. Basically, a guy who needs gas money will pick you up and drive you where you need to go. They're all over the city.

When I get down to Pigtown, I start looking for Antonio. Walking through the neighborhood I couldn't find him which wasn't abnormal. He was usually in one of over a dozen junkie houses in the huge neighborhood. I knew a few people in the neighborhood. So, it wasn't that I'd be alone. I'd hang in the hood until he arose from the crypt and surfaced to get high.

I noticed I was getting a lot of funny looks from people in the neighborhood, but no one approached me. (Antonio didn't allow everyone in the neighborhood to talk to me, even though everyone in the neighborhood knew who I was. If Antonio hadn't personally introduced me to you, he didn't allow you to talk to me. I didn't know this at the time. I found it out sometime later.)

I kept looking around for Antonio. I was there about an hour when someone came up to me. He asked me if I knew Antonio was arrested the day before. No, I didn't know. He told me a group of police cars ran down on him while he was walking down Scott St. (which is right off Washington Blvd). He said once the patrol cops handcuffed him they radioed. A couple of Detectives pulled up. Held a picture from a file up to Antonio's face and threw him in the back of the detective's car. I figured he'd been busted for drugs, either, selling or possessing.

It took a few days for me to get the info about his arrest from the jail. It took time for him to be booked into the system. I called the jail and the operator asked me for his name. I gave it to her. His charges were attempted murder and weapons. "WHAT?" He had no bond. I was devastated.

Later, I found out that he was arrested for shooting a young man from the neighborhood named Ryan. He didn't do it. I'm not just saying that because I'm his girlfriend. I know where he was when that shooting happened. He wasn't in the area. I went to the initial court hearing to get a grip on what was going on. Antonio wasn't an altar boy, but what I heard coming from the Prosecutor's mouth, put Antonio and his antics before I came into his life, into a whole new light.

In court his name was, Antonio Menace to Society. Another prosecutor at a later hearing called him Antonio Danger to Society. Yet another one called him, Antonio Threat to Society. That is who he is in the court system in Baltimore. Those were his last names. I was shocked. I'd never heard of anything like that before. It only fazed me for a moment though. It didn't make a difference if he had a record a mile long for robberies, extortion, murder and assaults. He didn't do THIS. I began the task of putting together the mental list of things I had to do to get him cleared of this.

Nowhere Near It

The night the shooting happened, Antonio was holed up in a basement apartment. Getting high. I tried to get him out of there. So we could do something fun. He wasn't moving.

His partner in crime was his cousin Nick. Nick was known for his gunplay. He was 6'3", milk chocolate, with black cornrows, weighing no more than 150 lb. with slanted eyes and an easy smile. He was THE MOST FEARED GUY IN THE NEIGHBORHOOD. Nick wasn't like Antonio. He wasn't approachable. He always wore a white or black T shirt with jeans. The shirts were so big on his wiry frame, you couldn't tell if he had a gun or not. And that was the point.

Nick was my guy. A raging junkie, but nonetheless my guy. Hanging with him was always fun and easy. He had a quick wit and he was generally a funny motherfucker. When Antonio wouldn't leave the house Nick and I went roaming around Pigtown on our own.

We walked up Washington Blvd toward all the bars in the neighborhood. When we got to the corner of Washington Blvd and W. Cross Street. We noticed an ambulance and police down by one of the bars three or four blocks down. Nick and I didn't want to be anywhere near that scene, so we headed to another bar on Scott Street closer to the Blvd. It was that shooting, Antonio was locked up for. Ryan had been shot seven times. Luckily he survived.

Ryan was in his early 20's, a good looking guy that stands about 5'10", built like a welterweight boxer. His mother is white. His father black. He was born and raised in Pigtown. He is well known and loved in his neighborhood. He has beautiful dark brown curly hair with olive skin and a bright smile that reveals a chipped front tooth. He has the kind of smile that gives you a glimpse of him as a little boy.

Ryan was in the hospital when he found out the police made an arrest in his shooting. He hit the roof when he found out it was Antonio who'd been arrested. Ryan and Antonio have always been very close. Ryan refers to Antonio as his brother. He called the lead investigator in charge of his case, Det. Claymore, to tell him they arrested the wrong man but, it fell on deaf ears. The police weren't interested in who shot Ryan. They were interested in getting Antonio off the street. You see, even though Antonio was an addict, he still had more authority in Pigtown than the police. One particular cop didn't like that. We'll call him Officer Puerto Rican Yo.

Puerto Rican Yo was a young up-and-coming beat cop who made it his business to know who was doing what in Pigtown. He's good looking and arrogant just like you'd expect. He stood about 5'10", a dark buzz cut, with an eggshell complexion and slightly slanted brown eyes. The neighborhood made up a rumor that he was half Puerto Rican and white. I later found out he was half German and Filipino.

When Antonio went to his first court appearance he was sick from withdrawal. He had a public defender. It was a quick hearing that didn't result in him getting out on bond. I was weak. I missed him and worried about his withdrawals. We couldn't talk on the phone because I had a cell phone. He couldn't make collect calls to it.

The public defender was a nice man. I don't recall his name, but I went to his office once. I called Ryan so he could hear for himself that Antonio didn't do this. He even let me look at Antonio's entire record as it appears to the prosecutor. I saw who snitched on him for his murder case. I knew by the name, Antonio didn't know who it was because the person was still around him. I wouldn't tell him because Antonio would kill him and that would be the end of us. The lawyer knew the police were after Antonio and not the people who actually shot Ryan. He told me that verbatim.

A month or so later, at Antonio's second hearing, Ryan left the rehabilitation facility to attend. Before the hearing, he approached the prosecutor on his crutches. He told him Antonio was not the person who shot him. The prosecutor stepped back from Ryan, looked him up and down and said, "Why do you want to let the guy who did this to you get away with it?" He refused to let Ryan speak at the hearing. He told the Bailiff outside the courtroom not to let Ryan in.

Puerto Rican Yo

One day I was leaving my house in West Baltimore, heading down to South Baltimore to work. I took a hack. When I got down on the Blvd, I went to my spot on the stoop right next to the pizza shop to begin working. The owner of the house allowed her nephew Nigel; his girlfriend, DeeDee, and I too sell drugs on her front stoop. We had a one-stop-shop. The nephew had crack. His girlfriend had weed. I had the heroin. We'd start at 3pm and be at it until late into the night. It was an excellent position because we had a reason to be there. His aunt owned the house. The traffic was acceptable because the pizza parlor next door was the neighborhood refrigerator. We were pulling it down.

On this particular day, when I got to the house, neither Nigel nor DeeDee was there. I didn't want to sit on the stoop alone. It was too hot around there for that. (And by "hot", I mean there were too many damn police around.) So, I decided to walk up the Blvd to the supermarket, about six blocks away from the stoop. I didn't want anything from the supermarket. It was just a distance away that I could walk giving everyone enough time to arrive without seeming like I was loitering. I had a few hundred pills of heroin in my bra. I didn't need to be stopped by anyone. I had never been stopped but, I'd like to think that's because I was stealth. LOL

I make it only two blocks from the stoop before I see Officer Yo and his partner. They had two neighborhood guys stretched out on a wall, frisking them. It had absolutely nothing to do with me. I kept walking. Yo and I locked eyes as he noticed me walking by. He said something to his partner. The partner looked at me. I'm thinking, OH SHIT. His partner leaves Yo with the guys on the wall and starts toward me.

"Hey, you." He says to me.

"Hey, you." I say back.

At this time, Yo is letting the two guys go on their way.

"My partner wants to talk to you." He says still walking toward me.

"Why? I don't have anything to do with that." I said referring to the guys being frisked.

"We know. He just wants to talk to you. Come here." He insists. I didn't feel like I had a choice. So I walked over there. My chest full of heroin and I are walking to the police. Grrrreaaat.

Once I got over to Yo, who was standing in front of some houses, I asked him what he wanted. I could tell by the smirk on his face, he was approachable. I could talk shit to him without being locked up. I knew this was his way of introducing himself to me. I also know he would never do this if Tonio was home. He asked me if I had I.D. I gave it to him. It was from Georgia, as was I. It immediately stood out to him. He ran my name. While he waited for information to come back on me, he asked me if I was Antonio's girlfriend. I told him I was.

"Have you talked to him?" He asked me.

"No, I can't talk to him. I only have a cell phone. Have yoooou talked to him?" I asked playfully trying to ease the situation. I'm still toting a chest full of heroin.

He told me he hadn't and laughed. He got the joke.

"We know he didn't do it" He told me. I was shocked.

"Then why is he still locked up?" I asked

"It's the system. He still has to go through the process. How long have you two been together?" He asked

"About nine months." I answered

"Do you love him?" He asked

"I'm in love with him." I replied

"How can you love someone like him?" He asked, dead serious.

"I don't know what you seem to know about him, and you don't know what I know about him." I said. We officially had an understanding.

I asked him if he was half Puerto Rican, like I'd heard? He told me he lets the neighborhood say what they want about him. He told me what he was actually mixed with.

The operator came back over the police system and said I was clean. Yo handed me my license and sent me on my way. It was a strange meeting. It left me with the sense that he's wanted to meet me and that was the only way he knew how to do it. Antonio had been gone for seven days.

The next day, I show up on the Blvd earlier than everyone else once again. I decide to walk around the corner and see if one of my friends is outside. I'd go hang with her and give the crew a little while to get there. As I'm walking down Rhinehart St. going toward Carroll St., I stop at the corner before I cross because I hear a car coming down the one way street. I look up to see how far away the car is. I see a police cruiser speeding towards me from about 30 yards away. I knew who it was. I stood on the corner as the cruiser barreled toward me. It came to a creeping pace as it got to where I was standing. Yo cut a left to go up Rhinehart. As he was cutting left he looked me right in the eye. I read his lips through the closed window. He said, "What about her?" I looked in the back seat of the cruiser. I saw one of the many neighborhoods snitches, Monkey. The name is self explanatory. I couldn't read his lips as they passed me but, he was saying something. The word FUCK flashed through my mind as I went on my way.

After leaving my friends, I headed back to the Blvd. This time the owner of the house's sister was sitting out on the stoop talking to a white guy. I felt comfortable enough to go over there and sit. I passed one of my customers on the way to the stoop. He told me Yo was on a tangent and watch out for him.

"Shit we don't have to worry about that for a minute though." I said, "He's on his way to take Monkey in." My customer informed me that Monkey was in the pizza parlor at that very moment.

That means he was just being driven around for information. Great! I went on to the stoop. Before I could grab a seat I see Yo driving past me. I flag him down like he's a cab. He stops in the middle of the street. I walk out to the yellow lines. I chat him up while I look in the back seat. It's empty. He watches me do it. He seemed amused. We say bye and I walk back to the stoop. Dude on the bike was right. Monkey wasn't in the back seat and he was not arrested. SHIT!!!! You have to understand, a heroin addicts motto is this, "I'm not getting sick for nobody." The fact that Monkey is a raging fiend and knows what I do puts me in a vulnerable position. If he's threatened with getting locked up, he'll rat me out without hesitation. Monkey isn't concerned about what Antonio would do. He can't see anything past his next high. Yo knows this. He had the opportunity to ask about me while he had him. It just so happens, Monkey owes me three dollars. That's enough to get me snitched out by itself. If I'm locked up he won't have to pay me. He can keep those three dollars, as of right now.

Once I take a seat on the stoop, the Public Defender called me. I'm the type of person that walks around when I'm in an intense conversation. So, while on the phone with the lawyer, I start to walk. I head straight up the Blvd. I get about 50 feet from the stoop and I hear someone call my name. "J.O.!!!!" I keep walking, listening to the lawyer. "J.O.!!!!!" The voice is louder. I thought it was Nick calling me. I turn around. I'm looking at Puerto Rican Yo, five other cops, patrol cars thrown in the middle of the street, as if they jumped out on someone and they had. The guy that told me Monkey was in the pizza shop is in the middle of the street, with them frisking him and searching the bike they pulled him from. I look at Yo; he's standing on the sidewalk motioning for me to come to him. I'm shook, but I can't let him see that. I quickly compose myself. I take the phone from my ear and wave it at him. He says,

"That's okay. Come here anyway." I have about 500 pills of heroin in my bra. I'm freaking the fuck out on the inside. Cool as a cucumber on the outside. I walk toward Yo as I tell the lawyer on the phone that the cops just pulled me up. I look at Yo, and say, "I'm on the phone with Antonio's lawyer. Do you mind if I stay on while we do this?" He looked surprised that I said I was talking to a lawyer. He told me I could stay on the phone. They were in front of a church. Once I got closer, Yo joined the rest of his squad in the street, frisking the customer. Still on the phone, I walked up to the crowd of cops and handed Yo my backpack. He looked at me and asked "What's this for?" I said, "That's what you want right?" He gave me a smartass look and said, "Yeah" sarcastically. He put my backpack on the trunk of one of his patrol cars. I took a seat on the step of the church. All while on the phone with the lawyer. The Public Defender wouldn't let me get off the phone with him. He wanted to hear everything that was going on. I knew as long as he was on the phone, they wouldn't do anything too crazy. I was scared to death. All they had to do was frisk me and I'd be going to jail for a long time. I had to continue to play cool.

Yo and another cop walk up to me. I'm on the phone, sitting on the church step, talking to the lawyer. Yo asks in an authoritative voice, "Who's that white guy over there on the stoop?" I look at him and with a fake stank attitude I say, "I don't know. I've been on the phone for, (I pull the phone from my ear and look at the timer. I read it as I show it to Yo) 28 minutes and 24 seconds, talking to a lawyer. I don't know who that is." He seemed stuck on what to do next. The second cop asked to see the pocket knife I had clipped on my belt. I un-clipped it and when I handed it to him my hands were shaking. The whole time the lawyer is on the phone listening.

"Have you talked to Antonio yet?" Yo asked me.

"Nope, that's one of the reasons I'm on the phone with his lawyer. Trying to find out what's going on." I responded

The second cop handed me my knife back after opening and

examining it.

"Alright then, talk to you later." Yo said and he walked over to his car. He grabbed my bag and brought it back to me. He never even looked in it. He wouldn't have found anything. They got in their cars and drove off.

The lawyer told me to walk away from the area and stay gone for at least forty-five minutes. I walked to the supermarket about six blocks away and finished talking to him. He told me to stay alert. Don't let the police talk to me about Antonio. I waited forty-five minutes and went to the stoop. Everyone was there and ready to work. As I'm walking past the church stoop the same guy who had just been frisked by Yo, rode up to me on his bike. He told me I needed to be careful. "Yo's got a Fuhin' hard on for you. You're all he was taw'in' 'bout the whole time they had me hemmed up. He was asking me questions 'bout you. Be careful." He rode his bike past me.

I was paranoid once I got to the stoop. I was watching everything around me. My coworkers were there and fired up for the money. I didn't tell them what happened. It would only make them paranoid as well. They could possibly ban me from the spot, if they were threatened with getting arrested. No customers had come yet. But, Yo did. He kept making circles around the block. He'd come to a crawl in his patrol car. When he got to me sitting on the stoop, he'd make eye contact with me. Then drive off. I don't know if anyone else on the stoop noticed it but, I sure did. It was meant for me to notice. The third or fourth time he made his lap, he had a female officer in the passenger seat. He came to a stop in front of me. I don't know if I heard him or if I read his lips but, he said, "That's her right there." I was fucking blown over. I knew what that meant. He couldn't frisk me, being a male officer, but she could. I panicked inside not letting anyone know around me. I didn't live in Pigtown, so I couldn't go put my stash in my house. My mind was racing. What am I going to do? I thought about the house that

Antonio was in the night Ryan got shot. The guy who lived there was a childhood friend of Antonio's named Poopie. I decided to walk the 4 blocks over to his house on Sergeant St just off the Blvd and stash my packs. I could give him a couple of pills for rent. I got off the stoop and walked in the direction of his house without saying a word to anyone.

Poopie rented a basement room from another dope fiend named Gary. Gary was a mechanic who worked out of his house. You got car trouble, pull up to his front door. He'll fix your shit right there in the middle of the street. The house didn't have any front steps. You had to go around the back of the house and enter through the alley. I called out to Poopie through the basement window in the front. He knew to come let me in around back. Once we're in the basement, I survey the room to see where I could stash the packs. Ceiling panels were as good a place as any. I told him I needed to stash the pack and why. He didn't have a problem with me using the spot and liked the fact I would pay him. It meant he wasn't going to get ill. I told him I'd be back to pick it up before I went home for the night. He was cool with that. I returned to the other side of the Blvd and the stoop.

Once I got back to the stoop I told my coworkers what was going on. They hadn't noticed. All the weed and liquor they were consuming didn't give them the opportunity to give a fuck about Yo. We just carried on without me selling for the night. I was kind of pissed because I needed the money but I couldn't take the chance of getting locked up. I had an unpaid day off. Fuck it, I'll smoke some weed and chill.

When I was ready to go home late that night, I got a hack I used to take me home every night. His name was Hutch. I'd just go to his house, no matter what time of night and he'd take me home. He was a nice man. He got high but he didn't cop from me that I know of. He could've had someone cop for him. I could trust Hutch knowing where I lived and not being robbed getting there. He drove me to

Poopie's first. When I got into the basement instead of giving me my dope, Poopie gave me money. He sold all the packs for me. I was HAPPY. I hadn't lost a day and I didn't get arrested. KEWL. We struck up a deal. I'd pay him $3 off every pill he sold for me. That way I wouldn't be hot on the block. Him being a junkie, he never had to worry about getting ill. It was a good deal for both of us. The only requirements I made were no fronting pills and he was not allowed to deal from the front window. He had to make everyone come to the alley to get served. He agreed.

The next day on the stoop, I directed all my clientele to Poopie's. He was one of them. Sort of a junkie celebrity among them. They were very comfortable with the new arrangements.

Hutch dropped me off that night. I was ready to relax and go to bed. As I got out of the car, I saw my neighbor Regina's sister, Leslie. Regina lived across the street from me, with her husband and twenty-two year old daughter.

Leslie and I were cool until recently. We used to hang out. She even came down to Pigtown with me a couple times. She had known Antonio for many years. He made the introduction. She was a little older than me but, still thought she was younger than what she was. You could tell she used to have things and lost them due to heroin addiction. She still had pieces of her old life, like a Louis Vuitton handbag that she always toted. I think she did it so people wouldn't treat her like a fiend. This was the first time I'd seen Leslie since she stole $100 and 10 pills of dope from me. I made the mistake of leaving her alone in my room while I went to the bathroom. She was on the steps of the neighbor three doors down from me, talking with them and drinking a forty. It was late, I was high and tired. I had every intention of going to bed. I had already made up my mind to stall her out on the money and dope because her sister was a good person. I didn't want to have Regina and her family looking at me like I was fucked up for beating her little sister up. Regina had already banned Leslie from her house when I told her about the theft. She thanked me for telling her. She said that anybody else would've tried to kill Leslie and everyone in her house for a stunt like that. I knew that was true.

Leslie and I gave each other the eye as I walked up the stairs. The people she was talking to were watching us watch each other. I saw Leslie say something but couldn't hear it. The people on the steps laughed. That irked the living shit out of me.

"So, when are you going to pay me the $200 you stole from me?" As soon as I said it the laughing stopped.

"What did you say?" She replied pulling the 40 from her mouth. I stop walking up my steps. She and I are level to one another.

"Bitch you heard what the fuck I said." I'm not so tired anymore.

"Come take it!" she shouted. The invitation was all I needed. I walked down the steps and over to her. As I walked, I heard the bottle break. I saw Leslie coming toward me. As we met, she swung the bottle in her right hand aiming for my face. I leaned back. She missed. As her arm came down, it crossed over her body. I leaned forward and punched her right in her forehead. She was lifted off her feet. She landed on her back in a flowerbed at the bottom of my neighbor's steps. The broken bottle was still in her hand. I climbed on top of her, straddling her. I grabbed her wrist, pinned it and the bottle down with my left hand. I punched her in the face with my right. Every time she tried to lift the bottle, I punched her harder with my right fist. I lost count of how many times I hit her when she finally let the bottle go. I used my left hand to swipe the bottle to the ground. When I heard it shatter, I let her wrist go. I started swinging on her with both hands feverishly. I pummeled her until one of the neighbors called on me to stop.

"Okay, okay that's enough. You proved your point." I heard someone say. No one tried to physically stop us. When I heard the voice I punched her one more time. Her head banged into the flowerbed with a heavy thud. I climbed off her. Without even looking back, I took her Louis Vuitton purse. I walked toward the entrance of the alley, two doors past my house. Under the streetlight I dumped the contents of the purse on the ground. I scattered everything looking for money. I found none. There was a pack of Newport's. I took them. I carried the purse into my house.

It was dark when I walked inside. Leonard was asleep on the couch. I threw the purse on the floor by the staircase. I walked upstairs to the bathroom. She hadn't hit me but, when I looked in the mirror, there was blood on the bridge of my nose. The cut was diagonal. There was blood on my shirt between my shoulder and chest. My T- shirt had a small puncture hole in it. I wiped my nose with a wet washcloth. She grazed me with the bottle. It looked like a paper cut. The cut on my chest went through my shirt, but it was the same as the cut on my face. The adrenalin was settling down. I heard the door being banged on. I went downstairs to see who was knocking. Leonard was awakened by it. I looked through the peephole. Two male uniformed officers, one black, one white with flashlights on the patio. I opened the door and they flashed their lights in my face.

"What's your name?" They asked me.

"My name is J.O. I'm who you're looking for." They were shining their flashlights on my face and clothes.

"Come down here with us." They ordered me. I looked at the street. There were several police cars and an ambulance in the middle of the normally quiet street. The entire neighborhood was up and out of their houses. I was humiliated. I had never had any trouble in all the years I'd been coming here. I walked down the steps followed by the two officers. When we reached the sidewalk in front of one of the police cruisers, they ordered me to take seat on the curb. Once I sat down they asked what happened.

"A couple of weeks ago she was at my house. While I went to the bathroom, she stole $200 from me. This was the first time I've seen her since then."

"Ok?" The white officer said.

"I asked her when she was going to pay me my money back and she came at me with a bottle."

"Right." the two officers said in unison.

"She swung the bottle at me. I kept hitting her until she dropped it."

"Right." they said again in unison.

"When she dropped the bottle, I quit hitting her."

"Right." They both said again. We all turned our focus to the voice that was yelling from across the street behind the ambulance. I could tell it was Regina. She was yelling at Leslie. I knew it was her because I could see the lights in her bedroom were on.

"What the fuck are you doing here? I told you I didn't want you back in my house in the first place." She yelled at the top of her lungs. Leslie was yelling incoherently. Another officer walked across the street towards me and said,

"She said you took her purse. Did you?"

"Yes, it's in the house."

"Will you go get it?"

"Yes, I don't want it."

"Come on, I'll go with you." We walked up the steps and into the dark house. Leonard was sitting on the couch pissed off there were cops in his house. I was mad at myself for having caused them to be there. I gave the cop the empty purse. He looked in it and asked "Where's the stuff that was in it?"

"I dumped it in the alley." We walked back out of the door and as we went down the steps he asked me, "Why'd you take it?"

"I was being an asshole. I was mad she came after me with a bottle."

"Right." He said. I sat back down on the curb. He went to the alley and shined his flashlight on the stuff I'd dumped on the ground. I could hear Leslie crying and yelling from the other side of the ambulance as I sat on the sidewalk. My next door neighbor,

Diane, was walking back from Regina's, giving me a dirty look and yelled at me, "Why the fuh' did you call the fuh'in' po-lice? We don't call the fuh'in' po-lice around here!"

"I didn't call the police." She was surprised at my response.

"Then who called the fuh'in' po-lice?" She yelled even louder.

"I guess she did."

"She did? Then I guess that bitch deserves to go to jail then. You know they taking her ass dontchu? " I just shrugged my shoulders. I was more concerned about them taking me.

Leslie was still yelling and crying incoherently on the other side of the ambulance. I was following the sound of her voice, which was moving to the back of the ambulance. I saw someone climbing into the back. The person had a grossly disfigured face. A bloody hand wrapped up in so much gauze it looked like a cast. Her eyes were swollen to the point of shutting. Her nose was just a tip where the nostrils were. Her mouth was bloody. I was thinking to myself 'Damn, who the fuck is that?' She was crying, screaming about her purse. The officer who walked me upstairs walked up to her, handed it to her as she climbed into the ambulance. That's when I realized it was Leslie. I was shocked. For a flash I felt sorry for her.

"Where's all my stuff?" she yelled.

"It's over there dumped in the alley." He replied.

"I want my stuff! I want her arrested for stealing my purse!" She shouted through tears and that jacked up face. The neighbors were rumbling as they heard her demand I be arrested.

"You better be glad you got the purse back." The cop snapped at her.

I still didn't know what they were going to do with me. I sat quietly on the sidewalk hoping they would forget all about me. One of the two cops who got me out of the house initially walked up to me, handed me an index card with a pen.

"Write your name, phone number, address and birth date down on this for me, please?"

"What's this for?" I asked

"It's a victim card. It goes with our paperwork so they can notify you if and when she makes bail, along with her court dates." I wasn't going to jail. I was relieved. I filled out the card. They wished me a good night and I was allowed to go back in my house. The neighborhood was still buzzing when I closed the door. I had no interest in hanging out. I had to apologize to my Godfather for bringing the police into his house. When I got inside I told him everything and apologized. He didn't hold it against me. He knew I didn't call the police. I wasn't responsible for them coming to the door. She stole $200 from me, but got her ass whipped and went to jail. I couldn't have asked for more. I smoked one of her cigarettes and went to sleep with a smile on my face.

Putting the Pieces Together

After everything that took place that week, I knew I had to get a private attorney to represent Antonio in a bond hearing. If a woman robbed me I could deal with it. If a man robbed me, I'd need Antonio for that. Plus I just wanted him out. We could fight a better fight if he was out on bond. I went to a law firm headed by two women. The one I hired, we'll call Renee Walsh. She was a young petite white woman, about 5'4", 130 lbs, in her mid-30's, with blond hair that hung to lobes of her ears. She's always sharply dressed. I liked her from the start. It was her energy. She has a fire in her that lets you know she likes combat in courtroom and she's good at it. As far as a lawyer goes, she's just what you want for your money. A pit bull guarding the yard. I LOVED her. I hired her on the spot and paid her for the bond hearing. We discussed her handling the whole case after we got him out on bond. First things first. Get Him Out.

It was at the bond hearing that the prosecutor called Antonio a threat to society. He talked about Antonio's prior record of having been convicted of a murder when he was 17. A home invasion and kidnapping, he did a few months after serving time on the murder. By this time the "last names" didn't faze me.

Ryan was out of the rehabilitation facility. He stayed in constant contact with me. He was hell bent on getting Antonio out. He went with me to see Renee. That was all she needed to get her juices flowing.

The morning of the bond hearing, Ryan and I sat in the gallery of the courtroom waiting for Antonio's case to be called. It was just like one of those courtrooms you see in the movies, beautiful dark wood all over the place, perfectly polished. I was excited because I knew he'd be home that night. I could finally kiss his face.

A sheriff's deputy brought Antonio into the courtroom shackled at the waist and ankles and sat him next Renee at the defense table. The case was called. The prosecutor gave all the reasons Antonio is a threat to society and why he shouldn't be given bond. He was angry and offended that Antonio would even think about getting bond. How dare he?

When Renee stood up, she was professional when she addressed the court.

"Your Honor, my name is Renee Walsh. I am representing the defendant in this case, Antonio Threat-to-society. Your Honor, we are here to request bail for my client. If I may ask, Mr. Ryan Thomas to please stand up for a moment? (Ryan stands up on crutches right next to me) Your Honor, this is the victim in the case my client is being charged with shooting. Mr. Thomas has told both the investigating officer, as well as, the prosecutors in this case, my client isn't the person who shot him. Mr. Thomas even left his bed in the rehabilitation facility, to go down to the courthouse in Cherry Hill at an earlier court appearance for my client to tell the prosecutor there that my client isn't the person who shot him. Your Honor, the victim is a defense witness in this case and based on that we believe there are enough grounds to warrant a reasonable bond for my client.

As far as his prior record is concerned, my client has done his time for that crime. His plea bargain was thirty years all suspended but ten. That should indicate the strength of the prosecution's case in that incident. We ask that you consider the evidence against my client in this case before you and grant him a reasonable bond. Thank You, Your Honor." With that she sat down next to Antonio. Ryan sat down next to me. I was super excited because I knew he was coming home.

The judge sat quiet on the bench for a moment. He pulled the file in front of him closer and began to read it. It felt like forever.

My mind was racing while he was reading. What would the bond be? I had a slight grin on my face, waiting to hear the amount. Then he looked up and started to speak.

"After going over the case in front of me and weighing the facts brought before me, it's the opinion of the court that this defendant should not have been within fifty miles of this incident. I am therefore denying bail." Shock. I had to keep repeating what he said in my head for it to sink in. Ryan was pissed. I was in shock. We couldn't believe it. Antonio sat at the defendant's table shaking his head. The courtroom officers walked over to him and escorted him out. Ryan and I just sat there stunned as Renee walked over to us in just as much disbelief.

"They have it out for him." She told us. We both just nodded.

"They're not even looh'in' for the dudes who shot me!" Ryan said angrily.

"It doesn't appear so." Renee replied. We all left the courthouse together. Ryan and I returned to Pigtown. Renee went on her way.

My mind was fucked up for the rest of the day. I still couldn't talk to Antonio because I didn't have a landline phone. I went to a crack house in the middle of Washington Blvd that we all went to. The owner, a guy named Stan, knew how to clone cell phone numbers. He was the hood AT&T. We all had one. You give him a Nextel phone and he could turn it on for you. He even taught me how to do it.

I went to talk to Stan, to ask him if I could use his phone to accept collect calls from Antonio. His boyfriend was in jail too. He could relate to my plight. Stan's house was where most of the dope fiend prostitutes lived too. They were a good portion of my client base and they loved me. I treated them like ladies and they paid me back with loyal repeat business.

Stan was a flamboyant homosexual junkie who lived in squalor. He had an air of prissy to him. His hair was over processed and never done. When he did pull it back in a rubber band, it was less of a ponytail and more of a receding Doberman stump. He spoke with a lisp through his chipped front teeth. I don't remember ever seeing him with a shirt on. He was a black man of medium build and stood about 5'7". His back was always arched. His bedroom was his palace. It was a dirty mattress on the floor with sheets that looked like they'd never been changed. Crack vials, dead cell phones, pieces of old crack stems and lighters were all over the floor as well. The rest of the three story row house was occupied by prostitutes, their junkie pimps and the johns they tricked with to get high.

I was always nervous going to Stan's house because you never know when something could jump off in there. The police could raid it. The john's could act up. The pimps could decide to beat their hoes. A random neighborhood dope boy could come by to kick Stan's ass because his phone wasn't ready or didn't work as long as he thought it should. Anything was liable to happen in Stan's house. So, I always made my visits brief.

I walked up the steps of the row house to the front door. Instead of knocking, I yelled up to Stan's bedroom, as was customary. It was located on the top floor in the front of the house. He knew my voice, so he yelled back through the window for me to come up. I knocked and was greeted by one of my prostitute customers named, Sarah. She was a very tall white girl with blonde hair. If she wasn't strung out on heroin and crack she would have been very beautiful. She looked like Daryl Hannah. She let me in; we shared a few cordial words as I made my way up to see Stan.

Once I got up to Stan's room, I got straight to business. I asked Stan about letting Antonio call his house and he didn't mind at all. He liked Antonio. Everyone liked Antonio. He told me about his boyfriend being locked up and said the phone company he used for some reason didn't charge for the collect calls. I wanted to pay him regardless but he refused. I was cool with that too. After agreeing on the times Antonio could call as to not interrupt him and his boyfriend's phone time, Stan would connect us on three-way so I didn't have to sit in the house and talk to Antonio. I bounced out safe and sound. I later called Antonio's mother to give her the number and information so she could relay it to Antonio when she spoke to him.

Steady the Course

Antonio's birthday is in July, the same week as the 4th. Even though he was locked up I still did something special for him. The jail was in East Baltimore. He told me his cell window was located on the side of the jail that faced the interstate. There was a two way street that ran alongside it with a five foot wall that separated the street from the expressway.

A few days earlier I bought a huge fireworks set from a guy selling them out of his trunk. It was nice, it had 85 colored flares. It stood about two and a half feet. The plan was to set it off in front of Antonio's cell.

Lockdown was 11 p.m.; everyone had to turn their lights off in their cells at that time. I asked a guy named Michael to drive me over there and explained why. He agreed. When we pulled up all the windows were dark in the jail. There were at least 60 windows on this side of the five story building. We parked right in front of the dark windows close to the corner that led to the back of the jail. I looked up and counted from the left side of the 3rd floor. He told me his window would be the 4th one. The light flipped on and off. I could see his silhouette through the painted glass. My heart raced. I looked at Michael "Are you ready?" I asked. "Let's do it." He replied. I jumped out of the car carrying this monstrous crate looking ensemble and ran across the street to the five foot divider wall and placed the fireworks securely on it. There was plenty of room, the wall was wide. My hands were shaking as I tried to light the wick. I didn't want to get caught out there. I finally got it lit and the spark from the wick let me know I could run back to the car. I took off running and could hear officers at the back entrance getting off work and talking loudly outside. I was controlled panicked. I could hear the hissing of the wick as I ran and knew the show was about to start immediately. I jumped in the car full of fright and adrenalin. I look at Michael and said, "Okay, we can go now." I wanted out of there. Michael looked at me and said, "Oh, no we're watching this." I was surprised he wasn't scared and all of a sudden I wasn't scared. Then we both turned to look at the fireworks show.

The start of the show was sparkles that shot up about 3 feet in the air in pink and silver. Before they could fizzle out there was a huge burst of green accompanied by a boom that soared about 50 feet in the air. It was followed by other bursts, booms and colors blue, purple, red, yellow and gold that shot out one after the other in glorious color. It was beautiful and bright. It looked like something you would see in a park on the holidays. I had no idea it would be that beautiful, big or loud. It was captivating. I then noticed a lot of yelling and I looked up at the jail to see all the lights in all the windows being flicked on and off repeatedly with the silhouettes of men yelling and banging on the windows. It was crazy. They were giving me their approval of the show I had put on. I looked at Antonio's window and I could see his silhouette looking down on me. The show ended with a blast of repeated shots like a machine gun hurling sliver in the air lighting up the night. As the box became a smoking mess Michael and I pulled off like it was no big deal. As we pulled up the stop sign at the corner I looked right toward the back entrance of the jail and saw a large group of correctional officers standing out there clapping and yelling too. Michael and I just cruised on by and made our way back to Pigtown.

By the time the phone calls were secured and I was in constant contact with Antonio two things happened. My business started going south and Nick was arrested on an armed robbery charge. Nick and I were very close, but his arrest caused a different type of problem for me. Antonio and Nick were partners in crime as well as conjoined dope fiends. They robbed dope dealers all over Baltimore and got high with the fruits of their labor. Out of his cut, Antonio would keep all the dope and give me all the money. With Antonio gone Nick still had my back. I didn't have to worry about being robbed because everyone was afraid of Antonio and Nick. The most dangerous thing in the world is a dope fiend with a gun who knows how to use it. Antonio and Nick were known as killers all over Baltimore and they were also known to get high as hell. No one wanted that problem.

At first, I was afraid of getting robbed by the neighborhoods guys. One of my friends in the neighborhood assured me everyone knows Antonio didn't shoot Ryan. Knowing that, no one would take the chance of having him come after them for doing something to me once he was home. Once home it wouldn't be a fistfight and only one person would walk away from it.

The hood where Antonio grew up developed a measure of respect for me during this time. He was gone yet I still held him down. He had money on his books, phone calls, I went to visit him every Sunday and I was faithful to him in his absence. Antonio and Nick wound up being housed together in jail so essentially I was responsible for the both of them in there, twice the money every week for commissary. I didn't mind. I loved Nick and worried about his withdrawals just like I worried about Antonio's.

The other problem was my trap house over at Poopie's. He was enjoying the celebrity of having the best dope in South Baltimore and he was indulging way more than he should. One day I go over there and the entire basement has been completely destroyed. The police had been there to raid the place. They went through every inch of the room looking for dope and didn't find any simply because I ran a night shop which means I don't load the trap until after 3pm. They'd come too early. I'd picked up the money like usual the night before and re-upped that morning. I spent the day mixing and had a few fresh packs on me. It was obvious that I wouldn't be working from there.

‘I’m glad you came in and saw it for yourself.” Poopie said to me as I entered the basement and saw the mess.

“What the hell happened?” I asked but, I already knew. I’d seen this destruction in my childhood. My mother sold drugs and our homes had been raided throughout my childhood.

“The po-lice came in here!” He said. “Yo an’ ‘em.”

Along with the destruction the police left behind the search warrant. Poopie handed it to me and as I read it I saw what brought them to the house. Poopie had been under surveillance by the undercover unit. Business had gotten so good that the steady traffic made Poopie lazy. They observed him serving customers from the front window of the basement. When I read that I was pissed. I confronted him with it and of course he denied it. He was adamant that he hadn’t been pitching from the window. I read him the warrant and he was silent. That was the end of our working relationship. Poopie was really mad that I wasn’t going to supply him anymore but, he knew he’d fucked up and I had every right to cut his ass off.

Poopie was a chili pimp on the side. A chili pimp is a one hoe pimp. Her name was Donna. She was a native of Pigtown, a short loud white girl with long brown hair and who was about 3 lbs from being pear-shaped. She was the neighborhood bully to the other junkie prostitutes in Pigtown. They feared her. She loved Poopie. She tricked all day and night and brought him drugs to keep him happy. Poopie would walk with her on the boulevard until she got a trick and then he would go back to the basement to wait for her. I enlisted Donna to be my new front person. She knew all the junkies and they were afraid of her so she wouldn’t have to worry about them being short on the money. Poopie was livid that I chose her and beat her up when he found out. She left him after that, which made him a no ho pimp.

Donna introduced me to a few of her friends. I met her at a friend’s house on the Blvd across the street from Stan’s house one evening. The woman who lived in the house was another white woman, with big boobs who was strung out as well. She had two kids, a boy about 11 years old, a girl about 6 years old. They were nice kids. The girl introduced me to her kitten. The woman seemed very excited to meet me. I assumed Donna told her I was her connect. They talked about all the money they could bring in with all the johns they had between them. They even told me about drugging johns and other prostitutes. They told me they'd give them a drug and when they passed out they'd strip the men of their wallets. The women they said usually kept their money in their bras so they would take a box cutter and cut the bra strap. I remember thinking, "That's fucked up." when they told me. With that introduction Donna was showing me the house she would be working out of. I didn't care so long as the money came back right. I made the same deal with her as I did Poopie, $3 off of every pill. Each pill sold for $10. I started her off with 20 pills until she moved up to 100. It happened rather quickly.

With Donna working and Antonio locked up I spent a lot of time in the neighborhood of South Baltimore, Pigtown. During this time I got a chance to meet the people who actually lived there and they got to know me. When Antonio was home people were generally afraid to talk to me fearing he may take it the wrong way. I knew the ones he introduced me to. With him gone and me having to make money in the neighborhood I learned the people in the neighborhood, those, who got high, those who sold drugs and those, who just lived there and worked regular jobs. I met some of my favorite people in the world in Pigtown.

I hung out in a bar on the corner of Cross St. and Carroll St. called Mom's Bar for the most part. I quit hanging on the stoop because DeeDee and Nigel broke up and she quit selling there. After I moved my operation to Poopie's their business suffered. The stress from that seemed to have caused the break up. I decided I didn't want to be in the middle of anything so I started going to the bar.

The entire neighborhood came in and out of this bar. The owner was a middle aged white woman who recently took over the bar from the previous owner. We could have a conversation. The bar was right in the middle of the action. So if Donna needed me she only had a 2 block walk to find me. I played pool with the other drug dealers in the neighborhood. I was the only girl though. The other girls hustled other things. Some dipped and dabbed in the drug game but for the most part they either worked a job or collected a government check and took care of their kids. I liked them, the girls. They weren't catty and they knew how to have fun.

Donna and I were doing well and it got to the point that her clientele came late into the night and into the early morning. I would collect from her before I went home for the night as I had done with Poopie. It became obvious that she needed more packs to last her through the night. I was happy to oblige. It only meant more money. Her packs got bigger.

I started hanging out with a neighborhood girl named Mickey. She was a pretty, perfectly brown, round, short girl with one of the most beautiful smiles I've ever seen. The only problem was she wasn't shit. She always stayed in some kind of drama and kept shit going. She didn't affect my relationship with others in the neighborhood because I hung with everybody. I got along with them all. I was very well aware that all of these people were from this neighborhood. Born and raised and I was an outsider, I stood on my own, no matter how cool I may have been and who my boyfriend may be that was always in the front of my mind. Even though Mickey stirred up shit, I took advantage of the fact that I could spend the night in her house whenever I didn't feel like going across town to go home. I wound up staying there so much that I had clothes there.

She lived in a row house that was only a matter of feet from where Ryan was shot. It was a two-story row house that was infested with roaches. I mean infested. There were so many roaches that they were brazen. They walked on you and weren't afraid of the light. Baltimore roaches I guess.

I spoke to Antonio nonstop on the phone. He always wanted something, more money, cigarettes, even a radio. What I did for Antonio I did for Nick. $50 for Antonio was $50 for Nick. Antonio had me meet a woman who worked at the jail as a nurse one night so I could give her two packs of cigarettes and two mp3 players for him and Nick. It also cost me $100 for her to deliver it. Money was pouring out faster than it was coming in. I only had one shop. And even though Pigtown was big enough to open a shop like you see on shows like "The Wire" Yo had a handle on just how wild that neighborhood would get, and it wasn't getting Wire wild by any stretch.

Seeing as I was in the neighborhood overnight Donna had a lot more freedom. If she had a problem I wasn't too far. I started letting her keep packs overnight and I'd collect the money when I got up and moving around the next day. One day I go toward the house early in the afternoon and I run into Donna coming out of the rooming house she lived in with her new boyfriend, Tony. She had mascara running down her face and looked like she was a victim of date rape. She couldn't look me in the eye. I knew something was wrong. She started talking and fake crying. She told me she was robbed last night. I didn't want to hear it. All I wanted to hear was, "Here's your money, J.O." I wasn't hearing that. I asked her what happened and where she was? She told me she was in the house she worked from and woke up with her bra strap cut. She didn't remember what happened. We went to the house. It was across the street from where she lived, 4 doors up from Stan. We went back to the workhouse and the owner was looking sheepish. Donna gave me a very dramatic rendition of the night before. She even showed me her cut bra strap that she was still wearing. I was furious. I had made the mistake of not picking up money from her before I went in for the night so she had about $1,000 on her last night.

I'm trying to stay calm and not beat the shit out of her. I look at Donna and tell her to walk outside with me. I don't want the woman who owns the house to hear what I'm about to say to Donna. As we step outside Donna is giving me drama. She's sighing like a little girl who knows she's in trouble but doesn't feel like it was her fault so she shouldn't be held responsible for it. As we cross the street back to the front of the house that Donna was living in, I started putting my words together in my head so that by the time we got to her house I wouldn't mince words or sound emotional. This was business after all. Once we got in front of her house Donna couldn't keep eye contact with me still.

"Donna, I understand you got robbed (I started.) But, you are responsible and you owe me money."

"J.O., it's not my fault I got robbed. They knocked me out. How am I supposed to know they were gonna do that shit? You should go after them about your money." She protested.

"Donna, you owe me the money because you knew what they do in that house and you took your chances going in there with the money. You told me what y'all were doing in there. As far as holding them accountable for it, that's your job. You get the money back from her and give it to me. I don't give a fuck how you do it but I want my fuckin' money and I don't want to wait all week for it. Do I make myself clear?"

She gave me a quick glance and looked at her feet when she nodded in agreement. "Donna!" I said very sternly so she would give me eye contact. She looked at me, "You're my girl and I fuck with you, so let's get this taken care of so we can go back to work." She knew what I meant; she was going to have to give me her money from tricking to pay for this mistake. She was weak from the thought. This meant she wasn't going to be getting as high as she normally would. I walked away from Donna really pissed off, more at myself than at her. I was lazy and it cost me. I now have to go into the little bit of savings I'd managed to put aside and get more work. I didn't have much because I had to keep Antonio and Nick up in jail and this was taxing me. On top of that I didn't have anyone to pitch for me and that meant I had to do it myself. I wasn't comfortable with that because the neighborhood had a lot of snitches and I was worried about Yo finding out and running up on me. At this point I didn't even bother going across town to my Godfather's house anymore. I was holed up at Mickey's and I was grinding to get my pack backup, not get robbed, and keep Yo off my back.

The Tide Shifts

The weather was changing, fall was fast approaching. More of the neighborhood guys were going to jail for selling dope. Yo had control of the neighborhood and it was showing. I'd see him around and we always said hello to one another. Yo was always approachable as far as I was concerned. He wasn't that way with other people in the neighborhood. Occasionally, he tried to be a hard ass with me but it always seemed to backfire on him. He'd actually laugh with me when it did. One day I had a traffic court appearance at the Cherry Hill courthouse. I ran into Yo there, he was in uniform we stopped and spoke as if we actually knew each other.

"Hey, what are you doing here?" He asked me as we walked up to each other.

"I'm paying a ticket. What are you doing here, fixing one? (He laughed) You on your way out?" I asked him.

"Yeah, are you?" He replied.

"Yup, you going back to the neighborhood from here?" I asked.

"Yeah, you?" He asked me.

"You should give me a ride back." I told him, he looked at me like I was crazy.

"Hell No!" He said laughing.

"I'm serious, (I wasn't) you'd save me hack fare. Come on?" He laughed and said,

"Hell no, I'm not giving you a ride to the hood. I hope you have enough hack fare."

"So you're telling me you're not going to give me a ride? That's what I'm to take away from this conversation?" I was looking at him dead in the eyes and he was trying his best not to laugh. He was blushing and nodding his head in answer to my question.

"Fine, I'll take the hack but, don't expect our relationship not to be affected by this turn of events." I said as I walked away from him and headed toward the exit.

"See you in the hood." He said over his shoulder.

"See you in the hood." I replied over mine.

Back in the neighborhood after court, I went and checked on Donna to get some money. She had been paying to my surprise. "I can't wait pay this bill off so, I can get another pack." She told me. She wasn't getting shit. A little fact she didn't know.

After collecting from Donna I ran into a friend of mine named Grace and we struck up one of our usual conversations on the front steps of her house which was on W. Cross St between Ward St and Carroll. She lived in the third house from the corner of Ward. I was sitting on the stoop with Grace standing in front of me with her back toward the street. We were enjoying our conversation as we always did.

She worked for a living and raised her son, Shane, alone. His father was the love of her life. He died when Shane was a baby. She was a former heroin addict who still enjoyed a beer. She only drank beer after work. Grace was off work this day and the weather was still warm enough to be outside with just a light jacket. So we sat at her house and chatted the afternoon away.

She was in the middle of telling me a story when Yo drove past. He pulled up nice and slow on the far North side of the street when he saw me. That brought him to a creeping pace in his cruiser. We made eye contact as I listened to Grace, she had no idea he was behind her and kept talking. I followed him with my eyes as he did mine. As he turned left pulling onto the Ward St, which is a narrow one way, he came to a dead stop. "Move!" He told me in an authoritative tone. I looked at him like he was crazy and told him,

"No, why do I have to move?" I asked.

"You don't live there that's why. Now move." Grace stopped talking and looked right at Yo and said,

"No, but I do so she don't have to go nowhere. Shiiiiiit." Rolling her eyes she turned her attention back to me and dismissed him in her own way. Yo looked at her and then at me. I was smiling at him pointing to her as if to say that's why I don't have to move. Yo knew he was beat but wouldn't let it go just yet. He looked at me and said,

"You're just mad I wouldn't give you a ride and you had to take a hack." I laughed when I replied,

"You're just mad you can't throw me off this stoop." He laughed at that and drove off telling me

"See you later."

Grace knew how to handle Yo like I did. The only difference, she wasn't doing anything illegal. She lived in the neighborhood and I sold drugs there. He may not have known that but I think he did. I think Yo had a lot of mercy on me. Grace and I continued on with our day. She was always good company. We always had good conversations and good laughs together. Yo had just provided another good laugh.

All over Baltimore heroin is the main drug followed by crack. To combat that problem Baltimore has the jump out squad, the narcotics unit, known as the Narcos, but pronounced "Knockuh's" by the locals. They were easy to spot. They always traveled in the same type of cars, a two door Chrysler Cavalier coupe. You could spot them a block away if you were looking and I was always looking. Yo would patrol the neighborhood and see guys he thought were selling drugs and tell the Knockuh's where they were and the Knockuh's would jump out on them. It was pretty much a daily thing. It wasn't abnormal to see them jump out on people and throw them on a wall and start frisking them. It never happened to me though. They knew who the dope boys were and kept an eye on them. Yo trying to throw me off the stoop made me very aware that he knew I didn't live in the neighborhood, which meant I could be arrested for loitering if I wasn't careful. That would turn into a major problem if I was dirty when I got stopped. I knew I had to be very careful down there.

Mickey lived on Nanticoke St. which was on the far end of W. Cross St. It was a rundown deserted street that had a lot of dilapidated houses and not a lot of traffic. People didn't hang out on the stoops as much on that street like they did on the others. It had a deserted feel to it. Kids didn't even play on the block like they did on the other blocks. My staying with her was really just a means to an end. I could come in and out as I pleased. It gave me a base in the neighborhood. A place that if I got stopped by Yo I could say that's where I was staying.

Mickey was not very well liked in the neighborhood by the other girls. She was always in some shit. Not always little shit either. She has two children by two different fathers, both of them in prison. The oldest son was named Donnie and his father is white. The youngest son is named Lil' David after his father. Big David was in prison for weapons after the cops couldn't convict him on the murder of a guy who wasn't from the neighborhood but was selling drugs there. Mickey's cousin Harv, killed the guy. Rumor has it; Mickey and Big David paid him $300 for the job. They then reportedly told the police on Harv, and Big David turned state's evidence against him. Mickey sold crack too. Not enough to make a life for her and her kids, but enough to make sure she had enough beer to get drunk and pass out every night, which she did. She'd mess with some of the neighborhood guys she knew had girlfriends and then start a fight with the girls. One night, in Mom's Bar, (on the corner of Caroll St. and W. Cross) such a fight broke out. I broke up the fight, but Mickey got at least five rows of her box braids snatched out of her the front her head for her troubles. It was a huge bald spot. It was laughable. Karma came a calling on that one. She was mad at me for not jumping in and helping her. I told her that she didn't need my help she was handling the girl well enough without me. The real reason was I didn't want to be known for jumping anyone in that neighborhood because I wasn't from there and if I'm jumping people then people could decide to jump me. I was also a grown up and if you mess with someone's boyfriend then you're on your own in my opinion.

Mickey was a bully, no question. That was evident anytime we saw Donna. As Donna got close to paying her bill with me off, the money started getting smaller and slower. It became harder to find her and she didn't come looking for me to pay me or when I'd leave a message for her throughout the neighborhood. When I did see her and I was with Mickey, Mickey would take it upon herself to throw Donna against the nearest wall and frisk her. Mickey would go through every pocket Donna had and if she had any money, Mickey would hand it to me. I did get a kick out of it. I never asked her to do this but, I also didn't ask her to stop either. When weeks had started to pass and the bill with Donna still hadn't been settled, I was getting irritated. Mickey was even more irritated. Whenever she'd throw Donna on a wall and didn't find any money she'd plead with me to beat Donna up. Donna was scared. I didn't want to beat Donna up. I wanted my money. Mickey was furious that I kept letting her get away with this. She told Donna the last time we had her on the wall that if she didn't pay me my money she was going to kick Donna's ass for me. Donna looked at me to give her some sort of sign that I wouldn't let Mickey beat her up. I gave her no such satisfaction.

A few days after that incident, it was a quiet day in the neighborhood and Mickey and I were sitting on her stoop. We weren't talking, just sitting. It was about 2pm. I just got up and walked away from Mickey and the stoop. Instead of turning left and going to W. Cross St toward the stores and bars I went right to Baynard Street which ran parallel to W. Cross St and headed toward the Blvd and Donna's house. I didn't say anything to Mickey and she didn't ask me where I was going.

As I walked up Baynard I saw Yo parked in his squad car on

Ward St., he was doing paperwork. As I walked up and leaned on his car I realized I hadn't seen Yo in the neighborhood in a while.

"What's up, girl?" He smiled when he saw me.

"Nothing much, where you been?" I asked

"I was gone for two weeks."

"Oh, yeah? Why?"

"I got married and went on my honeymoon."

"Congratulations! Where'd you go?" I was happy for him.

"Hawaii!" He had a big smile on his face, as if he was remembering his time there.

"I wish I would've known you were going. I would've asked you to bring me back some sand." He looked at me with a pleasant curious smile on his face.

"Why would you want sand?"

"I collect sand. I have sand from all over the world."

"Really?" I think it was the first time he'd heard of it.

"Yeah, I have sand from seven different countries in Africa alone. I collect sand." He seemed surprised to know something so personal about me. Maybe it was the idea that I did something so corny.

"I'll catch you later Yo."

"See you 'round the hood." He said as I walked away and continued on to Donna's.

When I got to the boarding house that Donna lived in and shared a room with her boyfriend, I knocked on the door. It was answered by an underage dope fiend prostitute named Crystal I saw around the neighborhood. She stood about 5'2" with honey brown skin, green eyes and sandy brown, curly hair. I was always struck by how beautiful she was and saddened by how young she was in this life. She wasn't even sixteen years old. She was on her way out when I asked her where Donna's room was. She pointed to a door at the top of the steps. We walked past each other.

I walked up the steps and reached the bedroom door. I listened for a second to see if I could hear any voices. I didn't. I knocked like a cop would, really hard and loud to wake them up. It worked. "Who is it?" Donna asked through the door. When I said it was me, there was a pause. "What do you want?" She asked. "I want you to open the door." I said with a fake laugh to ease her concerns. She opened the door enough to show her face. She looked like she just woke up.

"What's up?" she asked me.

"Open the door so I can come in." I said.

"I can't, Tony's not dressed." She tried.

"Then tell him to put some clothes on so I can come in." With that I pushed the door open and stepped in. Tony was standing in the back of the room by the window shirtless and wearing shorts. Tony and I said 'Hello' to each other and then I turned my focus back to Donna. We're standing in the room at the foot of the bed and in front of the door and I asked Donna for the rest of my money. Of course she didn't have it. Tony was minding his business getting dressed.

"Donna you owe me $150 and I know you have it." I said

'No, J.O. I don't." My anger starts to grow.

"Donna you're fucking turning tricks all night and you keep telling me you don't have my money. Are you telling me you haven't been working, or are you telling me you haven't been getting high?" I looked her in the face and I could feel the heat from anger hit my face.

'J.O........" before she could say another word I punched her dead in the forehead and the fight was on. She stumbled backward off balance and I stalked her and hit her again before she could regain any focus or balance. I kept punching her until she grabbed me as she was falling, which would've given me free range to stomp her out. Donna had given and received too many ass whippings so she knew what to do. She took me with her in her fall and we both wound up on the hardwoods grappling next to the heavy wood chest of draws. We landed on our sides facing each other and I'm using both fists to punch her in the face and head. You could hear them land. Tony is sitting on the bed putting his sneakers on while I'm beating the shit out of his girlfriend. I'm paying attention to him while we're fighting because he could jump in it. Then I'd have a different problem. With each punch I give her, Donna yells out in pain. After the 6th or 7th straight punch to her face she grabs both of my forearms and yells for Tony to help her. I'm trying to get her grip off my arms, she was strong as hell. I'm tugging my arms back and forth and my right forearm is scrubbing the floor and the base of the dresser. He says nothing. I'm watching him through the corner of my eye. She yells "Tony, call the police!" He stands up; I think he's going to pull me off of her. He steps over both of us and walks out of the room. She's yelling, "Tony! Tony! Help me!" as she continues to hold my forearms I continue punching her in the face. I get loose of her grip and still on our sides continue to pummel her with both of my fists not saying a word. I hear Tony walking down the wooden steps; I climb on top of her. She's yelling, "Tony, call the police!" I hear the door slam shut and really lay into her. She folds her arms to cover her face and as I'm swinging down on her she yells, "Okay, this means we're even." I keep hitting her relentlessly. When I finally stop, I leave her lying on the floor and walk out of the room into the hallway headed for the steps to leave. I see Joe, the owner of the house, looking at me from across the hallway standing in his bedroom doorway. I look at his Asian face and he looks terrified. I walk down the steps and leave the house.

On the walk back to Mickey's the adrenalin had started to leave me and the pain in my forearm had started to kick in. It looked like rug burn on my entire forearm. It hurt. Sitting on the stoop with Mickey I was looking at my scratched up arm pulling the rolled up dead skin off. Mickey asked me what happened to it.

"I just beat up Donna."

What?!" she yelled. I repeated myself. She seemed in disbelief and asked me why I didn't tell her I was going over there. I told her I just decided to go and it was something I had to handle on my own. She laughed her ass off. We went back to sitting on the stoop in silence.

Later that day I was on Carroll St. talking to some of the girls when this white woman junkie I didn't know came up to me and said

"If I had any money I'd give it to you."

"Why?" I asked her.

"Because, you beat up Donna." I was surprised and asked her how she knew?

"Everybody knows. Thank You." She said. I still didn't know how she knew, but I didn't want to get into a conversation about it with her.

Later on, I was in front of Mom's Bar and another junkie, this time a white man I didn't know, came up to me thanked me for beating up Donna too. I still didn't know how these people knew about the fight. I wasn't too concerned just curious. I went walking down Washington Blvd toward Stan's house and in the middle of the block was Donna talking to some people. She was back facing me, with her hair blowing in the wind. One of the people motioned toward me with her head as her mouth was moving. Donna turned around saw me and started walking toward me. She was wearing Ray Bans. When she got about 15 feet or so away from me she took off her sunglasses and revealed two swollen black eyes. She looked like a raccoon. I felt bad but not really. She deserved it and she knew it. She came up to me and put her arms out for a hug. I obliged her. After the hug she apologized to me for not giving me my money and I told her we were even. I knew I wouldn't get the rest of my money and would have to keep beating her ass to no avail.

What I didn't tell you is that Donna is one of Yo's snitches. It's known and not discussed. She's a prostitute and I realize that for her safety she has to have a relationship with a cop. Somebody may have to identify the body. I can only take the ass beating so far with her. If I bully her after I beat her up she'll put Yo on me. I decided to take the loss and keep it moving.

It was another warm fall day and Mickey and I were on the stoop again. We were laughing and joking when a young white woman came across the street from her house and approached us. I had seen her around the neighborhood and knew she lived across the street from Mickey. I'd even sold her drugs a couple of times over the months since Antonio had been gone.

Her name was Lisa and she was mess. She had on the filthiest clothes I've ever seen a person wear. Her dark brown hair was so dirty with oil that it stuck to her head. She was young. She may have been in her early twenties but was so small and petite she could pass for 16 physically. She was wearing a dark green sweatshirt that was shining from all the dirt that was piled on it. Her baggy blue jeans had dirt going up and down the thighs. Her white sneakers were so dirty they were brown. Her blue eyes were lost in the dirt all over her face. You could see her teeth were black and chipped. Her gums were swollen, exposed by her chapped lips as she started to speak. She said, "Hello" to Mickey first then to me. We said "Hello" back to her at the same time. I thought she was going to ask me if I was selling. I was prepared to tell her no because I wasn't at the moment. But that's not what she wanted. She asked me if we could speak for a moment and I obliged her. "Sure, what's up?" She glanced at Mickey as if to ask if it was okay to speak frankly in front of her. I told her Mickey was cool.

"J.O., I want to tell you I'm really sorry about Antonio."

"Thanks." I said.

"I didn't want to have anything to do with it and I still don't.'

(I was officially confused.) What are you talking about?" I asked her.

"The police, Puerto Rican Yo, he made us say it was Antonio who shot Ryan." My mouth hit the floor.

"Whoa, what are you talking about?" I asked in shock.

"It was Yo, he brought us to the station and made us point Antonio out in a lineup and sign statements." She said in a frightened voice.

"Who is we?" I asked.

"Me and my boyfriend, Bobby. We didn't have a choice. I'm just telling you so you know. Maybe you knowing will help Antonio in some way."

"It does help kinda. Are you willing to admit that on the stand? I asked.

"J.O., I'll do whatever I can to help out in the situation. Bobby and me talked about it and we both feel real fucked up about doin' it."

I didn't know exactly what to say. I knew that I had to walk a thin line here. If she was the one who identified Antonio to the police she was a witness. I couldn't make it appear that I was tampering with a witness. I pointed to the row house on Mickey's block I thought was hers and asked if she lived there. She nodded and said I could come by anytime. "Thank you for telling me. I know you did what you had to do."

I knew Yo didn't give her a choice and a dope fiend ain't getting sick for nobody. She seemed relieved that I wasn't mad at her and thanked me as she walked away.

Mickey and I just sat there until Lisa was out of earshot, before Mickey started to talk.

"That mother fuh'in' Yo, man. I can't believe it, but I can at the same time. That mother fuh'er Yo, man."

I was listening to her talk and trying to figure out how to make this situation work for us without catching a charge. I thought about the girl I used to sell with on the Blvd, DeeDee. Since her and Nigel split up, she hadn't been around the neighborhood much. Her hobby was videography. Over the summer I actually hosted a television show she produced that aired on the public access channel in

Baltimore. We would go and interview any rappers who were performing in Baltimore or DC. The show aired the interviews showing video's in between. It was fun. Then we'd go back to the hood and sell drugs. DeeDee answered the phone happy to hear from me. "What's up Nigga?" I could hear the smile in her voice. I quickly caught her up on what Lisa just told Mickey and me. She was bowled over. I asked her if she could bring her camera over and we could record the two of them recanting. She was game and said she'd be there in an hour.

DeeDee was a go getter. She always had some sort of hustle going and I respected her for that. Neither of us was from the neighborhood and we both understood what that meant. DeeDee on the other hand would beat a bitch down if she thought Nigel was cheating or flirting with someone. As far as looks go, I'll put it this way, my Godfather met her one time. He said she looked like Biggie with a wig. She was my friend though, a good one at that.

True to her word she pulled up to Mickey's house and found us on the stoop. Once again I gave her the rundown on what Lisa told us and expressed to her that I didn't want to chance tampering with a witness. She had it all figured out she said and the three of us walked across the street to Lisa's house.

I knocked on the door and Lisa's boyfriend Bobby answered. He squinted in the sunlight but managed to smile at me when he recognized me. He looked like he could be Lisa's boyfriend. He was white, 26, about 6'1", wiry frame, with what use to be sandy brown hair but, now was an oily glob on the top of his head. He looked like he hadn't washed the white t-shirt he was wearing in the same amount of time Lisa hadn't washed what she had on earlier. He was barefoot and his toenails were black. His brown eyes were drowned in his dirty face. His fingernails looked like he'd just rebuilt a transmission and the cigarette he was puffing on was shaking in his right hand as he pulled from it. He spoke to me as if we were friends. "Hi, J.O."

“Hey Bobby,” I replied as I smiled at him.

I heard DeeDee say, “Oh, hell no.”

“Bobby, is Lisa home?” I asked

“Yeah, she’s upstairs, I’ll get her.” He said as he made 3 steps back in the house and hollered her name. A few seconds later Lisa appeared at the front door with the same aversion to sunlight as Bobby.

She was a little more skeptical when she saw DeeDee with the camera but she knew DeeDee from around so she wasn’t skeptical for long. They both came out on the stoop and closed the house door behind them. I explained to them that we would like to get their account of what happened on video and they were quite willing to do it. I was relieved.

When filming started DeeDee took the lead. She asked their names and then asked them to tell their side of the story. The whole thing took less than 10 minutes. They had recanted. I was excited and sad at the same time. The police really had it out for Antonio. Yo was willing to become a criminal to get Antonio off the street.

Safety in Numbers

Winter was here and Antonio's case was at a standstill. He had been scheduled for a court appearance in December. The night before court, a blizzard hit the entire state. Court was closed and court dates were cancelled to be rescheduled for a later time. It was once again another disappointment.

Ryan was healing well, his crutches were gone and he walked with only a slight limp. He had gone into hiding; the police were threatening him to testify against Antonio. They'd been going to all of his friend's houses looking for him. He ran into a couple of cops from another part of town that detained him. They had him sitting on a corner handcuffed asking him if he was the one who'd been shot? They told him if he didn't cooperate, they would find him and throw him head first on the concrete.

Antonio needed a private attorney. I wanted to hire Renee but, Antonio blamed her for him not getting a bond. He didn't want anything to do with her. We argued about this for weeks. I reminded him what the judge said about him being 'within 50 miles of the incident'. It had nothing to do with Renee's abilities as an attorney. What it did have everything to do with was politics of Baltimore and his reputation in the city. He didn't want to hear it.

He had me go see the lawyer that represented him on his murder case when he was 17. He was an older white man by the name of Carl Davis. I called him to make an appointment regarding Antonio, he remembered him. I took Ryan with me.

It was dusk when we arrived at Mr. Davis' office. It was located in a building in downtown Baltimore. His receptionist had left for the day and Mr. Davis greeted Ryan and me as we walked into the office. He appeared to be a nice enough fellow but, I didn't get that same killer instinct I got from Renee. His black hair was receding and slicked back, he wore a white shirt with a black tie and dark slacks. He walked us to his office in the back and invited us to sit.

I began to tell him Antonio's situation. I introduced Ryan when we first walked in but, it wasn't until we were in the office that he realized Ryan was the victim Antonio was charged with shooting. He was taken aback that the victim was in his office on behalf of the defendant. We talked for awhile and I filled him in on the details of the case even telling him about Yo stopping me and admitting that the police knew Antonio wasn't the perpetrator. Before we left I gave him the one thousand dollars he told me he would need as a retainer over the phone. I didn't feel good about giving it to him. He didn't win his last case with Antonio, so I was of the mindset he wouldn't win this one, no matter how much of a slam dunk this was. I was running really low on money and this guy seemed like a waste of it to me. Antonio wanted to be represented by him and I was honoring that wish. I would've rather given the money to Renee.

I was stressed out and business was for shit. I hadn't really recovered from the Donna loss. Antonio and Nick needed money every week, plus my daily expenses and now I just kicked out a $1000. I was really broke. For days I stressed about what I should do.

Finally, I decided to call my mother back in Atlanta and ask her for advice. She had been home for many years by this time. She served more than 9 years in prison. She'd rebuilt her life and even remarried since being released.

She hadn't met Antonio. We'd never traveled to Atlanta. He was a heroin addict and couldn't be without heroin so traveling wasn't an option. She had no idea what was going on with me. We hadn't been talking a lot because I didn't want the judgment I deserved for being in this situation. I told her the truth, all of it. I told her I know girlfriends always think the boyfriend didn't do it. I told her about Ryan and what the judge said.

"Well, if the victim told a judge and a prosecutor that Antonio didn't shoot him and they still have him locked up, then they have it out for him." She said no judgment in her voice at all.

"My advice to you is to get him a great attorney and you need money for that. I know you're not making any in Baltimore just because I know Baltimore. So, my advice to you is to come back home and do what you do with the people you do it with here and get that money up. You have to do it fast because they're going to take him to court soon and everything has to be in place before then."

It was the first time my mother wasn't putting me down. She was talking to me as an intelligent person. I knew she meant it and that only reassured what I'd been already thinking, I had to go back to Atlanta and get with my old crew to make real money. I didn't want to leave because I didn't want Antonio to feel like I was abandoning him. I was the only person in his family that was helping him during this time. No one else did anything for him. I would call his mother and give her updates. I was the only one going to visit him every Sunday. I was all he had and I didn't want him to think I was leaving him too.

That night after I talked to my mother I spoke to Antonio who was now calling me on the house phone at Mickey's. I would just pay for the calls Antonio made. I told him about the talk I had with my mother and what decision I came to. He was upset and thought I wasn't going to come back. Antonio knew nothing of my life back home in Atlanta. He didn't know the people I knew. He didn't know the family I came from. He didn't know the money I made selling weed there. I assured him that I wasn't going to abandon him. I was strictly going back to make money for his defense and I'd be back before he went to court. He didn't believe me. I could hear it in his voice. I knew the only way to prove it to him was to show him.

Nothing I said would convince him.

I made all the arrangements I needed to before leaving. I collected all the money I had in the street from those that were selling for me. I went to Stan and arranged for him to 3way Antonio's calls to my cell phone. To my surprise Stan informed me he had a second line in the house. None of the other people in the house knew about it because there was no phone connected to the jack. He agreed to put a phone in the jack solely for the purpose to transfer the calls to my phone so Antonio could call me directly. I gave him $50 bucks for the favor.

The day I was returning to Atlanta I had an evening flight. I was in the neighborhood hanging out and I ran into Ryan who was out of hiding that day. He wanted to go to Foul Ball, which was the bar he was shot at. I told him I couldn't go get a drink because I was on my way to junkie's house who owed me $20.

I wasn't pressed about the money, it was the principle. This was an older white man who owed me the money. He was ill and I gave him 2 pills because he got a government check the next day. He assured me, I was more than welcome to come by his house and get my money. We had done it before, but this was the first time he was ducking me. Ryan walked with me to the guy's house. As usual, his girlfriend answered the door to tell me he wasn't there. I was cordial to her; after all she didn't owe me a thing. I told her to let him know I was leaving town and I'd be back before I left. Ryan was waiting for me at the bottom of the steps of the row house. She watched me as I left and saw Ryan. He and I stepped into the street and started walking toward Foul Ball when she called out to me. "J.O., hey." Ryan and I both stopped and turned around to look at her. She was speaking to me but looking at him when she asked me, "Rob owes you money doesn't he?" She never took her eyes off Ryan. I took advantage of that and said,

"Yeah, right now he does but in about an hour he's going to owe HIM money." Ryan jumped in the conversation and said,

"He sure is." The tall pretty black woman had a look of fear on her face never taking her eyes off Ryan. She said,

"Hold on a minute." and went back in the house shutting the door behind her. I looked at Ryan trying to figure out what was going on, he had a smirk on his face and a bit of a fire in his eye. Before I could ask him what that was all about the woman opened up the door and said, "Here" holding out a small wad of money. I walked back to the house climbed the steps and took the money. It was all there. She said still looking at Ryan,

"I don't know what you'd do to him about your money but, I know what he'll do." She was afraid. I looked at Ryan as I walked down the steps, he was ear to ear grinning, chipped tooth in full view, looking like a badass little boy with a goatee, nodding his head acknowledging her fear and giving her reason to have it. I just laughed and told him come on.

We walked to Foul Ball. I gave Ryan the money I got from the woman and I bought him a beer. We had a good laugh off of that. I always looked at Ryan as a little boy. Not in the physical sense but, in the cute, young guy sense. He was cute and slim. He was always laughing and smiling, being playful and silly when we hung out. He always calls me "Big Sis". He was so cute he couldn't be mean. At least that's what I thought. I now knew better. I should've known better all along. We have the same issue, being mixed kids in a black environment.

Welcome To The A

I arrived in Atlanta later that night. My high school friend Sheree came to pick me up from the airport in her brand new Cadillac Escalade. It was Burgundy and fully loaded. Sheree and I had been friends for 16 years. We met as sophomores at Northside High School in Atlanta. She's a paper brown skinned girl with sharp cat eyes. She has a perfect smile with perfect teeth that are accented by a slight front tooth gap. She's the same height as me at 5'6". She has a curvy figure with a small waist, ample breasts and a firm round butt. Her brown shoulder length hair was up in a bun.

She pulled up right as I was walking out of the airport and jumped out to greet me with a big welcome home hug. I was glad to see her. I was glad to be home. As we hugged it out, a friend of hers named Ray jumped out of the passenger seat, picked up my suitcase and put it in the back of the SUV. He offered me the front seat but, I declined, jumped in the roomy back seat and stretched out. Sheree got in the driver's seat and pulled away from the curb exiting the airport area. She formally introduced Ray and me while, proceeding to light up a blunt. I was home and I felt it. A sense of relief came over me as I inhaled the thick marijuana smoke and began to relax.

Sheree kept me in the loop as to what was going on with my old crew back at home while I was in Baltimore. She wasn't a drug dealer but, she hung out with the drug dealers. She was a member of my crew. She didn't sell weed, which is what we did but, she would hold money and occasionally work as a go between. It was Sheree that I called when I made the decision to return home. She had been trying to get me to come home for months, but I kept declining. I had a falling out with my boss some months back and that's how I wound up in Baltimore.

At the time there wasn't enough room for the both of us in Atlanta. So, I left and went to Baltimore to make money. When my boss wasn't mad at me anymore he told Sheree to call me to come back home. His name was Cuzn and he was a big time weed dealer. He was a millionaire and he only sold weed. Even though I didn't come home when he initially wanted me to, I knew I always had that door open and it would remain open until I chose to go home. It was an option that I knew I had. Antonio didn't know about it. It wasn't his business.

It was a warm winter's night in Atlanta. I was feeling more and more like my old self. As we drove up 85 North toward downtown Atlanta I saw the skyline of my beautiful city and as I inhaled the weed smoke I said to myself, "Welcome Home."

We had a stop to make before I went home, home being my mother's house. We were headed to Buckhead, which is north of midtown Atlanta. We were going to meet with Cuzn at one of my favorite watering holes, Intermezzo. It's a swanky dimly lit dessert restaurant that I have been going to faithfully for the last 8 years. I introduced Cuzn to it when we first started working together about 3 years before. Then he basically moved in there. He wasn't originally from Atlanta and had just arrived when I was introduced to him by a mutual friend of ours named SK.

We had to drop Ray off first. We didn't bring outsiders around Cuzn. We dropped Ray off at the Varsity restaurant on North Ave which was on our way to Intermezzo.

Cuzn was a good guy. More than a little fucked up in the head, but a good guy. He never told me his real name and in the business we were in, I wasn't really interested in it. Cuzn was just fine with me. He was a perfect chocolate brown with beautiful white teeth and he wore glasses. He was very unsuspecting. He didn't flash his money. He didn't frequent strip clubs like the rest of the out of town ballers who took up space in Atlanta. He hung out in the places I showed him when we first started hanging out. He was like my teacher in a sense. I looked up to him for being that to me.

We got along fine until we didn't get along. We made the

mistake of becoming intimate about a year after we began working together. When I wouldn't play his games of pitting his girlfriend's against each other. He decided the best way to fuck with me, was to cut me off and not give me any work. I took all the money I had to my name and went to Baltimore. I bought 15 grams of raw heroin from an African in D.C. that SK linked me into.

That's how I met Antonio. I needed a trap to set up in. I couldn't just walk out on a corner and start slinging dope. This is Baltimore. People get killed for nothing. I mean literally nothing. Selling drugs in someone else's hood is the easiest way to get killed. They wouldn't even think twice about it. They wouldn't even feel bad about it. They wouldn't have known me.

I got with a friend of mine named Darnell and told him what I was trying to do. He told me he had a good guy he could link me into. Darnell and I came from the same "family". We both learned the heroin game at the same time from the same person, Leonard. So, Darnell was protective over me. He wouldn't put me in harm's way. Whoever he was going to put me with was going to be the same way. I could trust that without having to ask for it. Darnell introduced me to Antonio.

Cuzn wasn't there when we arrived. We waited in our usual meeting place, which was in the parking lot of a fast food place next door. I was high as hell. I was ready to go into Intermezzo and order every cheesecake they had on the menu. This dude needs to hurry up.

Sheree and I were standing in the parking lot catching up when another member of our crew pulled into the parking lot. We called him Dougie Chin Chow. All of a sudden I felt like I was at a family reunion. I was glad to see him. He stepped out of his low key 1990's gray Volvo four door. We hugged like we were long lost family and it felt that way.

By no means is Dougie Chin Chow his real name. I gave him that name a couple of years back when we were at my house smoking weed and high off our asses. Now that I think about it, HE gave himself that name while we were at my house high off our asses. He was tall and brown about 6'1 with a slender build. Brown eyes, a small fro and a raspy voice. He had gaps throughout his entire mouth and he was always smiling. While the three of us stood in the parking lot waiting for Cuzn to show up we caught up with each other.

Sheree filled me in on what was going on with her two girls and husband. Dougie Chin Chow filled us in on his latest girlfriends. The time was flying by and after being out there for about an hour Cuzn finally showed up.

He pulled up in a 2000 black jeep Cherokee. As soon as our eyes met we smiled at each other. He pulled into the parking spot right in between Sheree's Escalade and Dougie's Volvo. It was about 11pm and we were just getting started, it felt good to be home. It felt good to be missed by my friends.

Cuzn turned the engine off in his car and got out. Sheree and Dougie were giving him hell about being the last one to show up, again. He didn't pay them any mind he just walked over to me with his big ass smile and we gave each other a huge, long hug without saying a word. It felt good to be home. After the long hug we separated and just gave each other a once over to make sure we still had all of our original parts. We did so I asked,

"Can we go inside now? I need a cheesecake, I'm high."

"Of course you are. I can see it all in your face." He said laughing at me. We all walked into the restaurant in a single file line.

Once we were at the table and had ordered, Sheree and Dougie carried on their own conversation giving Cuzn and me a chance to talk business.

"So, how's everything been with you?" He asked.

"I'm good. Glad to be back." I said

"You ready to work?"

"Yeah, I just need to get some sleep. I'll be good in the morning. Is what I smoked the project?"

We never referred to weed as weed. We only referred to it as the project. If you ever called it weed to Cuzn he would walk away from you and you would never see him again. He was very maniacal about his business. Even though he sold massive amounts of weed he was the only one out of all of us that didn't smoke it. He's never used a drug or drank alcohol in his life.

"Yeah, that's it. What do you think?" He asked me.

"I have no problem with it." I said still high.

"Is it a big project?" I asked which meant is there a lot of it.

He gave me this big smile and looked over his glasses and said, "Feel free to sell as much as your people will buy." That was all I needed to hear. It's about to go down.

We ended the night in the same parking lot. Before Sheree and I drove off Cuzn and I swapped numbers. It was the first time we would have direct contact with each other in almost a year. I was feeling more and more like my old self as the minutes rolled by.

I got to my mother's loft in midtown about 2am. I knew the security codes to get in the security gate and the front door to the building. The only time she had to get up was to let me in the apartment. She was glad to see me. I was glad to see her as well. I told her to go back to bed. I'd see her in the morning. She didn't put up a fight and went right back to her bedroom.

My mother lived with her second husband in a beautiful two bedroom, two bath loft apartment with exposed brick and a terrace the overlooks the old City Hall East building. The entire layout was open and warm. The kitchen was right out in the open on the right when you came down the short hallway which led you to the huge living room. My bedroom was the guest bedroom on my immediate right which was located right next to the second bathroom.

My mother's room was to the left of the hallway and it was massive. It had a huge walk in closet that is the size of actual bedrooms I've seen. At the closet entrance on the left is the master bathroom that looks like it belongs in a hotel. It has a double sink, Jacuzzi tub and a stand up shower. I love this place. It feels like I'm sleeping in a magazine. I get in bed and fall fast asleep. Tomorrow is my first full day of being home.

The next morning I woke up to my mother feeding her two dogs and talking to her chirping birds. She was in the kitchen when I came out of the bedroom and went to into the bathroom. When I came out the bathroom she asked me if I was hungry. I told her I was and she made me some scrambled eggs and turkey bacon. As I was eating an alert must've gone out over Atlanta that I was home because my phone started ringing off the hook. The first call was from SK the friend who introduced me to Cuzn.

"Hey there, are you here?" He asked when I answered the phone.

"Yup, I'm at my Mom's." Right around the corner, from where he lived.

"Good, I can't wait to see ya. I'll come and pick you up in a little while. How much time do you need?" He asked

"Give me about two hours?"

"Okay, I'll call you when I'm downstairs." With that we got off the phone.

The next call came right behind SK's and it was my friend Jennie.

"Hey, I hear you're back in town." She said in a happy voice.

"I am. I'm at The Carmen's. What up Slick?" I started calling my mother "THE CARMEN" when I was a teenager because of her dynamic personality. Most of my friends call her that too.

"I'm coming to see you tomorrow. I have to work tonight but, I'm off tomorrow." She said

"Cool, we'll get into something." With that we got off the phone.

The next call came from a friend of mine named Quid. He's a

rapper and a producer and we've been friends for a few years now.

"What's up Lil Mama? I heard you came home. What you got planned for tomorrow night?" He asked.

"Jennie's off tomorrow so we're going to get into something. I don't know what yet but, we're doing something. Why, what do you have going on?" I asked

"I'm gonna be in the studio with Mel tomorrow night. Y'all should come through and hang out. I want you to see the studio we're working out of. It's sick." He said.

"I'm in. We'll see you tomorrow. What time are y'all workin' 'til??" I asked.

"Shit, we'll be there all night. You know how we do. Y'all can spend the night if y'all want. It's big enough. Wait 'til you see it. It's sick."

"I doubt I'm sleeping in a studio but I'll definitely come hang out. I'll hit you later and check in witcha." I said ready to get off the phone.

"Do that. I'll hollah." He replied and we hung up.

I talked to my mother for a little while. "I saw Cuzn, last night." I told her. "Oh, really? How's he doing?" She asked. "He's Cuzn," I told her. My mother liked Cuzn. He was her type of guy, a hustler. Cuzn was a winner and everybody loves a winner. I also think he reminded her of the people she was friends with back when she was a hustler.

My mother is a small woman who stands about 5'5" with a petite frame. Her naturally thick black hair is dyed ash blonde. Her parents are from Puerto Rico but my mother was born in The Bronx, as was I. She was the oldest of 3 children. She met her first husband, my "father" when they were in junior high school. He was from Harlem, his name was Kenny and he was the second oldest of six children. His mother, my grandmother was a divorced single mother originally from St. Croix, U.S. Virgin Islands.

My parents separated when I was not even a year old. My

mother didn't wait for my father to get over his broken heart to take care of us. She carried on with me and my older brother Kenny Jr. She did what she had to do to make sure we were okay. Things weren't always good but, she did the best with what she knew and that's all we can expect in life. I appreciate my mother the older I get. The anger I had as a kid flees from me with each advancing year. I don't know if its maturity or Alzheimer's, but I'm good with it either way.

Another thing she didn't wait on was for Kenny Sr. to be a father to me. He had a relationship with Kenny Jr. but he and I never really got along. His Nation of Islam philosophy didn't settle right in my core from the time I was a child. It made him and I bump heads a lot because I was a strong willed child, who questioned what I was being taught.

My mother started dating a man named Legs in 1975. He was a big time drug dealer in Harlem. From the very first day he and I met our bond was forged. They only stayed together for about three years but, when they broke up it was as if my parents had broken up. Legs stayed in my life until he died in 1984 when I was fourteen years old. I was a Daddy's girl and my Daddy was dead. I feel that was the day I went crazy.

While we talked, I got dressed. My mother isn't an emotional mother. She doesn't show affection. That's my aunt Nicki, her younger sister. My mother shows her affection by buying you things. Material is her affection. It was very hard to grow up with that. I'm the opposite.

Her second husband is a great guy named Wayne. He's from the Midwest and we love him. Even though he's my stepdad, I love and respect him as though he were my real father. Wayne is 6'0 white haired man with more style and swagger than any young guy running around. For Father's Day one year my brother, Kenny, and his wife, Chelsea, bought Wayne a gold bracelet that said. "We Love Wayne", can't find guys like Wayne on the earth anymore-they don't make 'em. I'm privileged to have him in my life. He treats me like his daughter. He has since we met.

Wayne's out of town on business, so it's just me and my mother at home alone. We get along but our personalities are so much alike we can't spend too much time alone or we butt heads. That's why I'm bouncing out with SK in a matter of moments.

SK finally arrives and I buzzed him through the gate and front door so he can come up to see my mother before we go. SK and my mother like each other. He's a good guy and a hustler too. He comes in the house, after we hug; he greets my mother with a big hug as well. After a few minutes of them catching up, SK and I head out the door into the streets of Atlanta.

Its mid afternoon and we're hungry. SK decides to head to The SWATS (South West Atlanta Shawty). We go to a restaurant not too far from the Atlanta University Center, where all the Historic Black Colleges are. The restaurant is called Chantrelle's; it's a soul food cafeteria. We grab a chair and it's quite clear that in my absence SK has become a regular customer. As soon as we walked in the door the people who worked there greeted him as an old friend. He even had a specific server whose table we sat at.

While we were eating we got caught up. I've seen SK more recently than any of my other friends from Atlanta because he has an apartment in D.C. He makes frequent trips up there. When he does, he comes to Baltimore to hang out with me. We also speak pretty much every day. SK is how Quid knew I was back in town.

I told him about seeing Cuzn and he told me about the new characters he was meeting in his line of work. SK made fake documents like driver's licenses, birth certificates, tax forms, social security cards and during our meal he tells me he's added liquor permits to his menu.

A liquor permit is an I.D. that stripper's need to have in order to dance in a club. They cost anywhere from $50 to $350 depending on which county a young lady is trying to work in. If a person has a felony record within the last ten years they are ineligible for a liquor permit. That's where SK comes in.

He does quite well for himself in his line of work. He owns a 2001 white Jaguar S-Type 4.0 with cream interior. He owned a few condos and houses in a couple of cities including, Atlanta, D.C., Baltimore and Laurel, MD. He rented all of his properties with the exception of the one in a downtown high rise in Atlanta and another he owned in D.C. on 14th and N St.

SK is a 6'1" tall, brown, 185 lb. man with shoulder length dreads who wears glasses. He teeters on being nerdy and cool, favoring cool. We met some years back through my brother, Kenny's, former sister in law and have been very close friends ever since. When he bought his 1990 Lotus Esprit SE turbo he couldn't wait to drive it over to my house and show it off. I stepped outside my apartment and he was standing next to it grinning from ear to ear. It was all black with a peanut butter interior. It was his baby. The Jaguar was his everyday kick it car.

After we ate we headed back to his apartment to chill out. That's when I noticed I hadn't heard from Antonio all day. It was strange because he called me at the same times every day. I made a mental note of it and rode back downtown with SK.

When we got to his studio apartment I settled to the comfortable ultra-big futon that was in the living room. He pulled out some weed and I began rolling a blunt for us to smoke. SK was a nighthawk. He worked all through the night and was rarely up during the day. He used cocaine to keep him up. Well, he likes cocaine and it kept him up. He had all the equipment he needed to create all of the documents in his living room. It was a work at home business. While I rolled a blunt SK brought out a plate with a straw and razor. While I lit up my masterfully crafted blunt and took the first hit, he lined up his powder and did a line. We chilled and watched CNBC well into the night while he worked on orders for clients.

He dropped me off at my mother's just before 11 that night. I hung out on the couch with my mother until I went to bed.

The next evening Jennie came to pick me up and we headed to the studio to meet Quid and Mel. I still hadn't heard from Antonio but I was having too much fun to make the call up north and check on him.

Jennie and I stopped at the gas station not too far from the studio and loaded up on beer and blunts before reaching our final destination. The studio was in a small town called Douglasville. Neither of us was too thrilled about going down there, especially if we were going to be drinking and smoking. Douglasville, Georgia is a strict redneck county southwest of Atlanta. The only comfort we had about going down there was the fact that the studio was right next to the I-20 exit so we wouldn't be driving on the town's streets for any length of time.

Quid didn't describe the house. He gave us directions and following the directions landed us on a rural dirt road, which freaked Jennie and me out. The only thing we could see were huge houses and road signs that warned us of horses crossing. I called Quid to make sure we were on the right road. He assured us we were. He stayed on the phone with me until we reached the studio. What he neglected to tell us was that the studio was located in the basement of a multi-million dollar mansion at the end of this dirt road. We were pleasantly surprised when we pulled around a dirt corner and there he was standing in front of it.

The house was gorgeous. It looked like a Spanish hacienda you'd see in a movie about a rich old Spanish family. The house was a 5500 square foot home. We pulled into the circular driveway that had a massive fire pit in the middle. The house was the color of dark sand lit by the outside lights. It was dark as hell outside and I couldn't see anything past the house or the fire pit. Quid welcomed us with open arms and after hellos and hugs, we went inside.

Quid, Jennie and I met by chance at a hotel party about 4 years back. He is half Japanese and half black. He stands about 5'11" with a medium to large build with black curly hair, a mustache and copper skin. He's quite handsome if you like that sort of thing. We walk in through a large veranda into an enormous living room that had two huge beige leather couches, a large coffee table and a ladder leading to a library above the room, positioned above a double sliding glass door. We walked through there and into a professional chef's kitchen with all state of the art stainless steel appliances and a marble island in the center that matched the marble countertops. Quid offered us a drink and both Jennie and I raised our arms to show the alcohol we brought with us. He opened one of the doors to the refrigerator and we loaded the beer into it.

"We've been recording here all week." Quid said as we unloaded the bottles. "I can't wait for you to hear what we're working on."

"Whose house is this?" Jennie asked

"It's an investor's." Quid replied.

I was looking around while they were talking. The house was lit by candles and dim lighting. It was really beautiful. After putting the beer away, Quid walked us to a door leading to the basement.

Down in the basement was something you see in movies or documentaries about music. We were looking at a mastering board that stretched clear across the room. Over it was a LCD screen that showed nothing but waves of sounds that had been recorded. At the mastering board sat a young man by the name of Boogie. He was the engineer and he couldn't have been more than 23 years old. He was chocolate brown, with a welcoming smile and a humble energy. He welcomed us and offered us one of the three seats beside him. Mel was leaning on a speaker behind him writing in a notebook and stopped to greet us with hugs and hellos. It was Jennie and Mel's first time meeting. I'd known Mel for over a year. He's 6'2", chocolate brown with a muscular build. He has strong brown eyes and perfect smile.

With all the hugs and hello's out of the way they were eager to let us hear what they were working on. So we sat at the mastering board with Boogie and listened. It was an up-tempo beat with horns and heavy drums anchored by a deep baseline. Jennie and I were grooving while Quid stepped to the speaker Mel had been leaning on with his own notebook and started writing to the music.

After a while of listening it was time to start drinking and I ran upstairs to the kitchen to get us all a beer. When I got back to the basement Mel had poured everybody a shot of tequila from a bottle they had down there. We all toasted my return and the music and commenced to getting fucked up while the music boomed through the studio. After the toast the weed came out and seeing as Mel and I were the only ones who smoked, we headed out to a balcony that overlooked a wooded area, from what I could make out in the dark.

Mel is everyone's big brother, even though he's younger than me. He's very well grounded and he's a very caring person. So when the conversation between us outside lead to my wellbeing I wasn't at all surprised. It was chilly that late night and as we spoke we could see our breath in the air.

"I'm glad you're home J.O. It's good to see you." He started.

"Thank you, Mel. I'm really glad to be back. I'm glad y'all invited us over." I replied.

"How's Baltimore?" He asked

"It's Baltimore." I replied

"You home for good?" He asked

"No. Just here for a minute." I responded

"I know we don't talk about what it is that you do up there and I respect that but, I wouldn't be a friend if I didn't tell you we all would feel a lot better if you came home. There's always safety in numbers Baby Girl and your numbers are in the A." He looked me in the eye as he passed me the blunt.

I didn't say anything and I knew he was right but, I had a mission here and I had to complete it before I returned to Baltimore, being around my friends made me miss home even more. This is what I'm used to. Being with people who are being productive in what they're doing, no matter what it is they're doing. Whether it be music, drugs or working a regular job they were productive. They all could pay their bills and support their families. In Baltimore it wasn't like this. It was poverty. It seemed everyone there was struggling no matter what they did. The differences between the cities was so apparent to me I questioned how I wound up choosing the worse over the better.

After Mel and I smoked the blunt we returned to the studio and kept drinking. After I was really fucked up, Quid convinced me to get in the booth with Jennie and harmonize the hook on the song they were working on. All I have to say is, I have the range of a bullfrog.

Late into the night Jennie and I headed out. I was driving because I was the more sober of the two. We headed to her apartment in Gwinnett County, Ga., which was an hour's drive from Douglasville. We have to travel 30 minutes to Atlanta and then another 30 minutes north to reach her apartment. I was paranoid about driving in "Redneckville" but once we jumped on I-20 W my anxiety subsided.

Jennie and I shared a lot in common. The main thing being we are both mixed. She is half white and half black, stands 5'7 "with an hourglass figure, long sandy brown hair that just barely reaches her waist. She has olive skin and almond shaped eyes. She has supple lips and without a doubt she's a head turner. She can make a pretty woman feel like an ugly bitch just by walking in a room.

On the drive to her house we caught up on what was going on in Baltimore. Jennie is the only one of my friends that knows the whole story. I tell Jennie everything and she holds back on me. It's always been that way and I wouldn't expect anything different. She's more guarded than I am. I think it has to do with the fact that she's adopted. She has deep rooted issues about it. It manifests in her relationships with people. Jennie always thought she was put up for adoption because she was half black. Her adoptive parents are white; throughout her life she has battled her own demons on the issue. I can't say that I understand her plight. I appreciate the fact that she tells me the truth no matter what. In return, I do the same. We give each other the space to be ourselves. Jennie's distant, that's just her. But, no matter what, when I need her she's always been there for me. I can't ask for anything more.

Jennie and I met about 15 years ago when we were both bartending in a chain of strip joints in Atlanta. We became fast friends and never looked back. She's a real estate agent now and I'm, well I'm me. Once we make it in the apartment around 4am. I throw myself on her cream colored sectional and pass out grateful that we made it there safely, without being stopped. Gwinnett County is no less strict than Douglasville but only half as redneck.

The next day I woke up in my clothes around 10 am. Jennie was in the kitchen on the phone with a client. I went to the guest bathroom of her two bedroom apartment and jumped in the shower. When I came out of the shower, I left the bathroom wearing a towel. I walked through the living room to hear Jennie still on the phone. I went across the living room without saying anything to her, into her bedroom. She had a large room with a walk in closet, master bathroom with a garden tub and a stand up shower. I walked in her bathroom, grabbed her toothbrush and toothpaste and brushed my teeth. Then I walked into her closet, picked out a pair of jeans, a sweater and put it on. I made sure to match the jeans and sweater to the black Nike boots I was wearing. I found a pair of socks in one of the drawers of her dresser; I took them and walked into the living room, plopped down on the couch while Jennie was still on the phone in the kitchen. I turned on the TV with the remote. I was putting on her socks when she walked in the living room ending her call and took a look at me.

"Glad you picked those jeans, I was gonna wear them today."

She said.

"I don't think you want to wear them now, I'm not wearing any draws." I replied.

She scrunched her face up and said, "Niiiice."

"You're welcome." I responded with a smile as I put the last sock on.

Jennie walked into her bedroom, I heard the shower turn on and I put my feet on the coffee table and watched TV while she got dressed and ready to go.

I remembered I needed to find out why I hadn't heard from Antonio. While Jennie showered, I decided to call the number in Baltimore that the calls were transferred from. It just rang, that meant the calls weren't transferred. I was pissed. I called Stan's number, didn't get an answer. Of course I didn't, it was too early and he was probably asleep. I then called my mother to let her know I'd spent the night at Jennie's and started watching TV again. Cheater's was on.

About 15 minutes passed when I heard Jennie yell from the bathroom, "Did you use my toothbrush?"

"Yeah, I did and you wouldn't have known that had you used it before me." I replied

"I didn't know we were that close." She yelled back.

"It was either that or you'd be trapped in the car with me without me using it." I yelled back

"You have a point there." She said as she walked into the living room dressed in a pair of jeans and a v- neck gray sweater.

We did our last little bit of getting it together before we headed out the door. Food was the plan. We jumped on Hwy 316 headed to 85S going back into Atlanta.

It was early afternoon and we decided to eat by Lenox Mall in Buckhead. We chose Roaster's, the best rotisserie chicken in Atlanta. After that we'd go hang out with my mother for a little while. My mother looked at Jennie as a second daughter. We hung out with The Carmen until I got a call from Cuzn. He wanted to see me. He said he had a "picture" to give me so I could start work. A "picture" meant he was going to give me a sample of weed. We agreed to meet at a fast food parking lot in Decatur Ga. About a 15 minute drive from downtown Atlanta.

I had to make sure it was alright with Jennie first. One: she didn't like Cuzn. Two: she wasn't into illegal activity. She agreed to take me so long as it wasn't anything crazy. We left my mother's to head out to Decatur. As usual, we were there first. While we waited we listened to the radio and talked about how much she hated Cuzn.

When he finally arrived I exited Jennie's car and got into his. He was in a 2003 Black Mercedes S-550 coupe it took me by surprise because he never drove around in cars that were so flashy. I got in and sunk into the butter pecan leather interior. I immediately was overcome with the smell of marijuana. Good marijuana.

"What's up?" He greeted me as I closed the door.

"Shit, what's up with you, is the question?" I asked as I looked around the car even into the back seat.

"Just something I wanted for myself." He said with a grin.

It was strange and a little troubling to see Cuzn in such an expensive and noticeable car. The concept being, we've had such a good run selling weed because we've kept a very low profile.

"So, are you ready?" he asked. I nodded.

"I'm going to give you 2 different pictures to get you started. It's all you after that." He said as he reached under the passenger's seat from behind me. He pulled out a grocery bag that was tied at the top. He handed me the bag. When I looked in, I saw two different bags, a small Ziploc sandwich bag and a one gallon bag. I could tell I was looking at a pound and half ounce of two different types of weed. He began to explain.

"The pound is a high mid. That's what you smoked with Sheree the other day. The other is a hybrid of mid and blueberry Cush. See what your people think about that and get back to me. I'm testing it out to see if we need to start dealing with it on a heavy basis. The mid is what you can go crazy with though."

They both looked great. I knew I wouldn't have a problem getting rid of the mid but the hybrid was new to me. The word hybrid alone, said I'd have to do some major talking and educating to get it sold. Cuzn asked me if I had any money. As always I told him "No", he then handed me $500 and kicked me out of his car. I put the weed in my purse before I got out and headed back to the other side of the parking lot where Jennie was parked. I could smell the weed in my purse through the winter night and I knew that was going to cause me a problem as soon as I got into the car with Jennie.

I jumped in the car with her and tried to play it off as if it didn't reek. It didn't work. As soon as I closed the door she jumped and looked at me as if I was crazy. "Are you fucking kidding me?!" She yelled. "That shit stinks from here to high heaven!"

"I know." I said sheepishly.

"I thought he was giving you a picture?" That shit smells like 20 pounds!"

"I didn't think he was giving me a pound." I said in my own defense.

"Oh, hell no, I can't be driving around with that much weed in my car. Anything can happen. If we got stopped for anything we'd be telling on ourselves. Getting arrested, I can't take that chance. Oh, no."

One thing about Jennie, she didn't bend on things like this. I knew there was no arguing with her. I also knew I had over a pound of weed on me and I didn't have a car. If she left me I'd be stranded in Decatur with weed, no ride and the possibility of getting into some serious trouble. I stepped out of the car to make a phone call. It was dark. The streets were bustling with cars going up and down the streets with people on their way home from work. I called SK and hoped he was awake. As the phone rang I prayed he would answer and he did. Thank Goodness.

'Hey, you!" He answered with his usual smiling voice.

"SK, I need you" I said with calm urgency.

"Okay, what's going on?" He asked noticing the stress in my voice.

I ran down the situation to him and he was on his way. "I'll be there in 20 minutes, Sweetheart, don't stress." We hung up the phone.

I turned my focus to Jennie and saw that she had worked herself into frenzy. I told her SK was on his way. Without saying a word she pulled off. I could've sworn I heard her tires screeching as she pulled out of the parking lot.

You Smell Wonderful My Dear

It was cold and I wanted to go inside the restaurant but, I couldn't. The smell of the weed was way too strong for me to be inside of any place that wasn't private. I was cold, it was dark. I was praying that one of DeKalb County's Finest didn't pull up to me, standing in the parking lot and start asking me a bunch of questions. SK is a slow mover so, I knew I would be out there for at least 45 minutes, I was dreading it. I was relieved, happy and surprised when he pulled in, on time. The sight of that white Jaguar pulling into the parking lot was like seeing my knight in shining armor.

I jumped in the car as soon as he pulled up, from both relief and cold. As soon as I closed the door, he looked at me and with a big smile and said, "You smell wonderful, my dear." His car now reeked of the goodness. He liked it though. We jumped on I-20W and went straight back downtown to his apartment. Riding in the elevator up to his place on the 9th floor I hoped no one got in with us. My prayers were answered and we made it into his apartment safe and sound.

As soon as we got in I plopped down on the futon, opened up my purse and took the weed out to give it a good look. It was pretty, both bags. The small bag was green buds with blue coursing through out it. The pound looked like light green Christmas trees, all through the entire bag. I knew I had a winner. I show all of it to SK, he agreed. To celebrate our safe arrival home, I took some of the weed out of the blueberry hybrid and rolled us a blunt to smoke.

The pull was thick and smooth tasting like blueberries. I liked it and so did SK. I sunk further into the couch as the high settled in. I began to put the stress of earlier behind me.

With my high settling in nicely, I called the number in Baltimore that the calls were transferred to again. This time, someone picked up the phone. It was Sarah, the dope fiend Darryl Hannah.

"Sarah, this is J.O." I said

"Hi, J.O. how are you Honey?" she replied.

"I'm good. Why are you answering the phone?" I asked.

"I don't get what you mean?" she asked.

"This call is supposed to be transferred to my phone. Why isn't it transferred and why are you answering it?" I was pissed.

"J.O., my boyfriend got locked up and he calls on this line."

"I don't give a fuck where your boyfriend is. Transfer the fucking calls back and keep them transferred Sarah." I snapped at her in a low voice.

"J.O., Antonio has been calling and I'll 3way you to him when he calls again if you give me your number but I have to talk to Randy when he calls." She pleaded.

"Where's Stan?" I asked her.

"He's not here. He went to see his mother a couple of days ago. He's supposed to be back tonight." She answered.

"What time?" I asked, wishing I could reach through the phone to choke her ass out.

"I don't know. We're waiting on him to come in now." She replied and it sounded like fear in her voice. It wasn't enough fear to get her to transfer the calls back though. I hung up on her.

I went back to my high on the futon. SK asked me what my plans were with the weed.

"Sell it" I replied.

"I know that but, do you have it already sold or are you about to put the word out?" He asked.

"I can't sell anything I don't have. So, now that I have it. I'm about to put the word out. Why do you ask?"

"I have a friend I want you to meet." He said. I gave him a

straight faced look and he knew what I meant.

"He's cool. You don't have to worry about any funny business. I give you my word." He said knowing why I looked at him like that.

"Who is it?" I asked.

"His name is Black. I do some paperwork for him from time to time. But, his real line of work is what you do. If you meet him and you guys work together, I'll be responsible if he winds up owing you anything." With that I agreed to meet Black. SK called him to see if he could come over and Black was on his way.

I made a few of my own calls to guys that I did business with before I moved to Baltimore. They were all glad to hear from me. They were really glad to know I was back in town and working. It meant money for all who could pay my below market price. The benefit to being on Cuzn's team is, we made the price for weed in Atlanta. For example, if the market held a price of $1500 a pound, my price would be $1200 and Cuzn would get $900 of that. It was all money. Cuzn taught me that I could make cocaine money from weed. I was hooked ever since. When I couldn't sell weed, I sold heroin and the only place I felt "safe" doing that was in Baltimore.

Black arrived at SK's about an hour or two later. He was a tall dark skinned man, with short dreads with a mustache and full beard. With all the facial hair he looked to be in his mid-thirties but, his soft brown eyes told the tale of him being more along the age of mid-twenties. SK made the introductions; Black took a seat next to me on the futon. SK took his usual spot at his desk and went back to work.

Black and I started to chit chat, trying to get a feel for one another. After we'd felt each other out the conversation turned to weed.

Black spoke with a smile when he said, "So, I hear from my man you've got a good situation going on." He was rubbing his hand together. I laughed and asked him if he'd like to see it. He did, of course.

"I don't have to wait to open the bag to see what it smells like. I could do that by sitting next to you," He was laughing. I laughed because he had no idea what I just went through about the smell of the weed.

I didn't have to do any selling with this weed, it sold itself. It was a high quality mid-level weed. It was grown anywhere in either, California, Mexico or Arizona.

The levels consist of Low level, which is a brown, dirt like weed that has a lot of seeds, stems, almost no moisture if any and very little high. It has given me headaches. I won't smoke it.

Mid-level is what a lot of people call Arizona. Maybe because a lot of it is coming through Arizona, I don't know. It has 3 different types all being green. The darker the color green, the lower the level, it usually has more seeds. The brighter the green, the more expensive it is and the fewer seeds it has. The smell usually correlates with the color. The darker the less smell. If you get a dark green with a strong smell then you can get the same amount as a second level mid. The new thing is smell. Everyone wants strong odor.

The most expensive weed is Exotic. That's weed grown in Northern California, the weed grown with love. They have names like, Jack's Cleaner, Super Skunk, Headband, Cheese, Northern Lights, Lemon Freeze and my personal favorite, Nepal. You won't find a seed in any of it. I don't care if you buy a hundred pounds. The seeds are too valuable.

The blueberry hybrid is someone who crossed a high mid with blueberry Cush. I knew I had my work cut out for me with that one. The latest craze in weed is the exotics. A hybrid was just a fake version of that. It was clearly a strand of mid but it was blue and it reeked of blueberry. It had its selling points and it smoked well but it wasn't an exotic. I've decided to focus my energy on the mid.

Black asked me how much I wanted for a pound. I gave him my

price and let him know that price was for one or a hundred. The price was so low that there was no need to give discounted prices on bulk orders. I had bulk prices already. He told me to give him a minute and asked SK if it was alright if he stepped outside the apartment for a minute. SK said it was cool and Black walked out into the hallway. I assumed to make a phone call. He was gone for about 10 minutes when he knocked on the door and SK let him back in. Black sat down on the couch and pulled out a small wad of money. He counted out what I needed for the pound. Business was done for the night. It wasn't even 9:30 pm.

I called Stan later on and he answered the phone. I asked what was going on with the phone. He sounded a little defenseless and really not worried about it. So I decided to give him a reason to feel empowered and defensive about it.

"Stan, if I give you $150 will you transfer the calls back and make sure no one uses that line again?" I asked him. He was flustered by the amount. $150 to a junkie is a whole hell of a lot of money and if Stan had ever had that much money in his hand at one time it wasn't in the last decade. I'd put money on that.

He was stuttering and you could hear the smile on his face as he responded to my proposal.

"Uh, uh, yeah, J.O., I could do that, uh. How you gonna send the money?"

"I'll send it western union Stan. BUT, if I send you $150 and I have a problem with that phone again Stan, I'm going to feel like I'm wasting my money and I don't like to waste my money. Do we have an agreement Stan?"

"Yes, we have an agreement J.O. You won't be wasting your money. I promise you I'll take care of it. When are you gonna send it?" I could hear Stan's mouth starting to water over the phone. It was like playing with a little kid. Telling them you're going to take them out for ice cream.

I got all Stan's information I would need for the wiring. Before we got off the phone, I told him I wanted the calls transferred back to my phone immediately. He did it while we were on the phone. I just clicked over from the line we were on to the other line and that was all. I used SK's car to go to Western Union to send him the money.

No later than 10 minutes after Stan sent the calls back to my phone Antonio called. He was just as surprised to hear my voice when I answered as I was to hear his. We talked the entire time I was driving to wire the money and all the way back to SK's house. We caught up on everything that was going on in Atlanta. He needed money of course. I told him I'd take care of it the next day. We spoke until he had to lockdown for the night.

When I got off the phone with Antonio, I made two other calls, both to Baltimore. The first was to Stan to let him know I'd sent the money; the second was to one of the guys from Pigtown, named Quick, one of the many guys around the neighborhood that always let me know that if I needed them to handle something in Antonio's absence he would take care of it. Everyone loved Antonio and wanted him to know they were holding him down as best they could.

I told Quick I needed him to go into Stan's house for me and lay the law down about the phone. He didn't mind at all. He rather enjoyed the opportunity. Quick was a young wild "Hopper" as they are called in Baltimore. That's a young guy who is trying to make his name in the streets. Quick went into Stan's house, told all of the hangers on that if the phone was un-transferred again he would come back and beat the shit out of whoever did it and who they were fucking. That pretty much put everyone in the house in a pickle. I didn't have another problem with the phone. Stan was so elated to pick that money up that he called me just to chit chat from then on. I guess that made us friends.

With money coming in I felt less stress. The world was feeling a lot kinder to me than it had been over the eleven months since, I'd moved to Baltimore. I felt good.

The next day I went shopping for some clothes so I didn't have to keep going in and out of my mother's house, risking her asking a whole bunch of questions. She knew I was doing something, she just didn't know the details. That evening Cuzn had me meet Sheree to get more weed and give her the money I had from the first pound.

We met in a gas station in the Hightower area of Atlanta. We chit chatted for a moment and then made the exchange. We were sitting in her SUV when I gave her the money. She popped the trunk so we got out. I saw a huge black duffle bag and I grabbed it. I threw it into the trunk of SK's Jaguar and we said our goodbyes.

On the way back to SK's I made a phone call to a friend of mine named Scar who I worked with before I move. I let him know I was up and running. He needed ten pounds.

I went to SK's, took inventory of the black bag. I had fifteen individually packaged pounds. I took ten out, put them into another duffle bag SK gave me and went to Scar's house. I was back within an hour chilling on the futon, while SK did his paperwork. This time we watched the History channel and smoked another blunt. At that time, I had a little over three thousand dollars. It would've been more but I sent Antonio enough money to keep him cool for a few weeks and I bought clothes.

Black called me about 11 pm, asked if I was over at SK's? He showed up about an hour later, needing five pounds. Once again, I was done with work before the sun rose. I separated Cuzn's money from mine and called him to let him know I was done.

Long Nights

Normally, when I fell asleep on the futon, SK was up working. When I woke up, he was asleep. He didn't wake up until around two in the afternoon or so. He gave me full access to his car. So, if I needed to go somewhere while he was asleep or working, it was no problem. This made my life very easy. He had his own money so; anything I did for him was a gift and not a requirement. I appreciated everything he was doing for me. I tried to show it in ways that didn't necessarily mean money. I kept his house in order and kept him company. He was kind of a loner. In his line of work, he spent plenty of time alone. We would sit up and talk about everything under the sun.

Christmas was that week and that meant we were going to change things up a little. Cuzn has children; he was going to spend time with them. He'd leave me with enough work but, if I ran out or had a larger order, I'd have to meet one of the other members of the team. I preferred dealing directly with Cuzn.

Since work would be slowing down, I flew my daughter, Buttah in from Texas for the holidays. We stayed out at Jennie's house with her and her daughter Sidney, who was five years old. Buttah was twelve; I hadn't seen her since I moved to Baltimore. I usually had her for the summers and all school breaks but Baltimore was not the place to bring her. I was busy doing wild things to get him out of jail. I couldn't have my daughter running around the neighborhood while I was selling heroin on the corner. So last summer she spent in Atlanta with my brother Kenny, his wife and two daughters from his first marriage.

Antonio had received a court date; the trial is set for February. The lawyer he told me to hire, Mr. Davis, wasn't doing anything. Antonio was on pins and needles. I tried to talk to him about hiring Renee but, he was still blaming her for him not receiving a bond. No matter what I said he wasn't interested in her representing him. It really angered me.

I was paying for this. I should be able to pay who I wanted. I had already wasted a thousand dollars on Davis. I wasn't pleased at all about it. Antonio talked about a big time lawyer who defended one of his cousins in the past. His name was, Kevin Chase. He was the drug dealer's lawyer. All the big dope boys used him. I called him, told him about Antonio's case. He agreed to represent him for the fee of $18,000. I agreed. We made arrangements to mail him his retainer of $9,000 within a week.

Christmas was over. Although, I spent a good chunk of money on presents for my family and a spring wardrobe for Buttah, I still had money and I was still making more daily. I didn't have the full $9,000 but, I knew I would have it in a matter of days.

Black called me and wanted to meet for a bite to eat. He wanted to talk business. We met in a midtown restaurant called Murphy's in Virginia- Highlands. Black sat across from me. He told me he had a sale for fifteen pounds He asked if I would let him take the weed into North Georgia and bring me the money back. "Absolutely not" was the answer.

"I'll go with you. We can do it together." I said. He was hesitant but knew it was the only way he was going to get the sale. We were going to leave the next evening. He said it was an hour's drive from Atlanta.

Time Is Ticking

Scar was calling me nonstop. I would see him sometimes 3 or 4 times in a day, two pounds here, four pounds there. I wasn't mad at all. The money was flowing in. The plan to make sure Antonio had proper representation was well on its way to happening.

The night before Black and I headed up north, SK and I were chilling at his crib when Quid called him to see what we were doing. He said he was on his way and he had a friend with him, a rapper. It was about midnight when they arrived. SK and I were in the media room of his building, faxing some paperwork off to one of his clients. I went to let them into the building from the garage where he parked. I was happy to see him. We hadn't seen each other since the studio. I gave him a hug as he and his rapper friend walked through the door I held open. He introduced me to the rapper. He was from the Carolina's and had a hit or two in his career. We walked to the media room to meet up with SK and then headed back to the apartment. On the way up in the elevator I looked at Quid and said,

"SK heard from your girl Stephanie." Quid shot me a "fuck you" look. SK broke out into a huge grin holding back his laugh.

"Who, the fuck is Stephanie?" Quid asked lying through his teeth.

I ignored his attempt to not know Stephanie and said,

"Yeah, she wanted your number." The rapper is lost in all of this and SK is rocking back and forth holding in his laughter. We arrive on the floor and keep talking into the apartment. Once again, I ignore his attempt to not know Stephanie.

"She said she really needs to talk with you about soooomething" I said throwing my hands up as if to question what that could be.

"I think she misses you. SK has her number for you. You want I should put it in your phone?" I said batting my eyes with a girly smile on my face. SK has now started laughing.

"Shiiiiiiit, Fuck That!!!" Quid says in disgust.

I'm laughing, SK's laughing, Quid has a look on his face like he just ate a bug and the rapper is lost. I look at him and explain,

"Stephanie is a girl who tried to talk to SK."

"Oh, okay." He replies nodding his head. I continue,

"She also tried to talk to Quid."

"Oh I know that kind." Carolina said

"And she tried to talk to me." I shot back.

"Oh damn, okay THAT girl." Carolina said.

"Yeah, but I think Quid wanted to wife her." I said looking at Quid.

We all burst into laughter except Quid. He couldn't stand Stephanie and the three of us knew the mention of her name made Quid's blood boil. She was a toss around. They both tossed her around and then tossed her out. Quid has yet to admit that he and Stephanie had a thing to me.

For some reason, before I moved to Baltimore I got a call from Stephanie telling me she had just left a day's long fling with Quid. She was really feeling him. She then asked me to leave him alone so she could have him.

"J.O., I'm really feeling him and I need you to step back so I can get this to work."

The funny part about this conversation is that I had NO involvement with Quid in anything other than a friendship. I've known Quid for a long time and we've never even kissed. I didn't let on to Stephanie about that little fact, I was kind of enjoying listening to her sound like an idiot. I just let her talk and listened.

"J.O., I was with him when you called and y'all were talking about going to Jamaica. He told me you were going to pay for his trip. You shouldn't be paying for no nigga. I'm really feeling him and I need for you to not go anywhere with him and give me the space I need to get this nigga in my corner."

I was listening, not understanding why she was telling me this. This was the first time I was hearing they even knew each other outside of seeing each other when they were with me. I wasn't going to let her know that though. I told Quid I'd pay for the plane tickets to Jamaica but I was doing it for SK too. We were all going and I had the money to buy them when I saw them on sale. Everybody, I was paying for was returning my money. I wasn't going to explain this to her though. I just listened.

"I know you ain't feeling me like I was feeling you. So, I found someone who I think is feeling me. So that's why I'm asking you to leave him alone? I respected your wishes and backed off from you. I need you to do this for me? Please?" I told her I'd call her back, hung up and called Quid.

"Yo!!!!!! What's up witcha?" He asked answering the phone.

"I thought we were friends?" I asked. He heard the tone in my voice and settled down on the phone.

"I am your friend. Are you saying you ain't mines?" He asked seriously.

"No, that's not what I'm saying." I responded

"Then what are you saying?" He questioned

"If we're friends then why am I getting phone calls about things pertaining to you that I don't know about?"

"That's a very good question J.O. Somebody called you about something you have no idea about, I can empathize with your frustration. I recently found myself in the same predicament," he said. I caught his meaning.

"I just got a strange call from Stephanie."

"Who?" He asked

"Stephanie." I repeated.

"Who, the fuck is Stephanie?" He asked (I'm getting confused about now.)

"Stephanie, the tall leggy brown girl, Stephanie." I explained

"The chick with the short ass ponytail?" He asked growing

impatient.

"Yes her, she just called me talking about you?" I told him

"What the fuck she call you about me fuh?" He snapped

"She said you too just spent 4 days laid up and she wants me to back off of you so she can have you?"

"WHAT?" He yelled

"You heard me." I said

"She said what? You tell her Quid Pro Quo said she's a mothuh fuckin' liar and I don't know her." He was heated. I'd never heard him so angry.

"You're telling me she lying?" I was shocked but, didn't want to seem all into it.

"You're fucking right! I don't know her." He was still angry.

I hung up the phone and called Stephanie back and told her verbatim what he said, she burst into tears on the phone. She couldn't believe he would deny her. I was confused as hell and removed myself from the situation all together. I got a good laugh off of it then and I get a good chuckle whenever the opportunity presents itself.

Carolina asked SK if he had a phone charger he could use. SK showed Carolina the charger in the kitchen and he plugged his phone in. I sat on the futon and lit up a blunt I had already rolled. The four of us were kicking it for a while when Carolina turned to me and said,

"Who do you belong to?" What the fuck did that mean? I thought. I was taken off guard by it.

"What?" I asked. He took a seat beside me on the futon, I offered him my blunt.

"No thank you, Ma I don't smoke." He said then he continued

"Who is your man? Who do you belong to? You can't be on your own?" This must be some Carolina shit I thought.

I played along for the high of it. "His name is Antonio." I replied

"Where is he?" He asked

"He's indisposed at the moment." I said

"What does that mean?" Carolina asked

"He's a guest of the county." He knew what I meant.

"Oh, I *'m* sorry to hear that Ma."

Quid and SK were doing lines off the kitchen counter. All of a sudden, Quid focused his attention on Carolina and me. He came over and broke up the conversation, which I was glad for.

"Hey man, we've gotta get out of here. We've got to get to the club." He said to Carolina but, looking at me.

"We're cool man." Carolina replied

"Man, I've got some girls meeting us at the club. We've got to go." Quid insisted still looking at me. Carolina looked at me and said,

"I'm cool right here."

Quid and I looked at each other, as he continued to insist they head out to the club. Carolina then asked if I wanted to go to the club. I told him I didn't have I.D., so I couldn't go. It was a lie. I just didn't want to go. I had been up all day. I really just wanted to pass out.

"Ma, I'm not trying to be conceited. But, in my line of work, when I go to a club you don't need I.D. No one does. We just walk in the club. We don't even go through security checks." I knew this was supposed to impress me but it really just turned me off. Once again I declined his offer.

Quid kept stressing leaving. Carolina finally got off the couch and stood with SK and Quid at the kitchen counter, while Quid said his goodbyes to SK. I sunk into the futon feeling my high. Carolina focused his attention back on me. He asked if he could speak to me privately in the bathroom for a moment. I reluctantly agreed so we stepped into the bathroom away from SK and Quid closing the door behind us.

Carolina was leaning on the bathroom sink and I was leaning on the wall facing him when he started talking.

"Look, I like your style. You're not dressed provocatively and you look me in the eye when you talk to me. I like that. I know you know me and I'm diggin' you. I know you hook these guys up with girls and whatever but, I'm trying to hook up with you. Can we get together, Ma?"

I took one look at him and was unimpressed. I was now irritated and didn't want to be in the bathroom. I couldn't wait to get out of there.

"First of all, I don't know you. I know of you. There's a difference. Second of all, I'm wearing jeans and a sweater because it's comfortable and I don't need to show skin to get attention. As for you thinking that I hook them up with 'girls or whatever' I don't. They can do that on their own. They don't need my help in that field and we don't get down like that."

"I apologize if I offended you and thought the wrong thing but, I'd still like to spend some time with you." He replied with a slight smile revealing a gold grill. "Can I at least have your number?" That much I agreed to. We swapped numbers and left the bathroom. He and Quid left right after that.

SK went back to work. I fell asleep after putting on my pajamas. About an hour or so later I heard my phone ringing. I ignored it, but whoever it was kept calling back. I got up to see who it was. It was about 4 am. It was Quid, I answered the phone but it was Carolina on the phone. He told me he was back in the parking deck of SK's building. He'd left his phone on the charger. He wanted me to bring it down to him. I wasn't interested so, I asked SK to bring it down instead. When SK came back in the house he was laughing which, caught my attention. I asked him what was so funny. "When ya boy saw me and not you, he looked real disappointed." I rolled over to go back to sleep when my phone rang again. This time it was Carolina's number coming through.

"Hey, I'm in the parking deck. Would you come down and talk

to me for a minute? I really want to talk to you." He said

"I'm really tired. I didn't even go home because I'm too tired." I lied. "Can we meet tomorrow and talk?" I asked.

"I'm leaving town tomorrow, so can we talk for just a little while tonight? I promise I won't keep you up long. I promise." He said. Reluctantly, I agreed. SK found the whole thing funny and laughed at me as I walked out of the door. I'd thrown my clothes back on and grabbed the keys SK had given me to his house. I asked SK what type of car he was in so I'd know what to look for when I got down there.

"He's in a big blue jacked up Chevy Silverado. He's on the bottom deck by the exit. You can't miss it. Take the garage elevator down to the bottom floor and he'll be right there when you come off. He couldn't drive it up any higher or he would've fucked the top of his truck up."

I have to admit that I was intrigued with him. He was a rapper and I wanted to see what all the fuss was about. I had no intention of doing anything but the attention was welcomed.

Sure enough, when I stepped off the garage elevator there he was in his Carolina blue Chevy Silverado.

I climbed into the truck and gave him a 'what the fuck do you want?' look. He's smiling at me with a mouth full of gold teeth, top and bottom.

"I'm glad you came down. Thank you." He said

"Okay, you've got me down here. What's up?" I asked

"We went to the club and I couldn't stop thinking about you. Look, I'm staying in a hotel not too far from here. Can we go there and talk? I promise I won't try anything and as soon as you want to leave I'll bring you right back. No questions asked. I give you my word."

I was a little curious and he didn't seem like a bad dude.

"Right around the corner where?" I asked. He seemed pleased I was even entertaining him.

"Right, around the, corner. I don't know the street name but I know where it is. It's not too far from here." I admit I was curious to see what this was all about and I agreed to go with him. He slowly pulled out of the tight parking lot and I asked him,

"Do you go muddin' in this thing?" he looked at me as if I was crazy. I qualified my question.

"A friend of mine has one of these and he only bought it, so he could go muddin' in it." I was talking about Cuzn.

"No, I don't." He answered amused by me.

"Where are you from?" He asked

"I'm originally from New York but, I've been here most of my life." I answered.

"Where do you live?" He asked as we pulled out of the garage and onto the street driving toward midtown.

"I live between here and Baltimore." I answered. He gave me a look I couldn't pick up on.

The rest of the way we chit chatted as he drove and pulled up to a hotel in Midtown on 10th and Peachtree Street. Once up in his room he was a perfect gentleman. He was charming and funny. We were sitting on his bed with only the TV as light when he told me the entire time he and Quid were in the club he kept asking Quid questions about me. He said he must've gotten on Quid's nerves because at one point Quid looked at him and said,

"Nigga, that's J.O. You don't run through J.O. You just don't do it." 'That's my boy!' I thought. I lay on the bed while he was talking. He asked me if he could lay his head on my stomach while we talked. I looked at him like he was crazy. He assured me he wouldn't try anything. Don't ask me why but, I believed him. I hadn't been physically close to a man since Father's Day. I was willing to let him lay his head on me for the comfort of it

He kept his word and only laid his head on me. The next thing I knew it was morning, I woke up fully dressed with him spooning me, also fully dressed. I looked at the time. I had to leave before

Antonio called. While he was still asleep, I quietly put my boots on and headed out the door. I caught a cab back to SK's house.

That night, Black and I headed out to North Georgia to conduct our business. I was nervous because I was out of my comfort zone. I don't like leaving Atlanta to do anything illegal in "Georgia". The city of Atlanta, Fulton County is my safety zone. I know if I get arrested for anything I can get a low bond. Outside of that area I'm going to get a high bond and jail time. We were on our way to the sticks. I wasn't feeling it. I wanted to hurry up and get home.

We arrived about 7pm and it was dark. Black made a call to his client, to let them know we were in the area. We went to an Italian Restaurant for dinner while we waited. We talked during dinner it was a distraction for my nerves.

"So, do you have a man?" Black asked while we waited on our food.

I knew where this was going. When I initially meet men for business, they want to know if I'm fucking. I figured I'd nip this in the bud.

"You ever see a Ken doll naked?" I looked Black in the eye and asked.

"Huh?" He asked confused

"A Ken doll? You know, Barbie and Ken?" I explained

"Oh. Yeah why?" he asked smiling through his confusion.

"You know how a when you take all the clothes off of a Ken doll, he only has a triangle hump where his privates should be?" Black laughed and nodded to my question as I continued my point.

"Well, that's how I look at the guys I do business with. You're all Ken dolls. Feel me?" Once we finished eating Black made another call and we went to meet them.

I was still nervous. I thought we were going to meet his clients as soon as we got there. I played it cool though. We pulled onto a very dark back road. I almost pissed myself. I could be killed out here and no one would know. We had a gang of weed on us, on a road that didn't even have streetlights.

"What the hell?!" I said. Black laughed and assured me we were okay.

"This is where I meet them every time. How else would I know where this desolate motherfucker is?"

His words did little to comfort me. I couldn't see shit the headlights weren't shining on. We finally came to a stop somewhere in all that darkness. Black pulled in backward so we could see any approaching cars.

After about fifteen minutes of waiting another car came up beside us. Black got out with the weed. I saw a white woman and man in the car, when the headlights shined in the car as it approached us. The transaction took all of 90 seconds. Black was back in the car with a green plastic bag in his hand. He placed between his seat and the door. We pulled off, heading to the expressway.

Once we were on the expressway, well on our way back to Atlanta. Black reached into the bag, pulled out his money. Without letting me see what he pulled out, he handed me the bag. Inside were stacks of money, in what appeared to be separated into thousand dollar stacks. Each stack had a rubber band around it. I counted each rubber band and it equaled what I should've had. We were back in Atlanta before 10 pm. Black dropped me off at SK's. I went upstairs, counted the money and separated Cuzn's from mine. SK was watching me count all this money and said to me,

"You think Cuzn would let me get in on the action?" I was taken aback by the question because I never knew SK to sell drugs.

"I don't see why he wouldn't but, you'd have to ask him." I replied

"Can you ask him for me?" He asked

"No, but I can set up a meeting so you can."

I called Cuzn to meet with him to give him his money. I told him SK wanted to talk to him. He wanted to know what it was about. I told him he'd have to wait to talk with SK. We agreed to meet at Intermezzo in Buckhead later that night.

SK and I arrived at the restaurant about midnight and to my surprise Cuzn was already there. It may have had something to do with the large amount of money I had for him. We sat at the table with him Dougie Chin Chow and a young lady I didn't know. We all greeted each other. SK sat down at the table between Cuzn and me. They caught up with each other for a moment. Then Cuzn asked what SK wanted to talk to him about? I left the table to go look at the dessert display case. I needed to choose what I type of cheesecake I wanted. After I had placed my dessert order at the display case, I returned to the table and found Cuzn was waiting on me. I could tell by the look he was giving me as I walked back to the table. I sat down next to him as SK moved where I was sitting. He asked me if I knew what SK wanted from him.

"Yeah, I know." I replied

"Do you have anything to say about it?" he asked.

"No, it's none of my business." I said. I knew Cuzn was being my teacher again.

"You don't feel you need a tax in this situation? He asked me looking me right in the eye.

"I don't feel I do." I said

"You're bringing him to me for business. That's usually means you'd tax a person." He said showing me how to do business.

"He brought me to you in the first place, remember? He didn't get a tax off me for doing that. So, I don't feel I need one for bringing him to a person he already knows." Cuzn was frustrated with my point but didn't argue it.

"You're responsible for him." He said

"I am." I agreed. The conversation was over. SK would sell weed and Cuzn would give it to me. SK would have to deal through me and I wouldn't receive any money from his sales. If SK fucked up a package, that would be my responsibility too. I was cool with that. Cuzn wasn't.

The next day I woke up in the afternoon. SK woke up a short time later. We got up and went to get something to eat. SK had to meet a client, give them the paper work he'd done for them and get the remainder of the balance he was owed.

Cuzn called on our way back to the apartment. He wanted to meet in Decatur again. I was re-upping on work. SK let me use the car. I went to the designated gas station where Dougie Chin Chow met me. He had me follow him to a motel, a couple of streetlights away from the gas station

When I pulled up, I saw Cuzn in the passenger seat of an SUV. His partner Dex was in the driver's seat, parked in the lot of the motel. I parked a few cars away, as did Dougie Chin Chow. I walked over to where they were parked. I had on jeans, a sweater, a leather jacket and a pair of high heeled leather boots. Dougie made it over to the car with them before I did. I said hello to Dex as I walked up. They were parked backward and Dex was the closest to me. From the passenger's side Cuzn yelled for me to get my work out of the trunk of the SUV as he popped it open from inside the car.

I walked to the back of the car. Looking around first, to make sure no one was approaching or looking at what I was doing. In the trunk was a large block of marijuana, almost the size of the trunk itself. A BIG smile came across my face as I lifted it out of the trunk. It was a struggle. This thing was the size of a cello. It's covered in two large black trash bags on both ends that were taped together in the middle. There was no smell. I knew by the shape of it the weed was compressed and was still in its shipping package.

As I'm carrying this monstrosity in a bear hug to SK's car in heels, the three of them are watching me. Cuzn calls for me to come to him. Like an asshole, I turn around and start walking back toward him still struggling with the "cello". He and Dex both yell at the same time, "After you put that in the trunk!"

I turn around and approach the trunk of the car. I pop it open using the handset I'm holding. I get the block in the trunk, check my surroundings again and catch my breath. I walk back over to them. Dougie is standing on Cuzn's side of the car talking when I give Dex a hug through the driver's side window. I look at all three of them and thank them for the help carrying the package. They both look at Dougie and asked him why he didn't help seeing as he was already out of the car.

"She looked like she had it covered." Dougie said. We all had to laugh at that.

Cuzn turns to me and says, "You need to stop driving that car. It's too fucking noticeable."

"Yeah, it is" Dex said

"Yeah, it is but, what cop is gonna take the chance of stopping a light skinned, good hair motherfucker like me?" I said jokingly.

"I don't like it." Cuzn said.

"Alright, I'll work on it." I said knowing he was right.

"Good. Have it worked out quickly." He said. Then I bounced out of there and left them in the parking lot talking.

Carolina called me to tell me he didn't leave town after all. He wanted to see me. I told him I was working, couldn't that night, maybe tomorrow. When I got back to SK's house he was working, as usual. He stopped, as soon as, I came in lugging this huge package. I pulled it into the kitchen and locked the door.

I prepared to section the weed into pounds. The first thing I did was put a large pot of water on to boil. The moisture helps the weed decompress.

The next thing I had to do was, get the one gallon plastic baggies out. I'll put the weed in them while it's on a scale to weigh out each pound. I put the scale SK had on the countertop next to the baggie's. Once I had all of that ready it was time to start on the weed.

I took the two garbage bags, covering the "cello", off by cutting them so they were split. I'd lay them down on the floor so the loose weed would fall on it and not the floor. I had to unwrap the weed from its transportation wrapping. It looked like wood grain wallpaper. It was sticky on the other side.

Under that was a layer of plastic wrap. That was about 8-10 layers with some sort of detergent every so many layers. I had to cut through the wood grain and the plastic very carefully because I have to make sure the detergent doesn't get into the weed. That would cause a major problem.

I take a sharp knife and slowly slice through the layers. Pulling them back slowly, like a banana until I get to the final layer. I leave the final layer of plastic wrap on to protect the weed. This is a very tedious process. It takes patience.

Once I get to the last layer, before I remove it. I take the other layers and put them in a plastic garbage bag to keep them completely away from the weed. I then clean up any detergent that may have fallen out during the process. This usually takes about an hour. No need to rush. After all that, I'm ready to open the final layer. It's compressed, so there is very little to no smell. I ask SK to light a bunch of incense.

Once I start pulling the weed from its compressed state, the smell will start to bloom. The steam will help me pull it apart by rehydrating the buds. It will also make it puff back out from its flattened compressed condition.

This is a labor of love. You have to appreciate the bud to do this right. You also have to keep in mind; a big part of marketing is appearance. If the weed is just ripped from the compressed block the bud will be ripped and mangled. You will wind up with a large amount of "shake", which is the leaves from the bud that have ripped or may have fallen off due to dryness. This weed is moist. There's always going to be shake. You can't help that but, you can help how much by taking your time.

The cello is a solid mass of bright green loveliness. Every bud is clearly visible and I'm excited. I won't have any trouble getting rid of this. I give it 45 minutes for the top layer to start absorbing the steam and loosen from the brick. I check it every couple of minutes after that, by pulling on the corners of the block. Once the corners start loosening up I can start to gently pull at them peeling them backward. The first corner to soften up is the end I start with.

SK is working just a few feet away from me in the living room. The TV is on and we're both just tending to our perspective business. I check the weed for the 4th time and one of the ends gives me a little play. I start to pull the first layer back with ease. I work on it slowly because I have no choice. It will not be ready until it's ready. I just have to remain patient.

Slowly but, surely as the steam builds in the kitchen, the outer part of the cello begins to soften, as I pull piece by piece it begins to loosen up even more allowing me to pull larger chunks at a time. As I'm pulling clumps of buds off, I put them in the baggie's, with the mouth of the baggie opened wide, so the weed can still get the steam. By the time I get enough in the baggie to come close to a pound the buds are soft and fluffy. I keep pulling off the buds and weighing, as soon as I have a pound, I start on another bag. The smell was strong but the incense was keeping the smell from escaping into the hallway.

At one point, SK walked up behind me to see what I was doing and when he saw me pulling on the huge block of weed he looked at me and said,

"I can't do that shit!" That was the end of SK's drug dealing endeavors. I couldn't do anything but laugh and keep peeling.

All together the "cello" equaled 38 pounds. Carrying it felt like 70. I called Cuzn to tell him what it weighed. He picked up the phone and I said, "Hey, she's 38." And we got off the phone. I then took the pounds and put them in the black duffle bag I got from Sheree. I put the duffle bag between the TV and the wall of windows in SK's apartment. I was tired. The whole process took about 4 ½ hours.

Before I would be finished, I had to take the shake that accumulated on the garbage bags and put it in a baggie too. I picked up the ends of the bags and softly wiggled them until the shake had made its way to the center. I took a holiday greeting card of SK's and scooped the shake putting it in the baggie. I rolled the garbage bags up, put them in the same bag with the wrapping, swept up anything left on the floor and put it in the same trash bag. Once the kitchen was clean of any weed residue, I weighed the shake. It weighed in at roughly 6 ounces. This is the weed I would be smoking. I showed it to SK and let him know what its intended purpose was. He was pleased with it. I cleaned the scale, putting it and the baggies away. I cleaned the knife as well. I was finally done. I could sit down and relax. Back on the futon, I did just what you'd think, I rolled a blunt.

Carolina had been calling me since we spooned. I was always busy when he called but, he seemed to understand. He was in Atlanta recording his new album and made it clear that he wanted to see me while he was here. I had a different opinion of him after that night. He was a gentleman and he made me laugh. When I got some free time I would definitely be hanging out with him. I told Antonio that I met him but, I didn't tell him about the spooning. I'm not an idiot. It was something to talk about so I talked about it, just not all of it.

Antonio and my relationship has gone through a lot of ups and downs in the months we've been together. But, I've never been loved as hard by anyone, as I have been by him. For that reason I have gone through all the dope fiend antics like, him disappearing for days at a time, not having money because he's ill and had to get well. I will make sure I get him home in one piece. I keep him as comfortable as I can while he's there. I send him money. I talk to him on the phone and I Xerox books and mail them to him. For some reason Baltimore city jail doesn't allow inmates to have books. That's some ignorant shit right there. I do what I can to keep him in the loop of my progress. I can't give him too much detail but he knows for the most part.

The New Year came and business was going great. In the course of 5 days between Scar and Black I made $15,000. I would've made more but someone slid in a wad of counterfeit money into a couple of the stacks Scar gave me. I had to eat that lose. Scar lost out too. I didn't do any more business with him after that night. If I lose, you lose. Cuzn is the only one that doesn't lose. The time came for me to send the $9,000 off to Kevin Chase, Esq. I overnighted it to make sure he got it by the day I said I'd have it to him. He called me once his office received it.

"This is Kevin Chase calling for J.O." His voice was deep, authoritative and comforting all at once.

"This is me Mr. Chase. How are you today?"

"I'm doing okay, J.O. I hope you are as well? I wanted to let you know we received the retainer today and if you have a moment I'd like to talk to you about the next move we need to make."

"I'm all ears Mr. Chase." I settled in to listen to what he had to say.

"Good. Well the first thing we need to do is schedule a court date so Antonio can stand in front of a judge and formally end Mr. Davis' representation of him and put it on record that I will be his legal counsel."

"Sounds good to me Mr. Chase, but, you have to speak with Tonio about this too. This is about him."

"I'm already going to do that. I just wanted to touch base with you before I went down there to see him seeing as I received an envelope from you today."

"I appreciate that Mr. Chase. I really do. When can you go see him?"

"I'll be visiting him later on today. I want to get this done as soon as possible."

I was feeling good about this attorney. I wish it was Renee

instead but, at least he was going to see Antonio and had a plan in effect. That fuckin' Davis was useless.

We ended the conversation with me asking him to have Tonio call me when they were finished with their meeting.

Carolina called and wanted to see me. I told him I was working until about 8pm. He asked me to call him when I got off. I agreed.

Cuzn called too. He called SK and me back to back. He asked SK to drive me to meet him in Buckhead at 2pm. He then called me to tell me SK was driving me to meet him and not to make any plans. I didn't feel I had a choice so I agreed. I was very curious I must admit. I tried picking SK for any details that Cuzn may have given him. He was just as dumbfounded as I was.

We arrived at the designated place on time and found Cuzn already there with a chocolate young man named Raeford. Raeford was in his mid-20s and stood about 6'1. He had a serious yet engaging smile. Cuzn introduced all of us. Due to the fact that Cuzn will occasionally have a person I've never met with him. I'm respectful but, I never put too much stock into them. I'm not guaranteed to ever see them again. That's all a part of the being in Cuzn's circle. Pay attention to him and not the people around him. The four of us stood in the parking lot of the strip mall. I was still trying to figure out the reason for the meeting when Cuzn announced he had to meet with someone. I was still wondering why we had to meet. As I was about to head to SK's car, Cuzn informed me that I would be riding with Raeford.

"Huh?" I asked

"Yes. Raeford will be driving you around today. He has a license and a gun. He will be driving you around while you handle your business. Any questions?" Before I could respond he said, "Good, now get in his car. Have a great day."

I looked at Raeford who was smiling at me. I looked at SK who was shrugging and grinning. I looked at Cuzn as I headed toward Raeford's Black 2001 Nissan Maxima with tinted windows. Raeford was leaning on the trunk with his arms crossed. He walked to the passenger's side and opened the door for me as I took a seat. We drove off, following SK back to his spot so I could get my work I needed for the day. Raeford stayed in the car while I went upstairs to get my black duffle bag. When I came back down he put it in the trunk for me.

We ran around the rest of the day meeting Cuzn again and taking care of a couple of things I needed to do before I could hang out. I called Carolina at 8pm to let him know I wasn't going to be finished until around 10pm.

"Is it cool if we get together then?" I asked

"I'm over my cousin's house waiting on you. You tell me when you're ready. I'm on standby." He said with a smile in his voice.

I have to admit I liked that.

"Do you like to shoot pool?" I asked him.

"I do. I like that you want to shoot pool even more." He replied

"Okay, I know where we can go and have some fun. I'll call you when I'm done and tell you where to meet me."

"Whoa, whoa, whoa, what do you mean 'meet me'? I'm coming to pick you up. You call me back and tell me where to come and pick you up from. Understood?" He said that shit like a grown ass man. I liked that too.

"Alright, I'll call you around 10." I said and we got off the phone.

Around 7pm we met up with Sheree at our favorite pizza spot. I hadn't seen much of her since I'd been in town and we had to bond for a minute. As he had done all day, Raeford stayed in the car while Sheree and I met inside the pizza spot. We were sitting there eating and the conversation started.

"So what's been up with you?" She asked as if she already knew the answer.

"Shit, working." I replied

"Yeah, I know."

"What do you mean?" I asked genuinely interested

"I know you've been working. I hear you've been burning down the track on they ass." She was smiling

"Whoa, what? Where did you hear that?" I asked surprised

"Cuz." She answered

"Cuzn?" I was really surprised now.

"Yup, you're all he's been talking about. He's kind of rubbing you in everybody's face." She said

I was surprised by this because I really didn't discuss my business with Sheree. I don't discuss it with anybody and I was so busy working I didn't think about anything else. I didn't notice I was burning up the track. I guess I was too busy burning to notice. It made me feel good and exposed at the same time. People were talking about me, in my line of work it could be dangerous but, it was my boss talking about me and he was bragging about me to my team. After further consideration, I wasn't mad just surprised.

I called Carolina after Raeford dropped me off at SK's. I went upstairs to get ready to hang out for the night. I was in the bathroom putting eyeliner on about 30 minutes after I got there when Raeford called me. I answered the phone curious as to what he wanted.

"Hello?" I answered the phone.

"Ms. J.O., do you know how much longer you're going to be? I don't want to get a ticket." He asked very politely.

"How long am I going to be? I don't understand."

"Do you want me to circle the block until you're ready to leave?" He asked

"Are you still downstairs?" I asked surprised.

"Yes, Cuz told me I'm to drive you wherever you need to go. I can't leave until you tell me you don't need me anymore." He explained. All of a sudden it hit me. Cuzn had paid this guy to be my driver so I wasn't driving SK's car and risking getting pulled over. I smiled at the consideration he had for me.

"Raeford, I'm sorry. I thought you knew you were dropping me off for the night. Honestly, I didn't even know that he told you that. This is the first I'm hearing about it. I just thought, I don't know what I thought. You can go home. I'm sorry you've been down there all this time for nothing. I really am." I told him.

"That's okay, Ms. J.O., I understand. He told me not to tell you. What time should I pick you up in tomorrow?" he sounded like he was smiling.

"I'll call you when I get up and we'll set it up then." I said

"Okay, Ms. J.O., I'll talk to you in the a.m. then." We said our goodbyes and got off the phone. I felt secure in the thought of Cuzn caring that much about me. I finished putting on my makeup before Carolina got there.

A Transsexual Prostitute Once Told Me

He called me from downstairs to let me know to come down. He was parked outside the front entrance waiting. As I jumped in the big ass truck, he helped me in by holding one of my hands. He leaned in for a kiss, even though I hadn't planned on it I leaned in too and we kissed. It was warm, welcoming and personal. It was a great kiss. Still holding my hand he looked at me and said,

"That was our first kiss."

I was taken off guard because it was a side of him I didn't think about. He was a romantic. We headed to the Marriott Marquis right around the corner from SK. I knew everybody who worked there because I use to work there myself. I felt safe there. It was almost like being in my own living room. We had one of my friends who I use to work with serve us while we grabbed a pool table. We ordered drink after drink and talked the night away. Without my even asking a question he started telling me his story.

"The other night when you told me you lived in Baltimore I gave you a look. Did you notice?" He asked me

"Yes I did."

"The reason I gave you that look is because I used to live in Baltimore. I lived there when I got put out my Mama's house one summer when I got into trouble."

When he said that I instantly recalled Nigel saying Carolina was from Baltimore one night when we were on the block. I didn't tell him that though. I just listened. He went on to tell me how his own father turned state's evidence against him. He wound up doing a bid behind it. The only person he ever trusted and loved was killed. He had his name tattooed on him so that he was with him everywhere he went. He told me his real name and why he chose his stage name. I just listened to him while we shot pool and drank shots of tequila. He was good company and I was enjoying myself. After the 5th game I finally beat him and he was really salty about it. He wasn't the losing kind, I guess.

"Can I spend more time with you?" He asked looking me in my eyes.

"Yeah, I'm having fun. I wouldn't mind doing this again." I responded.

"When can we spend more time together?" He asked leaning in and coming as close to my cheek with his as possible without touching me. I liked that too.

"When do you want to?" I was officially playing the game.

"Tonight" He pulled back and looked me in the eyes.

"What's the plan?" I asked

"We can stay here and just hang out all night. Talk all night. Laugh all night." Before he could go any further I interrupted him.

"Do what else all night?" I gave him an "It ain't that easy" look.

"I'm not that kind of guy J.O. I'm really not." He said and I came back to reality. He continued.

"Do you really want to know what I really want to do?" He asked. I nodded while sipping my shot.

"I'd like to take you upstairs and chill out. I'd like to help you relax after a hard day of work." He clanked his shot glass against mine and took his shot. I was just staring at him when I asked,

"How do you plan on making me relax?" My interest was fading.

"I could kiss you all over." One of my eyebrows rose.

"Continue." I said finishing my shot.

"I could kiss you in some places longer than others but not miss one spot." He said as he leaned next to me on the pool table. I was thinking about the offer.

"What would I have to do in return?" I just got straight to it.

“I didn’t have a hard day. I’m relaxed right now.” He raised the empty shot glass.

I was thinking about this seriously. Not only was he fine but, he had a mouth full of gold teeth and the thought of being given head by a rapper with a mouth full of gold teeth was really helping sell his plan.

I make it a rule not to have sex with men right off. I like to think of it as a training program. I feel like if they give you head for a few weeks before you actually have sex with them, they understand that they can’t be selfish lovers when you do have sex. So I agreed and we left the bar. He got us a suite overlooking the skyline of Atlanta. I wasn’t mad.

True to his word once again, we talked, we laughed and he gave me head while I looked out over the city I love. Afterward we were both still drunk and enjoying more laughs together Carolina excused himself and went into the bathroom. He was in there for a while so I knocked on the door to check on him. I figured he was throwing up from all the liquor. As I knocked I heard the shower running, I asked him if he was okay. He said he was and I went back to lie on the bed.

While he was in the shower I thought about having sex with him. He was fine as hell and after getting head I could use the closeness of a man. The thought of sleeping with him didn’t turn me off, quite the opposite it turned me on. I decided I was going to do it.

He came out of the bathroom with a towel around his waist. His body was beautiful. He was deep brown, with muscles glistening from the water on his body. I was lying on my back leaning on my elbows watching him, picturing him naked. I noticed he washed his hair and had taken his braids out. As I was watching him walk across the room he suddenly stopped, put his hands in his hair and rubbed his fingers through it while shaking it like a woman would. I was instantly turned off. A voice in my head said, ‘That was gay’.

Immediately I wanted to leave. He was drying off. I was dressed, so all I had to do was grab my bag and make up an excuse for why I had to leave. I'd tell him I got a phone call while he was in the shower. I'll just grab my purse and bounce. I look around the room for my purse. I don't see it. That's when I realized, I left it in his truck. I rolled over and went to sleep.

A transsexual prostitute I once knew named Tuna La More told me that if a man does something that makes you say to yourself, 'That's gay.' Then he's gay. I never forgot it and that was the last I saw Carolina. The next day he dropped me off at SK's and that afternoon I heard his new song played on the radio. The song was hot. It eventually reached number one. He called me a few times after that night but, I was always busy, even when I wasn't.

Life went on and I met a guy who did alterations to cars. The alterations he did were the kind that fit quite well in my line of work. He installed secret compartments in vehicles. He showed me a car that if you saw it on the street you wouldn't look twice at it but, once he made a couple of sequential maneuvers in the car, you heard a motor start in the back seat, by the time you turned around the speaker in the back door panel was open. You could put about five kilos of cocaine in it and no one would be the wiser. I bought the car for $5000. I was driving back to Baltimore.

Antonio called to tell me about his latest meeting with the lawyer. He was pissed.

"Do you know what, he wants me to do?" He asked

"He wants you to go to court, fire Davis and hire him on the record." I answered

"Yeah, he also wants me to give up my right to a speedy trial." He said

"What? Where did that come from?" I asked

"I don't know but, I'm not gonna fuh'in' do it, hell no." He said with anger in his voice.

"Are you sure you don't want to do it?" I asked confused by the information

"Hell no, I'm not gonna to do it. If I give that up they will keep me locked up for three or four years behind this shit!" he yelled

"Are you sure?" I asked not believing they would ask him to do it knowing that.

"Hell yeah I'm sure! That's why it's called a speedy trial. If you give it up then they keep yo ass waiting for years!" He was about to blow a gasket.

We called the lawyer on 3-way so I could get in on the conversation. I couldn't believe this expensive ass lawyer wouldn't know he would be locked up for all that time, if he gave up his right to a speedy trial. Once Chase was on the phone I asked him about it and sure enough he did ask Antonio to do it.

"Antonio, I want to study this case until I dream about it in my sleep. I don't want to go to court until I've gone through the entire trial in my dreams. That way I would have seen anything the prosecution could throw at us. I'm telling you this is the right move to make." Chase explained.

I couldn't believe what I was hearing. It wasn't a hard case to prove. The victim is going to testify on behalf of the accused. How hard could it be to win this case? What could the prosecution throw at the defense that would trump that? I didn't like what I was hearing, I was getting upset. I asked Chase if he had another trial coming up, thinking maybe that was the reason he wanted the delay. He said he didn't. That made me even more pissed. We got off the phone with him and continued to talk to each other.

Antonio was livid and I was too. We kept snapping at each other because of it. He was mad they were asking him to do it. I was mad that once again, he chose a bullshit ass lawyer that I had to pay for. I was getting really sick of this shit. What made it even worse, Antonio had to make the decision over night because they were going to court in the morning. Out of nowhere Antonio asked me a question I wasn't prepared to answer.

"Have you slept with anybody since I been gone?" I didn't know how to answer the question so I answered it truthfully.

"No." I said

"Well, then let me ask you this? Have you gotten head since I been gone?" I was shocked that he knew me that well.

"This is not the time to discuss this." I tried to defuse the conversation.

"Look woman, I don't want to come down there and have some nigga looking me in my face knowing he's suh'ed my girl off and I don't know who he is." He said with anger. He always called me 'woman' when he wanted me to take the conversation seriously.

"You don't have to worry about that. I wouldn't put you in that situation." I said having admitted it at the same time.

"How do you know that won't happen?" he asked having got his answer.

"I know that because the person doesn't live in Atlanta or Baltimore so you won't have the opportunity for him to be in your face."

"Yeah, but he lives in the Carolina's though doesn't he?"

"Look, Tonio I'm not going to argue about this with you." I snapped using the game my brothers taught me.

"What do you mean you ain't arguin' about this? We're arguin' 'bout it now!" He yelled into the phone.

"I'm not going through this with you. For the simple fact that if the shoe was on the other foot. You wouldn't last 24 hours without getting your dick sucked and within 72 hours you would've moved back in with your baby's mother. So I'm not about to argue with you about it.

Let's get another thing straight while we're at it. If you had a rapper bitch with a mouth full of gold teeth wanting to give you head overlooking the skyline of Atlanta and you didn't have to give her anything in return, you'd do it! Shit, I'd kick you in the back and push you in the room myself. I'm not talking about this anymore so end it." I was done with the conversation but he wasn't. We argued until he had to lock down for the night. Not too long after we hung up the phone I got another call from, Kevin Chase. It was after midnight so I was surprised to be hearing from him.

"Hello?" I answered the phone.

'Hello, J.O., I'm sorry to be calling you this late. Am I disturbing you?"

"No, is everything alright?" I asked paranoid.

"Yes, everything is fine." He said with a chuckle. "I wanted you to know, I just got off the phone with a mutual friend of ours, Eric Wells." I sat on the phone in silence trying to figure out who Eric Wells was. Chase must've picked up on this so he continued.

"You may know him as Toe-Joe." He chuckled again. (Toe-Joe is Antonio's cousin, Chase's client.

Okay?" I asked waiting for the rest.

"Ever since the first time we spoke, I thought it was kind of outrageous, you would be footing the bill for Antonio's entire defense. So, I called him and kind of shamed him into paying the remaining balance owed. I hope you don't mind?" He asked calmly.

I really didn't know what to say at all. I just sat on the phone for a minute before I responded.

"I don't really know what to say about that, Mr. Chase. I can't say I've ever heard of a lawyer doing anything like that. At the very least I should thank you for being so chivalrous. I also might add that I haven't spoken to Toe-Joe since this entire thing started, even though Tonio had me reach out to him on a couple of occasions. Mr. Chase, Antonio picked you to represent him. I respect that. I honor that. I'm responsible for Antonio, have been the entire time. If Toe-Joe doesn't pay you, then what? Antonio's in the lurch?" I asked.

"I haven't had any issue of nonpayment from Mr. Wells in our history together. I don't see that happening in this instance either." He responded

"Then I guess I should stop being so skeptical and say thank you. Thank You, Mr. Chase. And when you speak to Toe-Joe thank him for me as well?" I said. Still feeling like Toe-Joe was an asshole either way. We hung up the phone and I watched television for the rest of the night.

Who You Talking To, Your Man?

I spent the night at Jennie's but, couldn't sleep at all. The next morning, the first call I made was to Raeford. Telling him I needed to be picked up by 3pm. The next call I made was based on a decision I'd made last night while I couldn't sleep. I called Renee Walsh's office. If I'm paying for this, I'm picking the lawyer I'm paying. She was in court. I left my number and a message for her to call me back. I was on pins and needles not knowing what happened in court. I had to wait for him to be brought back to the jail, before I found out what happened. Time was tight. His trial date had been set for late February. If he gave up his right to a speedy trial that date would be changed to indefinitely.

I needed Renee to call me back. I didn't care anymore about who he wanted to represent him. I was paying for it so I was going to pay who I thought would get the job done. As soon as she called I was going to hire her. My mind was made up. Antonio probably wouldn't get back to the jail until late in the afternoon. I was sure to lose my mind before then. I was caught off guard when he called me by 2pm. I was scared to hear what happened in court but, couldn't wait at the same time.

"Hey, what happened?" I asked afraid to hear he gave up his right

"I walked into court and both they asses was there. My name was called and we all stood up. Chase told the judge that I was there to take Davis off my case and put him on." He said frustrated.

"Okay, then what?" I asked not wanting to know out of fear for the worst.

"Then Chase told the judge that he was goin' to ask that I give up my right to a speedy trial. The judge asked me if I wanted to and I told him 'No, Your Honor, I don't.' Then the judge asked me if I knew what giving up my rights meant and I told him, 'Your Honor it means that the prosecution can leave me sitting in jail for up to 4 years before I go to trial' and he told Chase that I obviously knew what it meant and I wasn't giving up my right. The trial date stands." I was relieved.

"Bay guess, who was in the courtroom on another case?" He asked

"Who?" I asked

"Renee Walsh" He said

"You're kidding." I was surprised

"Nope, she took one look at me and asked me what I was still doing loh'ed up? I asked her if she would take my case and she said 'yes'. I asked her if she could be ready by the end of February and do you know what she said?" He asked

"No, what did she say?" I asked feeling like I was in a dream

"She said she could defend this case in her sleep. Can you believe that shit? She also told me to cut my hair off before we go to trial." He said.

"Hell, Yeah I can believe that shit! I told you she was the shit. I wanted her from the beginning!" I yelled in excitement.

"Guess who I called this morning as soon as I woke up?" I asked him

"Who?" he replied

"I called her." I said "I was going to hire her whether you liked it or not."

"You were right Bay, I should've stuh' with her all along." He said realizing he was wrong, at the same time feeling relief.

We called Renee on three-way and she was in her office. I think she was as glad to hear from me, as much as I was to hear from her. She said she got my message when she came in. She thought it was just as crazy as we did, I called and they run into each other on the same day.

I felt like everything was going to be okay. For the first time since this thing began. I had all faith in Renee. I could relax and let her do her job. We talked money. Renee said she would do the entire case for $5,000. I told her I would be there the following week. I would bring her the money in full. We were all feeling good about the trial. She wanted to know if we'd heard from Ryan. We assured her he would be there. It was all coming together. I knew Antonio was coming home for sure now. I was at ease. We hung up with Renee and continued to talk for a while. I was expecting him to bring up Carolina again but he didn't, I was relieved and surprised.

I called Chase to let him know, Antonio was going to be using Renee after all. He already knew. I asked him how much of the $9,000 was he going to charge me? He told me he wasn't charging me anything.

"It's your money J.O. I'll have it mailed to the address you give me." He said. I told him I would be returning to Baltimore the following week, to prepare for trial. I would pick it up then. We said our goodbyes and got off the phone.

This was going to be my last week in Atlanta for a while so I hung out and got fucked up as much as possible before I left. The time came and I packed my shit into my car, including 4 pounds of weed in the secret compartment. I drove all night to Baltimore. I arrived at 7am and went to Stan's house.

He knew I was coming. In the weeks I'd been gone, Stan and I became kind of close over the phone. So much so, Stan kicked out all junkies in anticipation of my arrival. It was not too far from the expressway. I would have to go through Pigtown to get to my Godfather's house. I just stopped at Stan's. It may have been crazy but, I laid my jacket down, on the very same sheets, I'd always seen on his bed and passed out for a good 2 hours. I got up and headed over to my Godfather's house. I finished my slumber in my room. He was happy to see me. Once I actually woke up that evening.

In Atlanta we had a winter frost on the ground in the mornings that would have melted away by noon. In Baltimore, it snowed not too long before I got there. The temperature difference was noticeable to me. I missed home already but, I was excited to be there to finally get this over with. Before I left Atlanta, I called Antonio's mother to give her the update on everything that was going on in the case. I told her about the lawyers, who was finally representing him and we were ready for trial.

'J.O., I have to tell you something.' She said to me

'What's that Mah Mah ?" I asked

"I want you to know, the reason I haven't been calling you like I should is, really because I'm embarrassed. I don't have any money to give you for Tonio."

It made sense, her telling me that. His mother Ronnie is a very proud woman who raised seven children as a single mother and was raising her granddaughter who belonged to one of Antonio's older sisters. I knew it was hard for her to say.

I said, "I don't need your money Mah Mah. I have him covered. He's my responsibility. All I need from you is to make sure we have as many people as we can show up for court every day. That's very important. It shows the judge and jury he's not some throw away. It shows them, he has family that loves and supports him. It influences the jury."

"I can make sure, the family's there." She sounded relieved in her reply. I knew she could do it because in her family, when Mah Mah speaks everyone listens.

"Then we're good." I said

Having been home in Atlanta, I felt like my old self. I looked like my old self. Now that I was back in Baltimore, I headed to South Baltimore to go shoot some pool at Mom's Bar. I paid the nurse at the jail money to bring Tonio a phone. Walking down W. Cross St talking to Antonio, I crossed over Carroll St... I heard someone call my name. I turned around to see a Chevrolet Cavalier Coupe with 4 Knockuh's in it. The one calling my name was, Puerto Rican Yo.

I took one look at him and started walking to the car talking at the same time.

"Oh, hell no, they made this nigga a knockuh!" I yelled. Antonio knew exactly who I was talking about.

"Who that Puerto Rican Yo?" he asked

"Hell yeah!" I replied as I walked up to the car.

Yo was smiling as if he were glad to see me.

"Who you talking to, your man?" He asked. I leaned into the car. Took a good look at all the faces of the cops I may need to watch out for in the near future. I took them in, one by one. Yo was in the front passenger seat. The driver was a white guy with a typical blonde buzz cut. The two in the back had dark hair. The one behind Yo looked Hispanic.

"Yup, what's up with you?" I asked

"Ain't nothing, how about you?" He asked in return

I told Antonio I'd call him right back and hung up the phone. Still leaning into the car I posed a question to Yo and the other cops in the car while laughing.

"How in the hell do y'all give everybody in this neighborhood hell for selling dope. Then let new nigga's come in here and set up shop? Can one of y'all answer me that?" I asked them all looking at Yo.

They all perked up at what I'd just said. Yo asked me the dumbest question he could've.

"Who are they?"

I laughed, "No, my Friends, you're going to have to do your job and find out on your own. I gotta go shoot pool. Catch you later, Yo." I walked away as I hit the send button on my phone and called Antonio back.

After hanging in the hood with my friends I headed back home for the night around midnight. I had things to do in the morning and couldn't stay out all night. It was good to be back but, only because I had a purpose for being there. If it wasn't for Antonio, I would be back in Atlanta where I belonged. I missed home already but, I couldn't wait to get him out.

The next day I went to the law office of Kevin Chase and picked up a check for $9,000. I took the check to Renee's office. We agreed to just have her deposit it third party and give me back the difference when the check cleared. She told me she needed to speak with all the witnesses involved in the case. I told her I'd make that happen.

I went to find the young man who was with Ryan on the night of the shooting. His name was Tucker. He like Ryan and I is mixed. I think his mother was Black. He is very tall, standing at 6'3" with big cat eyes and freckled honey skin with light brown curly hair. He has an easy disposition with a full lipped smile. He's not hard to look at. I brought him to Renee's office. Where they talked in great detail about the night Ryan was shot. I took him home afterward.

Before leaving the office, Renee told me she needed to speak with Lisa and Bobby too. I told her I would make it happen. I'd have to do things a little differently. I asked Renee if she would come to Pigtown to meet them, she agreed. The next evening she met me in front of Foul Ball where Ryan was shot. We walked down the street unannounced to meet Lisa and Bobby.

Renee was wearing a full length black cashmere coat with black leather cowboy boots. I watched her blonde hair, bounce in the cool breeze of the night. I loved it. She had so much style it made me want to be her friend. I walked up the steps first, Renee followed. I knocked on the door. Lisa and Bobby's roommate answered. He was a sweaty, middle aged white man with a pudgy build who stood about 5'10",who was balding, his hairline started at the crown of his head. He was wearing a loose dingy white v-neck t-shirt, dirty blue jeans and he was barefoot. I told him who I was and asked if they were home. They were. He invited us in as he yelled up the steps for them. We walked through a cluttered living room and followed him into a nasty kitchen. There were at least 6 cats standing around in there. I think 2 of them were on the kitchen table, which was covered with old food. As I looked around, I noticed Renee trying not to touch anything. She was holding her black leather purse close to her. As we were looking around the kitchen, we heard footsteps coming from the staircase in the kitchen. We looked up to see both Lisa and Bobby coming down in all their junkie glory.

They looked like they still hadn't bathed. Bobby had an open sore on his left cheek. By the way it looked, he was obviously picking at it. Renee was horrified by the sight of them but, to her credit she kept her composure and treated them both with the utmost respect.

They offered us a seat in the kitchen after I introduced them to Renee. I declined but, Renee took a seat across from Lisa in the middle of the kitchen. Bobby stood beside Lisa, I stood behind Renee and the roommate stood in the background by the kitchen sink.

Renee began asking about that night. Lisa did the talking. She said,

"I thought the whole thing was over when I saw Antonio going into 'Mom's Bar' the other night."

Rene's head snapped to attention when she heard this. My eyes opened wide.

"Who did you see?" Renee asked

"Antonio. I saw him the other night going into the bar. I thought the whole thing was over." She repeated. I wanted to jump out of my skin.

"You couldn't have seen Antonio the other night because Antonio is still locked up." Renee informed her

"Oh. Well I saw the guy who shot Ryan the other night going into the bar." She said looking at me.

Renee pointed at her and said "good I want you to say that when you get on the stand".

She asked them about their use and how often they got high a day. They said they get high about 10-15 times a day. That's about $300 between them. Renee looked at their dirty clothes and told them she wanted them to dress the exact same way for court. At one point Lisa started crying. Once again, Renee pointed at her and said, "Good, I want you to do that on the stand too." I almost burst into laughter.

After Renee got all she needed from the two of them, I walked her back to her car. On the way I asked her about the video of them recanting.

"I still have it but, I don't want to take the chance of anyone saying that they were tampered with." I felt relieved.

Once she was gone I drifted off into the neighborhood and hung out until I felt like going home.

The next day I went to Ryan's house. He was living in Fells Point by the Harbor with his girlfriend Erin. She was a beautiful brown haired, blue-eyed, Polish girl. She had the face of an angel and a body to challenge Hell for bad. I liked her. She was a stripper. She took care of her three year old son very well. She loved Ryan and he seemed to love her too.

We were glad to see each other. He gave me the rundown on what had been going on. The police had been going to every house he was known to stay, looking for him. The prosecutor went to his mother's house. He threatened to get a search warrant if, Ryan didn't call or come to his office. While I was gone, he was stopped by some patrol cops. When he told them his name, they told him if he didn't testify against Antonio, they were going to find him and dump him on his head on the concrete. He was officially laying low until the trial. We agreed that I would pick Tucker up in the mornings before court. They would meet us there seeing as Erin had a car.

The night before we went to trial, I went home early and watched TV with my Godfather, Leonard, who has always been in my corner. He moved me from Atlanta to Baltimore for the first time when I was 19 years old. I was alone while my mother was in prison and Kenny was in the Navy. He's a former Black Panther and still a revolutionary to his core. He's 6'1 paper brown skin with a bald head. He taught me how to hustle when my mother went to prison and I was on my own. His exact words were,

"I want to make sure you don't have to fuck out of both draw legs."

He taught me all about Heroin and how to mix it. It's a skill I have used very well.

We were sitting on one of the suede couches, when he asked me what was going on with the case. I told him everything. He was amazed that I was so intricately involved in all aspects. He warned me that the judicial system is fucked up and not to be trusted. I knew he was preparing me for the worst outcome. Truthfully, nothing could prepare me for a guilty verdict. I couldn't see how any jury could convict after Ryan got on the stand.

The Trial

Monday morning came and I was up before the alarm went off. I was nervous. I took my time getting showered and ready. I was trying to keep my cool. There was a lot riding on today and it was all I could think about. Before leaving the house, I called Tucker to let him know I was on my way to pick him up. He said he'd be ready when I got there.

I drove the area known as Cherry Hill to pick him up. Sure enough he walked out of the door as soon as I pulled up. We met Ryan and Erin in front of the courthouse. We all were nervous as we went through the metal detectors. We found Renee on the third floor in front of the courtroom Antonio was assigned to. We all greeted each other and walked in together.

As we walked into the courtroom, I noticed it seemed to have a red theme to it. The wood all over the room was red oak. It was quite beautiful and serene. It made a statement of importance. The walls and curtains complimented the wood with earth tones. As we walked in the prosecutor turned to look at us. He immediately noticed Ryan. He motioned for him to come talk to him.

He was in his mid-thirties with thinning blond hair, glasses, with a sour look on his pale, puffy face. Tucker, Erin and I took a seat at the front of the courtroom behind Renee who was sitting at the defense table. Slowly but surely Ronnie and some of Antonio's family started filtering into the room. I stood up and greeted her with a hug. Some of the family I knew and I greeted them as well. The ones I didn't know, Ronnie introduced me to. I then went back to sit with Tucker, Erin and Ryan who had finished talking to the prosecutor.

"What did he want?" I asked Ryan referring to the prosecutor.

"He asked me what I was gonna say on the stand." The three of us just stared at him for the rest of the conversation. He picked up on that and continued.

"I told him I'm goona say Tonio dihn't shoot me, cuz he dihn't. Then he told me, 'Look I really need your help to get this guy off the streets'. I told him I wasn't gonna help him put my people away for the rest of his life. He was gonna have to find a way to do that without me, for real." We were all shocked at what he'd just said. None of us said a word. Renee walked over to us and Ryan repeated what he'd just told us. She didn't seem surprised by it at all.

Ronnie came and pulled me to the side to talk. We walked a few feet away from the others and she looked at me with her Mama eyes and said,

"Look, Elissa is coming up here and I don't want no mess, here?" Elissa is the mother of Antonio's two children.

"You don't have to worry about me acting up, Mah Mah. I don't fight over men. I'm glad she's coming. We need all the people we can get here." She was taken aback by my response. Then she replied,

"Oh, okay then Bay." I think she was preparing for a fight with me. She called everyonne she loves "Bay" it's short for baby. I went and took my seat with Ryan and the others, waiting on the proceedings to begin. The family was sitting behind us a couple of rows back. All together I'd say about 15 people showed up to support Antonio. I liked that. When anything was being said between Renee and the prosecutor she would immediately walk over to me and quietly fill me in on what was being said. I would then tell Ronnie, she would relay it to the rest of the family. Bye the third time I was sensing a little tension from some of the other family members. I didn't care though. I had been waiting for this day and no one was going to get in my way. Elissa arrived with one of Antonio's sister's named Kim. Kim and I weren't close at all. You could actually say we didn't like each other. I nodded to them as they sat down with the rest of the family. I turned back to the front of the courtroom.

We all had to rise as the judge entered the room. After we sat down and some formalities were handled they called Antonio's name and I held my breath. A police officer escorted him into the courtroom from a door that was close to the defense table. He sat down next to Renee after smiling at everyone who came to support him. Both sides agreed they were ready for trial and that was all. The judge ordered the case to move forward that day. The next step was to get a new courtroom and judge assigned to the case. Renee came over to us after the proceedings were over and told me she was going back to her office.

"I'll call you as soon as they've assigned the trial judge. It won't be long so I wouldn't leave the area if I were you." she told me.

I told her I'd hang around until she told me it was cool to leave. As she walked out two sheriff's deputies walked in. We were the only group in the courtroom. We filed out into the hallway not giving it a second thought. Ryan and Erin were talking so Tucker and I walked into the hall with the rest of the family.

Once in the hall we were all talking, I was filling Ronnie in on what the next step was. That's when we saw Ryan being lead out of the courtroom in cuffs by the deputies. We were all confused. Erin was pissed. "They're locking him up!" she yelled to me as she walked behind him.

"For what?" I asked

"An old fuh'in' warrant, (Ryan answered) the fuh'in' prosecutor tol' 'em to do it."

I looked at one of the deputies; sure enough he was nodding his head, as they escorted Ryan through the hallway and into an elevator. We all just stood in the hallway confused as hell by what just took place. Erin got on her phone and called the jail to find out what the fine was going to be to get him out. It was $127. Before I could offer to give it to her she said she already had it and left to meet him at the jail.

The family was in a bit of an uproar. I was sitting on a table in the hallway with several of Antonio's family members standing around me. I decided to call Renee's office and tell her what happened. I called the office and the receptionist answered I told her what was going on. She told me Renee hadn't made it to the office yet and gave me her cell phone number. I was trying listen to the number when one of Antonio's cousins came up and started talking to me, telling me what to do. I held up my hand to indicate I was listening to what was being said. It didn't make a difference to him, he kept talking. I hung up with the receptionist. I thought I'd remembered the number she'd given me but, when I went to dial it, I drew a blank and had to call her right back. The cousin kept talking to me when I got the receptionist back on the phone. I walked away from everyone and went to a part of the hall where I could actually hear the number that was being given to me.

"I apologize for having to call you right back. There's a lot of commotion here and I couldn't hear the number. Could you give it to me again please? I'm sorry, I know you're busy." I said

"Not a problem, I understand." She said in a pleasant voice. I got the number and called Renee.

I told her what had just taken place.

"He's playing a dirty game." She said referring to the prosecutor.

"What can we do?" I asked.

"Nothing, his girlfriend is going to pay the money so he should be out sometime today." With that we hung up the phone.

While I was on the phone with Renee, Antonio's cousin took offense to me walking away and voiced his anger. He pulled Elissa aside and began bad mouthing me.

"Who she think she is? She ain't nobody. She ain't even

family." He told her

Ronnie saw what he was doing and jumped right in.

"I'll tell you who she is. She's the one footing the whole bill for all of this. So I'm going to tell you this once and only once. Let her do what she's been doing and leave her alone. She's got him this far and she'll get him the rest of the way. If you got a problem with it then I suggest you leave." She looked at the whole group of them and said, "That goes for all of ya." Mah Mah had spoken.

Once I was done on the phone with Renee I brought Ronnie and Tucker up to speed. Tucker and I left the courthouse and went to lunch across the street. We waited for Renee to call.

Before we finished lunch I received two calls, one from Renee telling me to be back at the courthouse by 1:30pm. The second from Erin, she went to the jail and was told that she couldn't post Ryan's bail until tomorrow. The prosecutor put a 24 hour hold on Ryan. Needless to say she was furious. I was too. I had never seen anything like this before in my life. I had never even seen this in a movie.

Tucker and I returned to the courthouse and the family had dwindled down to about 10 people. The cousin was still there though. Tucker and I took a seat on the same row as Ronnie and the other family members including Elissa but, we sat on the far end away from them. As I looked around the courtroom at the light colored wood, all the light green curtains, with pale green painted walls, Renee walked up with a smile and asked who everyone was. I started the introductions one by one and just as I got to Elissa, Renee interrupted me by laughing and said,

"Okay, okay everyone is a family member." She looked over the group and continued, "I'm glad you're all here and I hope you can come every day. It pulls a lot of weight with the jury when they see the courtroom is packed with family members." Then she went back to the defense table and started reading something.

I was beginning to worry. If they could pull at trick like that on

Ryan what else could they pull? Renee came back and sat with me after she was done reading. We were just chit chatting when the cousin came and sat behind us.

I'd heard about him from Antonio before. He was sentenced to 50 years in prison for an armed robbery. While in prison he mounted and defended himself in his appeal. His sentence was cut down and he was released from prison after serving 8 years. This made him a smart guy in the family.

"I think we should go with a bench trial." He said leaning his head between Renee's and mine. We both gave him a courtesy smile. I informed him that we were going with a jury trial. Renee and I continued to chit chat. He interrupted again.

"I think we should go with a bench trial." He was insistent. Renee and I both turned to look at him. He seemed pleased that he had gotten our attention and continued.

"We need a judge to rule on this and not let a jury have it. They could go either way. I done this before, I'm tellin' you we need to go with a bench trial. I'm telling ya." As he said this you could see the prison lawyer in him beaming with pride. I could see Renee was a little bit perturbed by him. I let her take this one. I just sat back as she started to respond to him.

"How long have you been trying cases?" She asked him

"I haven't." he responded sheepishly

"Good. I've been doing this for over 15 years and I have only tried one case as a bench trial, at my client's request. After that day, I swore I would never do it again. We are taking this to a jury. If they come back with a guilty verdict then we can still appeal the case. We give up that right with a bench trial, once the judge rules on the case there's no going back." Seemed pretty clear and simple to me but, the cousin still had an argument to make.

"Yeah but, the judge know the law. He has to go by it; the jury don't know the law. They can do whatever they want. I don't want to see my cousin go down for this." He had now turned into a militant black man.

"Do you think this case is about the law?" Renee turned her body toward him, "If this case was about the law, Antonio wouldn't have been locked up for this. At the very least, he would've been released when the victim told both the investigating officer and the two prosecutors that he didn't shoot him. Not to mention, the judge at the bond hearing who said Antonio shouldn't have been within fifty miles of the incident and refused to give him a bond. You want to go to a bench trial, with a judge who has his entire record in front of him, the power to put him away for life and not have it overturned on appeal? Let's not forget the prosecutor who just locked up the victim for not wanting to get on the stand and lie to help him out? I don't think so. I don't want a single person having that much control over his life. I don't think you want that for him either." She turned her back to him and I watched him shrink down to size. I wanted to laugh my head off but I felt sorry for him instead.

"Look, we've got this thing covered. Believe that. We go with a jury trial. No jury is going to listen to Ryan get on that stand, hear him say Tonio didn't do it and convict him. A judge would though. We're going to take our chances with a jury and watch him come home." I said to him.

(Now keep in mind, Ryan has told the Lead Investigator, a Judge and by the time of trial, FOUR Prosecutors that Antonio didn't shoot him. Antonio is STILL in jail 9 months later. This dude wants to give a Judge FULL CONTROL over the verdict.)

Still shrinking he said, "Well, I guess you got it covered." And with that he slid down the bench and left us alone. I got the feeling he thought he was going to show up at the trial and give legal advice to one of the top defense lawyers in the state of Maryland. He was outnumbered both in brains and strength. We were two strong women. We could handle this. He wasn't needed and he caught that hint immediately.

The judge came into the courtroom. Both the lawyers talked with him to schedule the trail and its process. Jury selection would begin later that morning. If the jury hadn't been sat by the end of the day, they would continue tomorrow morning and resume until it had been, with opening statements to follow. Antonio wasn't in the courtroom for this. He had been taken back to the jail. He rode there with Ryan and the two of them had a good laugh about being locked up together.

Tuesday morning when Tucker and I were about to walk into the courtroom Renee greeted us. She informed us that she'd just left a meeting with the judge and the prosecutor about Ryan. The prosecutor asked the judge to sign a material witness warrant on Ryan, to keep him locked up until he testified in the trail. He explained to the judge that his office had made numerous attempts to reach Ryan before trial, even going to several homes and couldn't find him. He was afraid he wouldn't come to court to testify if he was released. Renee didn't argue the point and agreed to keep Ryan locked up until the he testified. I was upset about that. I made it clear I thought she should've fought for him.

"First of all, I'm not his attorney. Second of all, while I was listening to his argument, I was picturing Ryan sitting in jail for two days and how pissed off he's going to be once he gets on that stand tomorrow. I want him to be angry. I want him to let his ass have it when he testifies tomorrow. I'm going to give him every opportunity to tell the jury what was done to him when he showed up to court as the victim in this case. That's how I'm going to represent my client." I wanted to hug her. I was witnessing brilliance. I love this woman. I wasn't mad at her in the least bit.

When I walked into the courtroom, I saw Puerto Rican Yo sitting in there. I sat behind him and said hello. He asked me where Antonio was. I looked at him like he was crazy.

'What do you mean, where's Antonio? He's locked up." I said with a smirk on my face and my eye's questioning his sobriety.

“He’s still locked up? I thought they let him out on a bond.” He replied faking complete surprise. Then he got up and left the room walking out into the hall.

Jury selection was boring. The family support had dwindled down to Tucker, Erin and me. Tucker couldn’t stay in the courtroom with us because he was going to be a witness. Erin and I spent most of the time in the hallway with him. Once the jury had been seated late that morning, my nerves went crazy. The judge broke for lunch with opening statement to begin as soon as we resumed for the afternoon.

They jury was made of mostly women. There were only two men, both white. One stuck out to me more than the other. He was a balding white guy, with a stank ass look on his face. The rest of the jurors were women, ranging in the age from early 30’s to mid-60s. They all looked like working class people. It was about 50/50 white and black. They sat in the far right hand corner of the courtroom. The judge was directly in front of me with Renee and Antonio on my left, the prosecutor sitting closest to the jury.

The opening statements started like you see in the movies. The prosecutor stood up and introduced himself to the jury. “The state will prove that,” Yada, yada, yada. You know the rest. When Renee stood up to talk, you could see the jury was waiting to see what kind of snake oil she was selling. She said what you would expect a defense attorney to say during opening arguments, “My client didn’t do it”. They were waiting for her to say it and seemed to give a collective, ‘Whatever’, look. I liked them for that. I knew this was my jury. If they were that obvious in their feelings about Renee, they would be that telling about their feelings during the case. At least that was my thought process.

Renee didn’t mention anything about Ryan testifying that Antonio didn’t do it. She made her statement short and sweet, ‘He didn’t do it’.

The first few witnesses were called to the stand. First, one of the paramedics that treated Ryan at the scene then the doctor that treated him. They testified about the severity of his wounds. He had been shot 7 times. It was a miracle not only that he lived but, he didn't sustain any life threatening injuries. Next, the patrol officer that was responsible for bringing the eye witnesses into the station house. It was Yo. His name was called into the hall. He walked in and sat in the witness box. After being sworn in the prosecutor started asking him questions.

Were you working on such and such a day?

Yes he was.

"Can you tell us about that morning?" The Prosecutor asked Yo

"I was patrolling the neighborhood and I was stopped by one of the residents of Nanticoke St. He informed me that he witnessed the shooting that occurred the night before. I asked him if anyone was with him, he informed me that his girlfriend witnessed it as well." Yo replied.

"What did you do once he said that?" He was asked by the prosecutor.

"I asked him to have his girlfriend come talk to me. He walked into his house. They both came out. She told me she too had witnessed the shooting."

"After confirming that there was a second witness, what did you do after that?"

"I placed both of them in my patrol car. I then drove them to the precinct in Cherry Hill."

"Did you just drop them off and leave them?"

"No, I introduced them to the lead investigator. I stayed with them through the entire process. I even drove them home after they were done." The black women jurors seemed to pay that some attention.

"Who was the lead investigator you introduced them too?" He asked Yo who then picked up a notebook from his lap and began to read through it.

"His name is, Detective Warren Claymore."

Yo, went on to tell how he was there when the eyewitnesses identified Antonio in a photo lineup. That he basically walked them through the entire process with Det. Claymore. Then he drove them home when all the paperwork was signed. He dropped them off and finished his shift. Renee asked him a few questions. There was one that stuck out to me. She asked him what the name of the female witness was and Yo replied, "Danielle." He looked at me right after he said it. Making sure he made eye contact with me. The reason this stood out, is because Danielle is the name of Nick's old girlfriend and Yo knows that. He intentionally gave the wrong name. He made it a name that was so familiar to us, Antonio and I had to pick it up. I broke my gaze from Yo, looked at Antonio who was already staring at me. He caught it too. Yo was dismissed from the stand and walked out of the courtroom. He didn't look at Antonio when he passed him. He looked me dead in the eyes once again. As he passed he gave me a wink. I subconsciously wagged my head, kind of stuck. He saw it. By the look on his face, he knew he caught me off guard. He'd won that round.

The next witnessed called was Tucker. After being sworn in the prosecutor asked him to tell the jury what happened the night of the shooting. He went through the entire ordeal. He and Ryan had gone into the bar to order a sandwich to go. While they were waiting they had a beer. Ryan bought a small bottle of liquor to go with them.

When they walked out of the bar they were confronted by two black guys, in their early 20's, one light skinned with a white shirt tied around his head like a turban. The other was dark skinned. They both stood about 5'10" with guns and demanded money. Tucker said before they could do anything, the guys started shooting. Tucker was closest to the door and was able to get back in. Ryan wasn't so lucky. When the shooting stopped, Tucker went back outside, to find Ryan lying on the ground in front of the bar, bleeding from all over. Another patron in the bar told Tucker to follow him to his car. The two of them tried to follow the shooters to get their tag number. They were unsuccessful. They returned to the bar to find the ambulance taking Ryan away and the police on the scene. Tucker said he was escorted to the lead investigator, Det. Claymore by a patrolman. Tucker identified himself as a witness to the Detective. The prosecutor kept his questioning bland and brief before letting Renee have a turn. Renee got up to question Tucker and asked him,

"Did you have anything in your hands when the shooting started?"

"Yes." Tucker answered

"What did you have?" she asked

"I had the sandwich I just bought."

"Can you describe the sandwich? I mean, what was it in? Was it in a bag? Were you holding the sandwich while you were eating it?"

"No. It wasn't in a bag and I wasn't eating it. It was wrapped in aluminum foil with tape holding it closed." He answered

"What happened to the sandwich when the shooting started?"

"I had it in my hand when I ran back into the bar. I dropped it on the floor when I ducked for cover with everyone else in the bar."

"What did you do when the shooting stopped?"

"I ran outside to see where Ryan was."

"What about the sandwich?"

"I picked it up off the floor on my way out." Tucker looked kind of embarrassed to be saying that.

I'm sure I wasn't the only one wondering why Renee was focusing on the sandwich. Where was she going with this?

"Did you get a good look at the person or persons who shot your friend?"

"Yes, I did."

"Is that person or persons in this courtroom?"

"No, they're not."

The prosecutor didn't ask that question of Tucker. The jury

seemed to pick up on that. One of the jurors, an older black woman, with short hair and glasses sitting in the 3rd chair, of the front row, closest to me, made eye contact with me. It was quick and deliberate. I was encouraged by this. My hope was growing.

Under Renee's line of questioning, Tucker was able to talk to the jury. He told the jurors that the investigator immediately started treating him as a suspect. He was interrogated on the corner feet from where the shooting took place. After repeated denials Tucker was punched in his face by the lead investigator. He was then taken to the precinct in Cherry Hill where Det. Claymore continued to accuse him of being involved in the shooting. When Renee had no more questions for Tucker, he was dismissed from the courtroom.

The prosecutor next brought out a TV and VCR. He played the surveillance video from the bar the night of the shooting. There was no sound. On black and white video we saw Ryan take a sip from what was clearly a liquor bottle. He put it in the side pocket of his cargo shorts. We saw Ryan and Tucker walk out after being handed a sandwich from the bartender. The two of them casually walked out of the bar. In a matter of seconds, all the bar patrons drop to the floor. They all look toward the door. Some start running for the back. Others cower under the bar where they were. You see Tucker run in and drop his sandwich as he ducked for cover. It appeared the shooting must've stopped because people slowly start to get up. Tucker gets up stumbling toward the door. Without looking down he bends over and scoops up the sandwich as he heads out the door still stumbling. The tape ends. The judge ended court for the day.

What Will Today Bring?

Wednesday morning Erin, Tucker and I were standing in front of the courthouse while Erin smoked a cigarette. A blue Crown Victoria, with tinted windows and two large white men wearing ties pulls up. It's obviously an undercover car. It instantly caught our attention. One cop got out of the front seat and opened the back passenger door. We were looking to see who would get out. First one out was Bobby. He had on a pauper suit, jacket, pants and shirt, not made to be worn together. It was different shades of green. I was pretty sure he didn't choose to wear it. His hair was washed and the sore on his cheek was now the size of a racquetball. It was covered with foundation.Then Lisa popped out of the car. She was pissed. The look on her face was pure anger. She was definitely ill. She got out of the car and saw me standing there. I was shocked when she walked right up to me and began talking as if, not only didn't the police drive her there but, they weren't walking up behind her.

"J.O., I'm sick o' this shit. The picked us up last night and kept us in a hotel all night. (Yup! She's ill) Tell your lawyer to make sure she asks me about how we chose him out of the lineup. Tell her to ask me, 'What did the police say to you when they asked you to look at the pictures?' Just like that. You got that?" I nodded as she said. "I'm sick o' this shit!" Erin handed her the rest of the cigarette she was smoking. Lisa just stood there puffing on the cigarette shaking, her head while looking at the ground. I made it a point not to utter one word. I just watched and listened. The two cops and Bobby stood about six feet behind her lingering. When she was done smoking, she tossed the filter to the ground, stepped on it, looked up at me and said, "I'm sick o' this shit." As she walked to the courthouse door the two plain clothes cops and Bobby caught up to her, escorting her in. Erin, Tucker and I just stood there, watched her go all the way in the building. We turned back to each other and didn't say a word. I mean really? What do you say after that?

Once in the courtroom, I walk up to Renee at the defense table. Court hadn't begun so Antonio hadn't been brought in yet. I ask her to step into the hall so we can chat. Once in the hall, I tell her what Lisa said. Renee was worried it was a trap. I reminded her there couldn't be a trap because he didn't do it. We agreed that Renee would ask the question.

When court began for the day, Bobby was the first witness called to the stand. The prosecutor stood from his chair as Bobby was being sworn in. He had an air of importance to him today. He was the only one thinking he wasn't obvious. He made you feel like this witness was going to clear up any confusion the jury might have. At least that's what I got. It was nauseating to watch. He stepped in front of the table as he started asking Bobby to state his name for the record and the other preliminary questions. He leaned on it as he began to get onto the night of the shooting.

"Can you tell us what happened the night of June 10th 2003? At approximately 7:15pm?"

"My girlfriend and I were walking up the street from our house."

"What street were you on?" he was asked

"We were on Nanticoke St in South Baltimore."

"How far did you walk up the street?"

"We were walking up to Washington Blvd."

"Can you tell us what happened while you and your girlfriend were walking up the street?"

"While we were walking across Cross St someone started shooting."

"Did you see the shooting happen?" the jurors perked up in anticipation of the answer.

"Yeah, we saw it."

"Did you see the person who shot the victim?"

"Yes, we saw him."

“When you say ‘we’, you mean you and your girlfriend, correct?”

“Yes”

“What is your girlfriend’s name?”

“Her name is Lisa?”

“Would you tell the jury about the shooting?”

“We were walking across Cross St and we heard someone yelling about giving them money. The next thing you know I hear shots going off.”

“So you saw the shooter in the act?”

“Yes.”

“Can you describe the shooter for us?”

“There were two black guys. One was light skinned with a white t-shirt tied around his head and the other one was dark skinned.”

“Bobby, can you tell us about the next morning?”

“Yes.”

“Did you go to the precinct with police?”

“Yes.”

“How did you get there?”

“The police drove us.”

“How did you come in contact with the police?”

“I was walking down the street when Officer Yo pulled up to me in his police car.”

“What happened next?”

“He asked me if I knew about the shooting that happened the night before.”

“Did you tell him you knew something about it?”

“I told him I knew about it.”

“What happened next?”

“He asked me where Lisa was.”

“What happened next, Bobby?”

“I told him she was at home and he told me to get in the back of his car. He drove me back to the house and told me to go get Lisa."

"What happened when Lisa came out of the house?" "He took us to the precinct in Cherry Hill."

"Did you have a chance to look at a photo lineup?"

"Yes"

"Did you identify anyone in the photos?"

"Yes" The prosecutor asks for permission to approach the witness and enter the photo into evidence. He then shows Bobby the photo lineup and asks Bobby if it was his signature on the document. Bobby acknowledged it was.

"Bobby, I'd like you to take a look around the room for me. Please tell the jury if you see the person you identified as the shooter in this document?"

Bobby looks around the courtroom and sheepishly identifies Antonio as the shooter. The jurors didn't give me much of a tell with this revelation.

The prosecutor relinquished the witness. Renee got up from her chair and went to stand in front of Bobby.

"You said you were walking across Cross St when the shooting happened, is that right?"

"Yes."

"How far were you standing away from the shooter?"

"I don't know." He shrugged his shoulders.

"Would you say you were 15 feet away?" She walked 15 feet from the witness stand. When she reached the distance she motioned with her hands asking the question again.

"No. Farther."

Renee walked into the empty seating area in the courtroom to the right of me across the room. She stopped at the first row of empty seats the distance being only two or three more feet and turned back to Bobby.

"How about this far away?"

"Yeah, that's about right." She remained in that spot for the next round of questioning. Pointing to herself she asks,

"Let's pretend I'm you. I want you to tell me what direction you're facing when the shooting started?"

"I was walking toward the Blvd."

"So which way is the Blvd if I'm standing where you were standing and you're standing where the shooters are standing?" She's facing him while she asks the question.

"The Blvd would be behind you."

"So you're both walking to the Blvd facing this way?" She turns with her back toward Bobby and the jury. She then turns back to him and asks, "Where is the victim? Is he anywhere near you?"

"No, he was in front of the bar." She's talking over her right shoulder.

"If you're standing where the shooters are and I'm standing where you are, where is Ryan standing?" With his thumb he pointed behind him. The jurors start giving each other glances.

"He would be behind me." The jurors start chattering among themselves, some nodding their heads to the others. They're all conferring with one another. Renee keeps going.

"So the shooting starts, which way were the shooters facing?"

"They were facing the bar." The jury is silent, watching Renee as if they know what she's about to do. Some of them are slightly nodding their heads waiting for it.

"So you and your girlfriend, Lisa right?" She turns her body at the waist to ask him this.

"Yes. Lisa." He responds.

"So you and Lisa are walking toward the Blvd in this direction (she slowly turns around while asking the question) when the shooting starts?"

"Yes" he replies. Without turning around she continues.

"The shooters are facing the bar which is behind you, correct?"

"Yes"

"What did you do when the shooting started? Did you run?"

"Yes, we both did."

"So you're running in the direction of the Blvd then?"

"Yes" The jurors were looking at Renee's back, shaking their heads. Renee then turns around, walks back toward the jury, makes eye contact with them and heads over to the defense table. As she approaches the table Antonio gave her an approving nod of the job she was doing so far. She picks up a few 8 by 10 pictures off the table and heads back over to the witness. She asks him to come off the stand. She invited him to stand with her directly in front of the jury. As he stepped out of the witness box, she held her full hands out to the jurors, inviting them to have a good look at him as she questioned him. The pictures were of the crime scene. One of them having been taken of the area Bobby was being questioned about. On the picture Renee had Bobby show the jury where he, Lisa, the shooters and Ryan were standing when the shooting started. The picture was taken at night so it reflected what he saw more accurately. The jurors weren't paying attention to the pictures. They were investigating Bobby instead. It didn't take them long to notice the open sore covered with foundation on his cheek. Renee made sure that side of his face was closest to the jury. I knew the moment they noticed it. The look on their faces told it all. They were disgusted. A couple of them even pointed at it. The whole time he stood there the entire jury looked like a bunch of monkeys eating lemons. I knew they got it. Renee was enjoying it. I wished I was standing right next to her, so I could feel what they were feeling. I had that burning in my body that comes when you want to scream but you can't. I was so happy.

After the jurors got their fill of him, Renee ended her questioning.

Once Bobby left the stand you could see a noticeable difference in the jury. In between witnesses they would sit patiently but after Bobby they seemed irritated. They looked at the prosecutor differently. They had contempt for him. They didn't hide it in the least bit. From that point on when he got up to talk they gave him attitude. They gave him dirty looks. They let him know they weren't buying his snake oil. Some of them fell just short of scoffing at him out right.

The next witness was Lisa.

Lisa entered the courtroom with a big attitude. You could tell she was angry. The jury seemed curious about this. They watched her every move as she was sworn in and the prosecutor began questioning her. She wasn't hiding how she felt about being there. The jury was particularly interested in her.

"Do you remember the night of June 10th, 2003?"

"Yes."

"Can you tell us what happened that night?"

"There was a shooting in front o' Foul Ball."

"Did you see the shooting?"

"Yes"

"Did you see the person who shot the victim, Bryan Thomas?"

"I saw the shooting."

"I understand that. What I'm asking you is did you see the shooter?"

"No" She rolled her eyes.

The jurors sat straight up in their chairs and leaned closer to her. The whole front row then looks at the prosecutor. I'm holding my breath.

"Lisa, didn't you identify someone as the shooter to the police the day after the shooting?"

"Yes"

"Then I'll ask you the question again. Did you see the shooter?"

"No, I didn't see what their faces looked like." With permission he entered the photo lineup Lisa signed identifying Antonio and handed it to her.

"Lisa, is this the photo lineup you signed identifying the

defendant as the person you saw shoot the victim Bryan Thomas?" Looking at the photo Lisa responded.

"Yes" She placed the paper on the stand in front of her.

"How is it that you identified the shooter in a photo lineup but you say you didn't see the shooter now?"

"I didn't see them." Lisa insisted.

"Lisa, are you afraid of something or someone? Is that why your testimony has changed?"

"No" She let out an exasperated breath and rolled her eyes again.

"Then can you please tell us why you've changed your statement?"

"The cops brought us to the station early in the morning. I was ill. I didn't want to be there and if I had to point someone out to get out of there then I would have and that's what I did."

My face hit the floor. Tucker was sitting behind Erin and me, I heard him say, "Oh, shit!" The jurors just stared at the prosecutor waiting to see how he would turn this into something that would benefit him.

"Are you ill now, Lisa?"

"Yeah, I'd say I am. They picked us up last night and I haven't been able to get well yet, so yes I'm pretty ill."

"So would you be saying anything to get out of here as soon as possible to go get well?"

"If that was the case I'd be saying what you wanted me to say, wouldn't I?" It was as if the jury was watching a tennis match. They would turn their heads to who was talking.

"Lisa, can you tell us what I just handed you?"

"It's the paper with the photo lineup."

"Would you tell me the name of the person who signed it?" She picked it up and turned it over to look at the signature.

"Me. I signed it."

"Would you turn the page over and tell me if there is any sort of marking on the page?"

"Yes, there's a pictured circled."

"Do you see the person YOU identified as the shooter the day after the shooting today in this courtroom?" He asked irritated with her. Before she answered him she looked over at Antonio and then looked back at the Prosecutor and gave him a look that could kill.

"Yes"

"Would you please point out that person you identified as the shooter to police the morning after the shooting?" She rolled her eyes at him. Turned toward Antonio, lifted her arm as if it weighed 100 lbs., barely pointing at Antonio, before dropping it in her lap, as if exhausted without saying a word.

"Your Honor, I'd like the record to show that the witness pointed to the defendant in this case?" The Prosecutor asked the judge and the judge so ordered.

"Thank you, Lisa I have your sworn statement right here. Are you telling this court that you lied when you signed this?"

"I'm telling you I didn't see the shooter."

"So your testimony today is you didn't see the shooter?"

"I Did Not See the Shooter." She was emphatic

"I have no more questions for this witness, Your Honor." He sat down and didn't look up from his lap as Renee got up. The entire front row of the jury started smiling when Renee walked over to them to question Lisa. It was as if they were rooting her on. They wanted to see what she could get out of Lisa. I couldn't wait.

"Hi, Lisa How are you today?" Renee asked in a caring tone.

"I'm ok, thank you."

"Lisa, I just have a few questions for you, so please bear with me."

"Okay"

Tell us how you came to be at the police station on the morning of June 11th, 2003?"

"My boyfriend Bobby left the house to go get our gate shot."

Renee interrupted her.

"I'm sorry, Lisa, what's a 'gate shot'?"

"It's the first high of the day."

"Are you an addict?"

"Yes"

"Is your boyfriend, Bobby an addict as well?"

"Yes."

"What drug or drugs are you addicted to?"

"Heroin and crack, mostly heroin, though."

"Please continue?"

"Bobby was gone about 10 minutes and when he came back in the house he said the police wanted me to come outside. I asked him for what but he just walked out of the door."

"Did you go outside to talk to the police?"

"Yes, it was Officer Yo."

"What happened next?"

"Yo told us he wanted us to go down to the precinct in Cherry Hill with him."

"Did you ask him why?"

"He said it was about the shooting last night."

"Did he ask you if you saw the shooting?"

"No"

"What happened next?"

"I told him I was ill. Bobby told him the same thing. Bobby told him we'd go with him after we got out the gate."

"What does that mean, 'out the gate'?"

"It means after we got high?"

"So you told him you were suffering from withdrawals and would go with him to the precinct after you relieved those symptoms? Is that correct?"

"Yes"

"What did Officer Yo say to that?"

"He said we didn't have time for that and if we hurried up we would be back before noon."

"What time of the morning are you having this conversation?"

"It was about 8am."

"So, he told you he'd have you back by noon? On an average day Lisa how many times would you have gotten high between the hours of 8am and noon?"

"3 or 4"

"You hadn't gotten high that morning, correct?"

"No we hadn't."

"When was the last time you two had gotten high prior to that morning?"

"When we got back from the Boulevard, after the shooting, we got high for the rest of the night, 'til we went to sleep."

"How many times a day do you and Bobby use heroin Lisa?"

"About fifteen times a day." The jury is shaking their heads.

"Fifteen times each or the both of you total fifteen a day using heroin?"

"Each."

"Turning back to the officer, Lisa did you agree to go with him?"

"We didn't have a choice. Yes."

"Why do you feel you didn't you have a choice?"

"If we didn't go then he would've waited for us to go cop and he would've arrested us." The prosecutor objected and the judge sustained. Renee kept right on going. The jurors already heard it. They knew she was telling the truth.

"When you got to the precinct were you shown a photo lineup?"

"Yes."

"Who showed you the lineup?"

"Yo"

"What did he say when he showed you the lineup photo's?"

"He gave us the paper with the pictures on it and asked us to point out the person we recognized." The jurors were staring daggers at the prosecutor.

"Lisa, are you sure that's what he asked you?"

"Yes, I'm positive."

"How did you come to pick out my client?"

"We didn't know any of the other guys on the page."

"You recognized my client though?"

"Yes, he was the only one we knew."

"How do you know him?"

"Tonio's from the neighborhood. I've always seen him in the neighborhood."

"Earlier you said you didn't see the shooter. Why didn't you see the shooter?"

"I took off running when I heard the shooting start. I did look to see who was shooting when it started but I only saw the back of 'em."

"Can you describe what you saw as you ran away?"

"I saw a guy with a shirt wrapped around his head. I think he was the one shooting."

"Which way was he facing while he was shooting?"

"I saw the back of him."

"What about Bobby? Did you see what he was doing when the shooting started?"

"He was running ahead of me." The jurors started grumbling.

"Lisa, is it your testimony here today under oath, that you never saw the shooter and the only reason you picked my client out of a photo lineup is because you were instructed by the police to pick out the person you recognized?"

"And I was ill."

"And you were ill. Is that your sworn testimony here today?"

"Yes ma'am."

"Are you ill now Lisa?"

"Yes ma'am."

“I apologize for keeping you so long. Your Honor, I have no further questions for this witness.”

The judge gave the jury their lunch break.

A Smile and a Wink

Erin, Tucker and I went to smoke a blunt in the parking garage and grabbed something to eat before we had to be back. To combat the laziness from the weed we each drank an energy drink right before going in the courthouse. I was nervous. I didn't want to take anything for granted. The jury seemed to have shifted completely to our side but, I wasn't ready to let myself celebrate just yet. I couldn't, I had to be prepared for the worst. I tried to keep my head focused in case the worst happened. Erin and Tucker were celebrating already. They were convinced the jurors smelled the bullshit we'd smelled all these months. They tried to convince me to relax. I wanted to but, I couldn't. I was high, so I'll substitute that for relaxed.

Once the three of us returned to the courthouse we waited in the hall for court to start. The prosecutor walked passed us on his way in but wouldn't look at us. We were the only ones in the hallway. When Renee got back we went over Lisa's testimony.

"Can you believe her?" Renee asked me.

"I was shocked. What about her telling you she saw the shooter going into the bar?"

"Once she said she didn't see the shooter I was happy." Renee said.

"I was too." Erin interjected

"I thought the jury was going to walk out of the room when she said it." Tucker added

"I have never seen a jury this animated. I like it." Renee said with a big smile on her face.

"I think all of us do except the prosecutor." Tucker said. We agreed by laughing.

Court began once the jury was seated. There was a noticeable difference when the jury came back from lunch that day. It was the first time most of the women acknowledged me. They didn't speak to me but, as they were being seated about four of them made eye contact with me. Each held their gaze until I was aware it was intentional. It was the first time I felt good enough to give them all a slight smile to let them know I was acknowledging them back.

The judge stopped the prosecutor in the middle of calling the next witness and asked the attorneys to approach the bench. On Renee's instruction Antonio went with them.

The judge was an old angry, tall, lean white man. The entire trial he sat on the bench with a menacing look on his face. He had the same look as he spoke to the attorneys as Antonio listened. He was focusing on Renee while he spoke. We couldn't hear him. Antonio turned to me in the middle of the conversation and mouthed something. The only thing I could understand was that the judge was talking about Antonio to Renee. He was angry, he made that very clear. He dismissed them.

The next witness to be called was Ryan. The prosecutor asks the judge for permission to approach him and with permission he, Renee and Antonio returned to the bench. He just listened intently as they spoke among themselves. After they were done talking and left the bench the judge gave the jury a ten minute bathroom break.

Once the jury was out of the room Antonio turned around in his chair and told me that the judge told Renee that he had been receiving threatening looks from her client. If Antonio didn't stop immediately, the judge would make him watch the rest of the trial from a television monitor in a room outside of the courtroom. Antonio denied giving the judge dirty looks.

With the jury out of the room Ryan was escorted in by two officers. Ryan was wearing leg irons. They escorted him to the witness stand with Ryan taking little short steps to accommodate the shackles. Once he was seated in the witness box and the escorts had left the room, the jury was allowed back in from break. It was then I realized that the jury was given a break so they wouldn't know Ryan was shackled. If they had it could've prejudice them against him. You could only see Ryan from the waist up as he sat in the box. I was angry that they couldn't see his feet. As the proceedings began Ryan looked directly at Antonio, gave him a smile and a wink. The jurors saw it.

The prosecutor started questioning him as soon as he was sworn in. Ryan recounted the night he was shot by repeating what Tucker had already said. His story separated when the shooting started. He was first out of the door, trying to fasten the button on his cargo shorts, making sure his bottle of liquor didn't fall out. Two black men, described the exact same as Tucker described them demanded money. Ryan said when the shooting started he ran for the door but, when the first bullet hit him, he couldn't make it from the sheer force. The next 6 hit him as he tried to head in the opposite direction to Nanticoke St. He testified he tried to hide behind one of the support beams to get cover from the shots. He never even cleared the awning before falling. It was as if Ryan was at home plate and the bullets were being fired from the pitching mound. He was cornered.

Ryan went on to talk about being whisked away in the ambulance to shock trauma. He said he woke up in Shock Trauma with paper bags on his hands. The nurse was arguing with the lead investigator on the case. He said Claymore ignored the nurses' demands that he leave and shouted questions at him. While he was laying on a bed fighting for his life with 7 bullets in him, he was being treated as a suspect in his own shooting. You could see the anger growing in Ryan's face with each prosecution question.

As Ryan answered the next question, I heard it.

"Did you get a good look at the man who shot you?"

"Yeah, I saw them." Ryan emphasized his by stomping each foot.

The two stomps made the chains rattle. I looked at the jury and they heard it too. The sound was magnified in the big, marble room.

The prosecutor was visibly thrown off by the sound. He took a moment before he asked the next question. Out of sheer frustration with the pause in questioning, Ryan stomped his feet again and rattled the chains. The chains were louder. You could tell they were coming from the witness box. The jurors started moving around in their chairs giving each other long looks as they all realized it at the same time. They knew he was wearing leg irons. Some of them started watching Ryan's movements to make sure he was the one responsible for the noise. He watched them watch him and deliberately stomped his feet two more times consecutively to give them confirmation. Once the jury had their confirmation, they turned to the prosecutor, who like the rest of us watched it all go down. Erin and I were sitting together. We grabbed each other's hand and held tight.

The prosecutor knew he had a problem. He didn't let it affect his line of questioning. He continued,

"Can you look around the courtroom and tell the jury if you see the man who shot you?"

The jurors leaned forward waiting on Ryan to answer as he glanced around the courtroom. Then he shook the chains one more time before answering the question taking his time, he replied.

"No." the jury erupted to my surprise. The first woman who locked eyes with me earlier leaned over to the woman on her left and said loud enough for me to hear across the room,

"He didn't do it." I thought I was going to pass out when I heard her.

"Would you take a moment to look around the room again and tell us if you see the person who shot you?" the prosecutor asked him again. The jury leaned backward this time knowing the answer wouldn't change. This time Ryan made a show out of looking around the courtroom. He stretched his neck out to look at the section of the courtroom with no one sitting in it. He stood up in the box making sure that the chains rattled some more, looking behind the jury. He sat back down in the chair, stretching his neck to look behind the judge sitting on the bench before, returning his glare to the prosecutor sitting at the table in front of him. He answered the question again.

"No."

The jurors were now giving the prosecutor their own glare but, he's not done yet.

"Would you take a look at the defense table please?" He asked Ryan still not giving up. Ryan looked right at Antonio and then back at the prosecutor.

"Yeah?" Ryan replied.

"Do you see the person who shot you sitting at the table?"

"How many times do I have to tell you he didn't shoot me?" Ryan snapped at him. The chains are BOOMING from the marble acustics.

The jurors started twisting in their chairs, grumbling amongst themselves, some shaking their heads while doing it. The prosecutor finally gave up and Renee took over.

"Do you know my client?" was her first question.

'Yes." He quickly replied he seemed relieved he was about to tell his story. The chains weren't as loud.

"How do you know him?"

"He's my brother!" the jurors started chattering again.

"When you say brother, do mean you share at least one parent?" Renee asked matter of fact.

"No, we're not related at all. I've known Tonio since I was a little kid. We grew up in the same neighborhood. I was a little light skinned kid growin' up in the hood; he was a big light skinned kid growin' up in the hood. We're both light skinned in the hood. That kinda makes us brothers." The jurors laughed. Then Ryan looked at Antonio and said, "What up Light Skin?", once again rattling the chains. Everybody but the prosecutor and judge laughed out loud. Then Renee brought things back into focus.

"So if my client was to have shot you, you would know it was him who did it and be able to identify him to the police wouldn't you?" Renee asked standing right next to the jury box in front of Ryan.

"Shoot me? *(chains)* He would never shoot me. *(chains)* He would never do anything to harm me. I never have to worry about him doing anything to me. He's my family." The jurors looked at Antonio with soft eyes. They quickly turned their gaze to the prosecutor with hard eyes.

"So you're telling this jury and this court that my client is not the person or persons who shot you?"

"That's exactly what I'm saying again!" he shook the chains again by stomping his foot to emphasize, 'again'.

Renee picked up on that.

"You said again. Is this the first time you've said my client wasn't the person who shot you?" the jurors were all ears.

"No, this is NOT the first time I've said he didn't do it."

"When was the first time you told someone my client wasn't the person who shot you?"

"The minute I found out he was arrested for shootin' me."

"Who did you tell this to?"

"I called the lead investigator, Det. Claymore."

"Where did you call him from?"

"I was in the hospital."

"So, let me get this straight? You find out your friend was arrested for shooting you, you called from your hospital bed to report to the lead investigator that they had the wrong man? Is that right?"

"Yes." *(chains)*

"What did the Detective say to you when you told him my client didn't shoot you?"

"He told me he was going on vacation for a week and when he got back he would drop the charges and get Tonio out o' there."

(chains)

"Did you hear back from him after that?"

"No. I called but he was never in and he didn't return the messages I left for 'im." *(chains)*

Renee let the jurors take it all in before she continued.

"Did you tell anyone else other than Det. Claymore?"

"Yes." *(chains)*

"Who else did you tell?"

"I left the rehabilitation center and went to one of his preliminary hearing. I told the prosecutor at the courthouse in Cherry Hill. That dude looked me up and down and asked me why I want to let the guy who did this to me get away with it. I started yelling at him. He wouldn't let me talk at the hearing. He told the cop outside the courtroom not to let me in."

It seemed the jurors were with us all the way. They sat back in their chairs taking in everything Ryan had to say.

"Was anything done after you told that prosecutor?"

"No" *(chains)*

"At any time have you ever indicated my client was the one who shot you?"

"No, never." *(chains)*

"What is that noise?" Renee directly asked Ryan.

"They're the chains on the leg irons I'm wearing."

The jurors already knew.

"Why are you wearing leg irons Ryan?" He turned his body completely toward the jury, making sure to rattle the chains before answering.

"I'm wearing 'em because when I showed up for court on Monday and told the prosecutor here, I wasn't gonna lie on the stand and say Tonio shot me. He had me arrested and won't let me pay the fine to get out. I've been in jail for the last 2 days." Some jurors nodded with sympathy. Others just dropped their heads, shaking them.

She asked him about the night at the hospital and how he was treated by the lead investigator. Was he in a lot of pain while being peppered with questions? He responded "yes". We all felt for him. The jurors seemed to be amazed he was sitting in front of them. He said the Detective refused to leave Ryan alone when a nurse requested he leave the questioning for a later time. He told the jury about his injuries and how painful they were. His hip had to be replaced. He'll have a bullet lodged in his back for the rest of his life. It was either that or risk paralysis removing it. He walked them through everything he had to go through during his recovery. You could see their empathy for him. Renee ended her questioning. The prosecutor just wouldn't let it go and began his redirect.

"Bryan, isn't it true you had an outstanding warrant for your arrest and that's why you were arrested?" He asked from his chair. The jurors perked up at the question.

"Yeah, an open container warrant from two years ago. It's a $127 fine and you put a hold on me so my girlfriend couldn't pay it! I've been sitting in jail for 2 days for nothin'!" the jurors sat back in their disgust. The prosecutor finally gave up and ended the questioning.

Seeing as the jurors knew Ryan was in custody, the judge didn't send them out of the room. Ryan eased from the witness stand and waddled over toward two approaching officers. As he baby stepped out of the courtroom the jurors leaned forward to take a look at his leg irons. They gave the prosecutor the dirtiest looks once they were done watching Ryan waddle away. It was then I felt I could start chilling the champagne. Ryan's testimony went well into the afternoon. After he was done the judge sent everyone home for the day. I thought it was a good idea. It gave the jurors the night to go over not only Ryan's testimony but Bobby and Lisa's too. Tucker and I followed Erin over to the jail to get Ryan out. She paid the fine and I paid for dinner once he was released.

The Beginning of the End

We went to Sabatino's in Little Italy, the best Italian restaurant in Baltimore. We laughed about how the day in court went. We filled Ryan in on all he'd missed. Tomorrow he'd be able to go in the courtroom and listen to the rest of the testimony. He wasn't going to be called back to the stand. We laughed, we ate and Ryan assured me that Antonio would be coming home. I believed him.

I spoke to Antonio later in the evening and he was excited. He couldn't wait for the trial to be over.

"The jury sees what they tryna do." He said

"I know. Did you hear the lady in the front row say you didn't do it?" I asked

"Hell yeah, she yelled that shit. They was lookin' at me all day. I know they know I'm innocent. I can't wait to hear 'em say it." He was pumped.

"Me either." I responded

Once again we talked until he had to lock down for the night but, this night was different. It was the first time we knew he wouldn't be there much longer. It was the beginning of the end to this nightmare.

The next morning court started late. The judge had some things he had to do before continuing the trial. He didn't sit on the bench until after noon. He spoke with Renee and the prosecutor, informing them that we wouldn't begin testimony until 130 pm. Erin, Tucker, Ryan and I went to Pigtown after we found out and smoked a few blunts until court started. I was more relaxed that day than I had been before. I felt the end coming. It felt good. The thick smoke from the weed made it surreal. I drank another energy drink on our way back to the courthouse. Renee met us in the hall when we arrived. She was in a good mood but, you could see she was still in battle mode. She knew she was winning but, she still had work to do. She wasn't leaving anything to chance.

"How are you guys today?" She asked as she approached us.

"Good and you?" We all responded at the same time.

"Ryan, I want to tell you that you did a great job yesterday. I'm glad you FINALLY got the chance to tell your side of the story."

"I am too. I hope the jury see what these mother fuh'ers been up to and go ahead and let my man out. He should'uh never been loch'ed up in the first place."

"I agree." She replied

"Well, I guess Lisa and Bobby finally got their chance to go get well." I said

"Yeah, the way she was looking yesterday, she's probably still high from last night." Tucker said. We all laughed.

"Well, she deserved whatever high she got out of it. She helped us out tremendously yesterday. She made my job very easy." Renee said

We all walked into the courtroom to wait on the day to begin. Ryan, Erin and I sat together while Tucker sat in the row directly behind us. A friend of Antonio and mine came with his infant daughter, to sit in for a while and show his support. He sat next to me when the trial started for the day.

His name is Darnell, and he's a dead ringer for the rapper T.I. He was wearing a kufi, a beanie worn by Muslim men. Once proceedings were underway the judge stopped everything to tell Darnell to remove his hat. When Darnell tried to explain that it was for religious purposes and could be worn indoors, the judge forced him to remove it. It was very obvious the judge was in a pissy mood. He scowled at Darnell until he removed the kufi. The judge continued talking to the lawyers from the bench. Once finished, the next witnessed was called.

The jurors were more receptive to us this afternoon. They were even cordial when they came in. They seemed genuinely pleased to see Ryan in court sitting next to me. Most of them greeted me with a nod and a smile. I returned each one I received. They did the same to Renee and Antonio too. They noticed Ryan was sitting on the defense side of the room. They noticeably took it all in. Smiling and nodding at him too. When the judge reprimanded Darnell they didn't seem to like it very much. It felt like an "Us" against "Them" type of thing. The jurors seemed to be on the "Us" side of things. I was hoping they ALL felt the same way. The women were the ones making their feelings known. The male juror in the back far corner seemed to stick out to me. He hadn't been responding to the testimony like all the other jurors. He wasn't easy to read. I got the feeling from him that he was an asshole. If there was going to be any kind of glitch with this jury, it was going to come from him. He'd looked at me a few times during the week but, its meaning wasn't anything I could put my finger on. The women jurors kept my spirits high. They all looked like mothers, grandmothers and aunts. Each of them had an energy about them that said they could be the matriarchs of their individual families. They seemed to have grown protective of Ryan and Antonio. They watched them with caring eyes and looked at the prosecutor as the boogie man they weren't afraid of. Sitting there taking them all in, I felt like Antonio was in a good place. I felt he was safe in their hands. I knew they would take good care of him. But, then again I was high as a kite and could be mistaken too.

Fuh'in' Claymore

They called Det. Warren Claymore to the stand.

This was my first time seeing him as he walked into the room. The first thing I noticed was how big he was. He was massive and bald. Intimidating didn't even begin to cover it. He's Green Mile big, only paper bag brown. Cute knows nothing about him. Watching him walk across the room to the witness box, I imagined him being a former football player who couldn't make the pros. He probably became a cop to have a funnel for his aggression. Once he was sworn in, it wasn't hard to see I was at least right about the aggression.

Under direct examination he answered short and direct but, with arrogance the jurors didn't seem to like. When he answered some of the questions he would stomp his feet just like Ryan had. I knew the jurors were being reminded of Ryan with each one. Claymore joined the Prosecutor in calling Ryan, Bryan. It infuriated me every time I heard it. I felt they were continuing to be disrespectful to him and what he went through. I wondered if the jurors caught on to it. If they did, I hoped it would work in our favor but, it still pissed me off.

The prosecutor walked Claymore through the questioning and it all seemed very professional. It also didn't ring true. His demeanor was daring the jurors not to believe him.

He testified being called to the scene and talking with Ryan before he was taken away in the ambulance. He then testified about Tucker returning to the scene. He left out hitting him.

When Renee got up to question him you could literally watch his entire demeanor get worse as she walked toward him.

"How many times was the victim shot?" Renee asked

"7" Claymore answered

"Was there a lot of blood in the area he was shot?"

"I would say there was." He responded as if it were a stupid question.

"When you met Tucker at the scene did he identify himself as a witness and a possible victim to you?"

"Yeah." He stomped his feet.

"How many times did he tell you he was a witness?"

"I don't know a few." You could clearly see he was irritated with the questioning.

"Why did he have to tell you repeatedly that he was a witness?" Renee asked him from about five feet away looking directly at him.

"I don't understand the question."

"The question is simple Detective. Why did the witness have to repeatedly tell you he was a witness?" Claymore didn't know how to answer the question so he didn't. Renee continued.

"Did you not believe him the first time he told you? Did you not hear the officer who introduced you to Tucker tell you he was a witness? Did you not believe him when he told you, so you kept checking to see if his answer would change? Why did Tucker have to keep telling you he was a witness?"

"No, I didn't believe him." He snapped with a sneer on his face.

"What had he done to make you not believe him?"

"He left the scene for one thing." He answered sarcasticly

"When did you find out he witnessed the shooting and then left? Who told you that?"

"He did."

"So if he hadn't told you he left and came back you wouldn't have known?"

"Yeah, I would've found out."

"How?"

"Somebody would've told me." More sarcasm

"Did anyone else tell you, Detective?"

"Huh?" He seemed caught off guard by the question.

"Did anyone else tell you that Tucker left the scene and returned?"

"No."

"So then it's safe to say that you wouldn't have found out if he hadn't told you." All of the women jurors are covering their mouths to hide their laughter.

"Did he tell you why he left the scene?"

"Yeah, he said he and another patron from the bar tried to follow the suspects to get the tag number but lost them." He seemed annoyed.

"Did anyone else tell you why he left the scene?"

"No" He stopped looking at Renee when he answered her.

"Was there another witness who contradicted Tucker's reason for why he left the scene?"

"No."

"But you didn't believe he was a witness?" She faked curiosty.

"No"

"Did he give you a description of the people who attempted to rob him and Ryan?"

"Yes."

"What was the description Tucker gave you?" She perked up with this question.

Claymore read the exact same description from a small notebook he had in his lap, given by all the others.

"Where was the initial questioning taking place?"

"It was in front of the bar."

"Where the shooting happened?" She asked mocking horror.

"Yes." He replied rolling his eyes at her act.

"So you're questioning a witness who just saw his friend covered in blood?" She asked pointedly.

"Yes" He leaned into the microphone in front of him.

"Would you say you were putting him through an interrogation?"

"I would say I was questioning him." He was officially disgusted with her.

"You were questioning him while his friend's blood is all over the ground in front of him?"

"Yup," he replied almost bored. Renee gave a quick nod to his attitude and quick answer. She glanced at the jurors to see if they noticed it too. A couple of the women jurors on the front row nodded to her to give her the answer she sought from them.

"So, I'll ask you again Detective, what about Tucker made you not believe him?"

The detective seemed ready to be done with this line of questioning and gave an answer he thought would end it.

"I watched the video of the bar and he had something when he left. I thought it was a gun."

"Are you talking about the video from the bar as the shooting was happening, that video?"

"Yes, that video. He picked up something when he walked out of the bar. It looked like a gun. So when he came back to the scene I didn't believe him." The look on his face told her he had outsmarted her. She then walked over to the TV and played the video again for him and the jurors to see up close.

"I want you to show me on the video what you thought was a weapon as soon as you see it."

The video starts to play and Claymore sat quiet all the way through until Tucker goes to pick up the sandwich off the floor.

"There, right there. It looks like a weapon." He pointed to the sandwich. Renee froze the screen and pointed to the sandwich to make sure that was what Claymore was referring to. She then looked at the jurors and asked them if they thought it looked like a gun. They knew not to answer.

"What kind of gun looks like that?"

"Huh?" He was stuck.

"What caliber of gun is about foot long, silver, with no handle or trigger on it?" She asked bluntly.

He was stuck by the question and couldn't answer. She moved on.

"When did you get a chance to look at the video?"

"When I got back to the station?" He answered with attitude.

"Wait a minute? Didn't you just testified that you interrogated him at the scene because you watched the video and saw him pick up what you thought was a gun?"

"I thought he had a gun. Yes" He sounded nervous. I sat up straight.

"You testified you interrogated him at the crime scene because you saw him run from the bar with a gun on the surveillance video? Am I correct, Detective?" She was standing directly in front of him.

"Yes" He responded reluctantly.

"But, you didn't see the video until you got back to the station? Do I have that right, Detective Claymore?"

"Yeah" he was angry.

"Why did you hit him?" She asked out of nowhere. My head snapped.

"Why not?" Every mouth in the courtroom dropped on the floor. His arrogance was swelling inside him and it was about to blow. Renee left what he said hanging in the air and changed direction.

"Detective, did you search Tucker at any point?" She walked back and forth about four feet in front of him and the jury.

"Yes, I did."

"Where were you, when you searched him?"

"We were on the street."

"You searched him at the scene?"

"Yes."

"Did he have anything on him?"

"No, he didn't have any weapons."

"No, Detective I want you to listen to the question I asked. Did he have ANYTHING on him? In other words, did you pull anything from his pockets or retrieve anything from his person?"

"Yes."

"Can you tell us what that was?" The Detective looked down at his lap and you could see him trying to gather his composure. He was angry. He seemed insulted that he had to go through this. Then he answered the question.

"He had a sandwich in his hand."

The jurors erupted again murmuring among themselves. The disgust was written all over their faces. They were muttering to themselves.

"Can you describe the sandwich for us please, Detective?"

"It was a sub wrapped in foil, the kind you get from a carry out."

"Did it look like a gun when Tucker first walked up to you at the scene? Did you pull your gun when he approached you?"

"No."

"But, it looked like a gun on the video you hadn't seen yet? Is that right Detective?"

"Yes"

"So, you used the information you saw on the video you hadn't watched yet to determine that Tucker was uncooperative?"

"Yes" He rolled his eyes. She just stood in front of him, holding him to his answer. The jurors soaked her in.

"When you got to the hospital to see the victim did you tell the staff to place paper bags over his hands?"

"Yup"

"Why?"

"I wanted to make sure he didn't have gunpowder on his hands."

"Did you think he shot himself seven times?"

"No"

"Did you have any witness statements saying that the victim had been shooting too?"

"No."

"So what made you think he needed to be tested for gunpowder?"

"He wasn't cooperative." He was pissed.

"He wasn't cooperative, Detective? Is that what you said?"

"He wasn't cooperative." He mocked with a stank attitude.

"In what way wasn't he cooperative, Detective?"

"He didn't want to answer my questions?"

"Did you ask him for a description of the people that shot him?"

"Yes, I did."

"Did he give you that information?"

"Yeah, he did."

"Did he tell you who was with him at the time of the shooting?"

"Yes."

"Did he tell you what he was doing at the time leading up to the shooting?"

"Yes."

"Then tell us how he was being uncooperative?"

"He wouldn't answer my question, that's how?" He snapped.

"Would you please tell this jury what questions he wouldn't answer of yours?" He was quiet for a moment. The jurors waited for the answer.

"I didn't like his attitude!!!" Claymore yelled out. The jurors are in an uproar. They're talking to one another and pointing at the Detective.

"You didn't like his attitude? Is that what you just told the jury, Detective? You didn't like his attitude?" She was on the brink of hysterical laughter, so were the jurors.

"Yeah, that's what I said." Remarkably, his arrogance had survived his stupidity.

"What attitude did the victim display to you in the early hours after he'd been shot seven times, Detective? Would you please share that with the jury, as well Sir?"

"He just had a bad attitude, that's all." He barked.

"He had a bad attitude. (She's shaking her head walking back and forth in front of him and the jury.) That's what he did? He had a bad attitude. Can you give the jury one example of Ryan's 'bad attitude'?" She stopped to ask the last question. He looked at his lap and seemed to be thinking before he answered. We all waited patiently.

"No, not really."

"Did the hospital staff ask you to leave him alone and save the questioning for another time?"

"Yes, they did."

"Did you do as they asked?"

"No, I kept questioning him."

"Were they not doing their job helping a patient who'd been shot seven times?"

"Yes they were."

"What condition was the victim in when you asked them to put the bags over his hands?"

"He was shot."

"Was he bleeding Detective?"

"Yes"

"Did he appear to be in a lot of pain?"

"I don't recall."

"Do you recall if he was sitting up and moving around?"

"He was lying on the bed."

"Do you recall if he was laughing and joking?"

"No, he wasn't."

"As far as you recall, Detective, did Mr. Thomas seem comfortable to you?"

"I don't recall."

"Would you say he was fighting for his life?"

"I'd say he was shot a lot of times."

"Did he look like he was in the position to get up and leave the hospital?"

"No"

"Just a shot in the dark here, Detective but, was Ryan conscious when you walked into the medical bay?"

"No."

"When did he wake up after you walked into the room?"

"When I woke him up." The jurors are churning in their seats.

"Wait, so you walked into the room, where a shock trauma team is working on a patient who's been shot seven times and you go wake him up?" Renee is looking at the jury.

"Yeah!" His voice boomed.

"Why did you feel the need to interfere with the doctors and nurses working on Mr. Thomas, not saving your questions for a later time?"

"I had a job to do." He was indignant.

"Did you feel like your job was more important than that of the doctors and nurses?"

"Yes, I did."

"Was your job going to save his life?"

"He looks alright to me." He pointed his chin at Ryan. The jurors were offended.

"Excuse me?" Renee snapped at him

"No, I wasn't going to save his life."

"Did he give you any indication that he was withholding information?"

"Yes he did."

"What kind of indications was he giving you?"

"It took him too long to answer the questions."

"What do you mean 'too long'?"

"When I asked him questions he didn't answer me

immediately."

"You're saying a person who'd just been shot seven times, who was in horrendous pain, couldn't answer you immediately?" She's mystified.

"Yes, I'm talking about him!" and he pointed at Ryan sitting next to me. The jurors didn't like it and started talking among themselves while giving him dirty looks. He watched and listened to them. He gave them a dirty look of his own and rolled his eyes at them.

"So you see the victim lying bloody, unconscious, in pain, fighting for his life and because he couldn't put THAT aside to answer your questions you deemed him suspicious? Is that correct?"

"He could've answered me. He wasn't shot in his mouth." The jurors seemed disgusted by his response.

"Did you ask him if he saw the people who shot him?"

"Yes."

"Did he give you a description of his assailants?"

"Yes he did."

"Did that description match the one you got from Tucker?"

"It seemed to."

"How old did the victim think the assailants were?"

"He said they were in their early twenties."

"So, once again, he did answer you. You just told us he described the two men who tried to kill him. Did you not?"

"Yes" You could see he hated having to give her that answer. His face was balled up with anger. Renee continued with her questioning.

"They', you said Ryan said 'They' meaning more than one, correct?"

"Yes, 'they'." he stomped his feet again and bobbing his head in anger.

"Did you ever look for or identify the other assailant?"

"No."

"No, you didn't look for him or No you didn't identify him?"

"Neither."

"How many times did you interview the victim that night?"

"Twice."

"Twice?" She acted confused.

"Yeah, twice." He was bored

"When was the second time?"

"At the hospital." He looked at her like she was dumb.

"If the hospital was the second time, where was the first time?"

"In the ambulance."

"That's right Detective, I remember now. You testified to that earlier. What did you ask the victim while he was in the ambulance?"

"I asked him if he saw who shot him."

"Did he answer?"

"Yeah."

"Did find you out any new information from the second interview that you didn't know from the first?"

"No." The jurors are over him.

"How long have you been on the force, Detective?"

"Eight years. I've been a detective for three of 'em."

Renee walked over to the defense table, made eye contact with Antonio, and picked up a piece of paper, then walked back over to the jury box in front of Claymore.

"Detective Claymore, when the two witnesses came in the next morning to identify the shooter how long did you interview them for?"

"I didn't." He said. The jurors looked at us, and we looked at them at the same time, all in disbelief. Did he just say he didn't talk to the witnesses? We all turned to Det. Claymore.

"I don't understand. What do you mean you 'didn't'?" Renee probed.

"I didn't interview them. That's what I mean?"

Renee asks the judge if she could approach the witness. After getting permission, she handed Claymore the paper in her hand. She asked him to read the printed name of the person who filled out the report and the signature of the person who signed it. While he's reading it Renee asked that it be submitted into evidence. Once it had been, she continued her questioning.

"Warren Claymore." He read.

"Isn't that your name?"

"Yes"

Darnell's baby started cooing. In the middle of the testimony the judge started yelling at Darnell.

"The courtroom is no place for a baby! Either quiet her or leave the courtroom immediately!" His voice boomed. While Darnell tried to quiet her, the judge had no patience and yelled at him again, "Remove yourself and that child from this courtroom or I'll hold you in contempt!!!" The baby wasn't crying, she was cooing in happiness. I'm sitting next to Darnell watching his face turn red with anger. He composed himself and quietly rose to leave.

"Call me and tell me what happens." He said to me as the judge started yelling at him again, "Sir, you're testing my patients. I've ordered you to leave or face the consequences! This is the last time I am going to speak to you before I have you hauled out of here!!! Now leave immediately or else."

No one could believe what just happened. We were all in shock, everyone except the judge and the prosecutor. The jurors were infuriated. They just kept looking at me shaking their heads. Once Darnell and the baby left, Renee picked up where she left off.

"Detective Claymore how is it that you filled out and signed this report but you never talked to the witnesses?"

"My Sergeant filled it out for me."

"I'm sorry did you say your superior filled out this report for you?" She snapped.

"Yup"

"So who signed it?"

"He did." He stomped his feet.

"You're a police officer Detective, what is it called when a person signs another's name on a legal document?"

"It's called forgery!" his voice boomed in the courtroom.

"So who interviewed the witnesses if you didn't?"

"My sergeant did I guess. I don't know." He said as if she were getting on his nerves.

"You don't know? Why would he interview witnesses and sign your name? Can you tell the jury why he would do that?"

"He was looking out for me." Renee snapped at him hearing this response.

"You mean he falsified a police report for you, isn't that right?"

"I guess he did, then." Claymore shouted in anger. He had lost control. He was burning in that seat and couldn't do anything about it. She wasn't done with him yet.

"Did the victim call you from his hospital bed?"

"Yeah he called me."

"Did he tell you the wrong person had been arrested?"

"Yeah he told me." He was looking straight at her.

"So once again, the victim is being cooperative in the investigation, wouldn't you say, Detective?"

"He was lyin'."

"How do you know he was lying?" Renee asked with a sarcastic grin.

"I had a hunch."

"That same hunch you used to determine that a sandwich was a gun? (She laughed at him.) And what did you do with that information?"

"I went on vacation."

The jury had finally had enough of Claymore. They were openly displeased with his attitude and his answers.

"Did you need a vacation from having other people do your

police work for you? I have no further questions, Your Honor." The prosecutor objected and the judge sustained it. She was too quick and got it all out before he had the chance to react. Claymore was dismissed and the judge ended court for the day.

What Can Go Wrong.........

Friday came it was the last day of court. If things went well Antonio would be home tonight. I got up that morning controlling the excitement that swelled inside me. It wasn't over and I didn't want to act like it was. I was keeping myself in the mindset of Murphy's Law. What can go wrong, will go wrong. I couldn't let myself get ready for an acquittal only to have him convicted or a hung jury. I was expecting the best yet preparing for the worst.

Tucker and I smoked a blunt he already had rolled on the way to the courthouse that morning. I needed it. I felt like I was about to jump out of my skin. It calmed me down a lot. When we met with Erin and Ryan in front of the courthouse, they told me I looked high. So we went across the street to a store. I bought some eye drops and another energy drink.

Renee was sitting at the defense table when the four of us walked into the courtroom. She was the only one there. We walked up and talked with her while we waited on everyone else to show up. She was nervous too. We all were. Ryan was ready to hear the verdict because he felt it was his verdict too. I asked Renee if I could speak to her alone for a moment. The two of us walked into the hallway leaving the others to talk amongst themselves. Once in the hallway, I told Renee how I felt.

"I'm kinda pissed off Renee."

"I can understand that. What are you pissed about?"

"They keep calling Ryan, Bryan. It pisses me off because it only proves that this case isn't and has never been about him. The prosecutor doesn't even have enough respect for him to know his name. He's the victim in this case and neither he nor the Lead

Investigator gave a shit enough to learn his name."

"You're right. What should I do about that?" she had a smirk on her face as if she already knew what to do with it.

"I think that should be pointed out to the jury."

"Then it will be. Don't worry about it." She touched me on the arm and I felt understood. We went back in the courtroom to continue waiting for the prosecutor, judge, jury and Antonio to come into the courtroom.

I sat with Erin, Tucker and Ryan in our usual spot. Antonio was brought in a few minutes later. The prosecutor came in a few minutes after Antonio. Then the judge came in. He greeted the attorney's and asked if they were ready to continue. After both agreed they were ready the jury was brought in. Once again they greeted us with nods and smiles. I took a deep breath and thought, 'Here we go again.'

The judge asked the prosecutor to call his next witness. The prosecutor rose from his chair and announced, "Your Honor the State Rests." It was almost over. With that announcement, the judge asked Renee if the defense was ready to proceed with its case. Renee informed the judge, she wouldn't be calling any witnesses. She asked that the case be dismissed because the prosecution didn't prove their case against her client. Some of the jurors seemed to agree with her request. Nonetheless the judge denied the request and Renee rested for the defense. The only thing left was the closing arguments.

The judge gave the jury a fifteen minute break before the arguments began.

During the break I was a nervous high wreck. I wanted to skip this part and just give the case to the jury. I was sick of hearing lawyers talk. What I really mean is, I was sick of hearing the prosecutor talk. He would have two chances during closing arguments to get his point across. He would speak before and after Renee. I felt that was too much time for him. What could he actually say anyway? Renee should be the one with the most time. She had the best shit to say. That's my opinion and it holds no water.

We stayed in the courtroom during the break. As we sat around talking someone walked in the courtroom and we all looked to see who it was. We were surprised to see Detective Claymore sit across from us in the audience. I just sat there looking at him, taking him in. He was a massive asshole and it seemed he liked being one. It was written all over him. I couldn't see how a woman would want to be with a guy like him. He seemed hateful. He reeked of anger. He was the worst kind of cop you could be. He was a liar and a bully. I just looked at him and kept looking at him even after he noticed I was looking at him. We just sat there looking at each other not saying a word. He cut his eyes at me and ended the stare down by looking away to the empty jury box.

Ryan began talking.

"He's a pussy ass nigga." I was shocked as he kept talking.

"This punk ass hole didn't even look for the nigga's that shot me. Fuh' him, Fuh' all them cops. They all dirty anyway, I can't stand they asses."

Claymore heard everything Ryan had to say and continued to look at the empty jury box. Ryan just stared at the side of Claymore's head waiting on him to look at him. He wanted to have eye contact but Claymore wouldn't turn. Ryan decided to force him to turn and look at him.

"You coward ass nigga. You can't even look at me while I'm taw'in' shit to you. You ain't shit." Claymore turned his head and gave Ryan a blank stare. Ryan looked at him while he got the rest off his chest.

"You's a coward whore, nigga, you know that?" He waited for a response but, didn't get one. Claymore just kept looking at him.

"Nigga you so ain't shit, you make ya mama not shit." Ryan had to laugh at the one and that was the end of his tirade. I just looked at him while he laughed. It seemed to feel good to him. His laugh became contagious and I started laughing with him. It did feel good. He deserved that and more in my opinion. I was glad Ryan did it. He didn't lie in the least bit. Claymore was a whore and he wasn't shit. He had to get it from somewhere so, his mother is the most likely source. Fuck It and Fuck Him. Claymore just turned his head away again and it was over.

As all the parties gathered back in the courtroom tension filled the air. The prosecutor wasn't as inflated as he had been. The judge was just as cantankerous as he'd been through. The jury seemed like they were ready for the case to be given to them. Renee was raring to go. I felt like this was going to be the longest part of the trial. The judge called us back into session. The prosecutor got up from his chair and began his closing arguments.

"Ladies and Gentlemen, this week you heard from one of the doctors and paramedics who took care of the victim in this case. You heard them describe how severe his wounds were. You heard from the neighborhood patrolman, who the eyewitnesses flagged down the next morning to identify themselves as witnesses. You heard from those witnesses themselves. Bobby sat in that chair under oath and identified the defendant as the shooter. He told each and every one of you that the man sitting in that chair across the room was the person he saw shooting the victim, Bryan Thomas.

You also heard from Tucker who was with Bryan when he was shot. You heard Tucker testify that he tried to chase the defendant down with a person who was in the bar at the same time but, the defendant got away from him. You heard him say that. He was being a good friend. He was a good witness. I thank him for being so forthcoming.

Det. Claymore told you how he got the description of the shooter from both Bryan and Tucker. They both described the same person, to the tee. The same person Tucker chased to no avail, the same person Bobby identified as the shooter. That person is the defendant.

Ladies and Gentlemen, he shot his friend seven times, *seven times*. This is his friend? It's clear to all of us that Bryan is a better friend to Antonio then Antonio is to Bryan because he got on the stand and covered for him. I wish I had a friend like Bryan Thomas. What he needs is a friend like you, the jury. Bryan needs for you jurors to do what he couldn't do. Hold Antonio responsible for trying to kill him. That's what he did. Antonio tried to kill Bryan in cold blood. You heard the witnesses. You saw them one by one point him out under oath. You know as well as I do that Antonio is guilty and needs to pay the price for almost killing his friend. *His friend.* I ask that you return a verdict of guilty in this case. Send the message to the other "Antonio's" in Baltimore that we're tired of this going on in our city. Thank you very much." He sat down at his table and the jurors watched him. They looked at him as if they were asking him if he really thought they were buying what he was selling.

When it was Renee's turn, the front row of jurors adjusted themselves in their chairs and gave her a welcoming smile. She approached them as if they were friends at this point and they received her as such. This was very encouraging for me to see. It gave me more hope.

"Ladies and Gentlemen, I don't know what case the prosecution's been watching over the past week, but it hasn't been the one you and I have been watching. (A few jurors seemed to quietly chuckle)

He mentioned the witnesses who identified my client as the person who committed this crime. Let's revisit that part of the trial, shall we? The first was Tucker; he didn't identify my client as the person he saw shooting Ryan. He was the only other person who saw the culprits face to face other than Ryan. As I recall the Prosecutor didn't even bother to ask Tucker to identify my client as the shooter. Why is that?

Next was Bobby, he testified under oath, he was running away while the shooting was going on. You saw him instruct me on the position he was facing when the shooting happened. Did any of you see a way that he could've seen the faces of the shooters that night? I don't.

The next witness was Lisa. I liked Lisa, I must admit. She was brutally honest. She admitted on the stand that she's a heroin addict. She admitted to being sick from withdrawals on not only the day she testified before you but, on the morning she was intimidated into going to the precinct to identify my client in a photo lineup. She admitted that she would've said anything that morning to get out of there and get high. She also admitted that if she were doing the same thing here in this courtroom she would've just said what the prosecution wanted to hear, so she could be done with this whole process. I respected that about her. She didn't identify my client under oath. I want to point out the difference to you all. She didn't get on the stand and identify my client as the person who shot Ryan that night. She identified the picture she signed after being told to pick out the person she recognized. There's a difference. Lisa testified that she couldn't see the shooters because she was running away from the area and who did she testify was running ahead of her? Bobby.

Then we got to hear from the most important person in this entire trail. We heard from Ryan Thomas, the victim. This case is about him. He is who needs justice. Ryan is who almost died that night. The prosecution seems to have forgotten that. The prosecutor is so unconcerned about him and what happened to him that he didn't even make it a point to remember his name. During the entire trial he kept calling him Bryan. (Renee turns to the prosecutor.) His name is Ryan not Bryan.

Ryan told you my client isn't the person who shot him. He told you Antonio is like a brother to him. He told you he would NEVER worry about Antonio doing anything to harm him. Do you believe him? I do. I found him and Tucker to be the most credible witnesses that were called to testify. They were also the only ones that had the best view of their assailants.

Finally, we heard from the lead investigator, (Renee dropped her head and just shook it while she let the jury soak in the memory of him.), Detective Warren Claymore. Where do I start with this guy? (She paused again before continuing.) Detective Claymore did a terrible job in his investigation. I'm being kind when I say terrible. He was criminal in his investigation. He was unprofessional, abusive, derelict, and arrogant. He was all of those things while he was investigating. His Sergeant, according to Detective. Claymore was committing felonies by "looking out" for him and falsifying legal documents. To make it plain and simple for you all, (She pointed at Claymore while turning away from the jury and they turned toward him too.), he should be in jail. If he's telling the truth about his superior, then they both should be in jail. We pay them to falsify reports and ignore the facts of a case. We pay them to ignore the victim. We pay them to just randomly pick a person to arrest and charge with horrible crimes. We pay him to treat the victim as the suspect, then make up a suspect and arrest him. They should both be under investigation. (Claymore didn't take this too kindly and scoffed at her and the jury once he became the focus of their attention.) This is where our tax dollars are going. To a police officer who doesn't do his job. Then he goes on vacation, while my client sat in jail for a crime the lead investigator knew he wasn't responsible for. How did he know? Ryan called him from his hospital bed and told him. That's how he knew.

He called both Tucker and Ryan uncooperative and suspicious, but he couldn't give us an example of how he came to that conclusion. I guess the only way he would've deemed them cooperative is if they would've gone out and arrested the true culprits themselves. We know Detective Claymore wouldn't have minded. His Sergeant is already doing his work for him. I think he came to the conclusion they were uncooperative because they wouldn't lie right along with him. He may have come to that conclusion about Lisa or Bobby but he wasn't there for that interview even though the report says otherwise. Simply put he's a disgrace.

Ladies and Gentlemen, Antonio didn't do this. The witnesses and the evidence prove that. I'm asking you on behalf of my client and Ryan to return a verdict of not guilty."

Some of the jury looked at Antonio while others looked at Ryan. Ryan nodded his agreement while giving a slight smile. Renee thanked the jury and took her seat next to Antonio.

After Renee was done, the judge called for a lunch break before the prosecutor had his last crack at the jury.

It was 1:30pm when court got back underway. The prosecutor gave his final closing argument to the jury. They looked bored and irritated with him. He didn't say anything different than he did earlier which seemed, in my opinion, to only bolster Renee's argument. As I listened to him talk, I hoped that the jury saw through this entire thing, as easily as I could. I didn't want to assume anything though. I wasn't going to assume anything involving this case. I wouldn't allow myself to think for a second that this was in the bag. I wouldn't allow myself that luxury until I heard from the jury that I could. The only one who seemed to be the slightest bit interested in the prosecutor's final statement was the balding white guy, sitting in the furthest upper seat from me in the left hand corner. He seemed to want the prosecutor to give him something he could bring into the jury room. I don't know if he got anything out of it but, I didn't and the rest of the jury didn't seem to either. His last plea to the jury lasted about twenty minutes.

After the prosecutor was finished, the judge explained to the jury that he would next charge them before giving them the case. He explained that "charging" them, would be explaining all the rules they were to be made aware of, before they were allowed to go into deliberations. He said charging them would take a while. He would rather charge them and let them go immediately into deliberations. Since we had already gone into the afternoon, he decided to let them go home early for the weekend. On Monday he would charge them and allow them a full day of deliberations if they so needed it.

I was kind of mad but, not really. I mean I got mad for a second because this was going to be another weekend he would be locked up but, after I had a second to think about it, I realized this worked out in our favor. If the jury went into deliberations late in the afternoon it could be stopped until Monday anyway. The jury could have the weekend to let everything sink in. They could come in Monday with their own arguments ready for deliberations. I liked the idea after thinking about it.

Less Than 72 Hours

Antonio called me that night with drama. His kid's mother, Elissa wanted to visit him in jail, for what we were expecting was his last visitation that Sunday. I wasn't in the mood for the drama and told him to let her come see him. He didn't want her too. He told her not to come, she started threatening him with the usual he wouldn't be able to see his kids. I knew what all of this was about but once again, I didn't care. I knew this was only an issue because Antonio thought I was abandoning him when I went back to Atlanta. He started pillow talking Elissa while I was gone, just in case I didn't come back. Of course, when I asked him about it he completely denied it. . I didn't really care if she came. I told him I didn't want to be the excuse, for him not seeing his kids when he came out. I told him it didn't matter who came to see him because he would be out Monday anyway. He still wanted me to come on Sunday. So, I minded my business and showed up to see him.

When I got there I asked the female officer who signed me in if I could look at the computer screen she was on, to see who'd been visiting him while I was gone. She said I could, so I turned the computer monitor toward me. Both she and I both read that Elissa had been visiting him since the first Sunday after I left Baltimore. It only confirmed what I was thinking. He was playing. I confronted him about it during visitation. He said it was only so he could see the kids. I knew better but, there was no need to argue the point, it wasn't going anywhere. As far as I was concerned, he could've gone back to her as long as I got back the money I put out for his defense. I'd get it back in cash or in the ass whipping I'd put on Elissa. I figured, if he went back and tried to stiff me on the bill I'd beat the shit out of her. I'd inflict at least $5,000 worth of damage to her person. I didn't tell him any of this. I just sat back in the cut and watched how it would all play out.

Once I left Antonio after visitation I headed over to Pigtown to see Stan. After court, when I was in the neighborhood. I'd park my car in front of his house, so he could keep an eye on it, while I was out and about. I'd drop in on him before I went to hang out. He had two guys selling out of his house. I didn't know them. One was a tall brown skin guy. He wasn't anything to look at. He was about 6'2" with cornrows and slanted eyes. The other one was a little shorter. He had long black curly hair. He kept in two long braids falling passed his shoulders. He looked like he was either mixed or of Latin descent. He was the more respectful of the two. I didn't speak to either of them. The uglier of the two always seem to have something to say to me every time he saw me. I didn't speak to them the first few times I saw them. I didn't want them to mistake me for one of the working girls around the house. I didn't want them to say anything that I would consider disrespectful. If they had, I wouldn't have been able to let that pass. It would've quickly escalated into something very big and very dangerous. They weren't from the neighborhood, this much I knew. In this neighborhood, even if I don't know YOU, YOU know me. These guys don't know me, which means they don't know Antonio therefore, they're not from here. That would cause a problem with anyone from the neighborhood who knew. Although, I knew their presence wasn't known to the local business boys, it wasn't my place to let them know. I was busy with the trial and that was the only business I cared about.

The Sunday before going back in court I offered Stan a business proposal. I wanted to open a night shop in his house. My hours would be 9pm to 6am, Stan agreed. He did mention that the other guys were working out of there. I told him I wasn't concerned about it.

Poopie had gotten out of jail a few months before I came back from Atlanta. He'd been assisting me on a couple of things in the neighborhood. I was preparing to set up shop all during the trial and Stan was the last link I needed. Poopie had already been spreading the word that I was coming back to work and the neighborhood was buzzing. They all knew the updates from the trial that Antonio was expected to come home.

I had secured my heroin and crack sources in the evenings after court. I was waiting until Tuesday to get things together. Over the weekend I purchased all of the cutting materials I would need for the heroin. I already owned the other things like scales and strainers. The 3 and 1 as we call it is a combination of Quinine and Benita. Quinine is a powdered tonic that was used to treat Malaria. Benita is a chalk like baby laxative. For every three ounces of Benita, you match it with one ounce of Quinine, hence 3 and 1. I had all of that secured at home. I also went and bought empty gel caps for the packaging, that's what we sold it in. $10 a pill, each pill the size of a vitamin. The crack I would buy already cooked. I didn't know how to cook it and I didn't want to know.

I had to wait until Antonio was home before I made the coke and dope purchases. He would have to be there when I set up shop. He would have to put the two guys out of the house. I couldn't do it by myself without making a spectacle of the house and blowing the spot up to the police. Heroine is perishable and I wasn't going to buy it to sit on it so I waited. No need to waste good money on good dope just to sit on it and have it "fall" while you're not using it. Buy it, mix it, sell it.

I wasn't trying to turn the neighborhood out but, I couldn't just live off the money I brought back with me from home. I had to make money. Antonio had to work when and if he came home. I was only buying enough of both to start a shop. If it was going to get any bigger it was going to have to grow from the bare minimum.

Monday Morning

Monday morning came. As we arrived at the courthouse, Erin, Ryan, Tucker and I were all excited. By the look on Renee's face when we ran into her in the hall, she was too. When they brought Antonio in he had the same look on his face. The judge charged the jury that morning and didn't finish until around 11am. It was so long and boring. I thought I was going to run out of the room screaming. He broke early for lunch. The judge told us we had to be back by 12:30.

Once we came back from lunch the jury went directly into the jury room to start deliberating. I received no looks from the jury as they filed out of the courtroom. I wished I had.

Erin, Tucker, Ryan and I hung out in the hallway during the deliberations. We cracked jokes to make the time pass. I kept trying to imagine what was going on in there. Time, was moving fast and slow all at once. So many emotions were running through me. I was excited the jury had the case. I was scared the jury had the case. I knew it was about to be over but, I didn't know what the end result be. I had a feeling it would go our way but, was afraid it wouldn't. I couldn't keep still but, I had too. I was on the verge of having an anxiety attack. An hour had passed and not a word. I felt it was a mixed signal. If they all thought he was innocent then they would've been back already. I felt someone was holding out. I was afraid that if they deliberated late in the day then our chances of him coming home were grim. For the life of me, I couldn't see how they would convict him. I wasn't a juror though. After an hour and a half the bailiff came into the hallway and announced the jury had reached a verdict.

I Held My Breath

We all loaded back into the courtroom. The four of us sat together. Renee took her place at the defense table, when Antonio was brought into the courtroom. Ryan sat between Erin and me with Tucker behind us as usual. The prosecutor was at his table when the judge entered and we all stood up. It was a few minutes before the jury was brought in. I was nervous as hell. Antonio seemed excited and relieved. He didn't seem to have a doubt in his mind. They slowly filed in. I watched them for any hint of what they had decided. As I was scanning them the lady from the front row with the short hair and glasses walked to her seat. Just as she sat down, she looked directly at me. She gave me a wink and a smile. I grabbed Ryan's hand and whispered through my held breath, "Antonio's coming home." He didn't see what the juror had done and didn't know why I'd said that. He looked at me shocked and asked, "What?" but, before I could tell him what happened court was called to order and the proceedings began. No talking was permitted. I sat there with one hand gripping Ryan's and the other hand over my mouth.

Antonio was called to stand, as the foreman of the jury, the white man from the front row, stood in the jury box, to read the verdicts. The foreman had to read each verdict one by one for each count.During the reading of the FIRST NOT GUILTY verdict, the judge stopped the foreman, and began yelling at Erin, "This is a court of law! I will not have these proceedings interrupted with outbursts! Remove yourself from this courtroom Madame before I have you escorted out by the authorities!" It came totally out of nowhere and left everyone dumbfounded as she walked out. She was sitting to my left on the other side of Ryan and hadn't uttered a sound. As she left she yelled over her shoulder, "That's okay, he's coming home. I'll see you outside Tonio."

The judge had the foreman continue with the reading of the verdicts. Before he could complete them, the judge targeted someone else in the audience. He interrupted the jury foreman and turned to me. He started yelling at me for talking while the verdict was being read. Mind you, I'm sitting in the seat with my hand over my mouth as I had been since the jury was seated. I just stared at him, with my hand over my mouth, while he yelled at me and threatened to throw me out too. Before his rampage was over, I turned to the jury and waited for him to finish, so the rest of the verdicts could be read. Not guilty on all counts. It was over. He was exonerated. He would be home that night. It was finally over. Once the verdicts were read we all filed out into the hallway and celebrated with Erin. I hugged Renee as hard as I could. I knew this was all her doing. She was brilliant in the way she handled this case. We all had a laugh about the judge throwing Erin out. We filled her in on my scolding.

The jurors started filing out into the hallway. Most of them approached Renee, asking for her card and treating her like a celebrity. I was a few feet away when Renee called me over to them. I looked over and saw the very same group of women, who had been giving me eye contact during the trial, standing together waiting for me. All had welcoming smiles on their faces. I gladly joined them. As I walked the four or five feet to them, they held out their arms to me. I thankfully walked into the group hug I was invited to. I thanked them all individually. There were no words that could adequately express how grateful I was. After the group hug I hugged them all individually. When I hugged the woman with the glasses she whispered in my ear, "You keep him straight. Hear me? They want him gone." I looked her in the eye and told her I would. I talked with the jurors for about 10 minutes. They told me the things that they noticed during the trial; one of them being the photo lineup. Of the six people, Antonio was the only light skinned man. They told me they would've finished earlier but, they had one person holding them up. I asked them if it was the white man, with the bald head, in the far left corner seat. They said it was. I introduced them to Ryan, Erin and Tucker. When they met Ryan they asked how he was feeling. They seemed genuinely concerned about his health. They were a very warm group of people. I was not only glad they were the jury, I was also glad I had a chance to meet and thank them all.

The prosecutor walked out of the courtroom while we were all in the hallway talking. You could hear a pin drop from the silence. Every last one of us including the jury just stopped and stared at him, as he took his walk of shame passed us. As soon as he was out of sight, our conversation picked right back up. We said our goodbyes. Once again, I thanked all of them. As they were leaving, Renee told me that Antonio would be released from the courthouse and not the jail. It would take a couple of hours before he would be processed out for release. I decided to leave and go home to tell Leonard about the day's events.

I Can Breathe

When I walked into the house, Leonard was in the kitchen making a sandwich. His eyes were wide as he looked for some sort of sign as to what happened. I told him about the acquittal and he was elated. He was proud of me. He knew how hard I worked on this. Now I had been rewarded with the correct decision. I told him I had to go back and pick Tonio up. He offered to go with me so I didn't have to park.

We got back to the courthouse right before dusk. I went to the entrance that I was told he would be released from. Leonard got in the driver's seat and circled the block until we came out. I entered the building and told the officers at the entrance why I was there. They pointed to a door just passed the metal detector and told me Antonio would be coming out of there. I went through security and the officers offered me a seat at the security area. I found a magazine and read it while I waited. It seemed like it was taking forever. I kept checking my watch. I had been there about 30 minutes when something told me to turn around. When I did, I saw Antonio walking toward me. It was the first time in almost a year that I was looking at him without him being behind glass or wearing shackles. He was pale from not being in the sun. His big afro was gone. His hair was cut into a Caesar. He was fat but, he was free and that was all that mattered. I finally let out the breath I'd been holding all these months. I walked up to him and we hugged for what seemed like a lifetime. Then we said goodbye to the officers and stepped out into the cool spring night. Leonard pulled up. Antonio and I jumped into the back seat.

Leonard was thrilled to see Antonio. He exploded with good will as soon as the door closed. As we pulled off, Antonio looked at me and said, "Thank You". I laid my head on his chest and we rode in silence back to the house in West Baltimore.

The first few days Antonio was home were like a honeymoon. We spent a lot of time alone. We did go to see his family. He eventually got to see his kids after feuding with their mother. We went to eat at every restaurant he missed while he was away. We just enjoyed being back together. Things were good.

Business didn't get started on the exact date that I originally planned. During the time Antonio was gone, he ran into a lot of people he knew in the street from all over Baltimore in there. He had made some business plans with them. They were to bring them to fruition once they were all home. I just played the background at these meetings. I never talked. I just listened. Once we were alone we'd talk about their content and I'd tell him what I thought.

Let me say this about Antonio, he is not the average dope fiend in the sense you may imagine. He is not the type of addict that you see begging for money. You will never see him not fly. You will not see him unkempt. I don't care how high he gets. He's the best dressed drug addict I've ever seen in the hood. He has an eye for fashion and he's very vain. His appearance is always together. Even when he goes to rob people his "caper gear" is always sharp. You will never see him not looking good. The irony of it is, he will be fly as a motherfucker, nodding out in a dilapidated row house. He's so brazen with his aggression and power that he once didn't feel like leaving the dope house to go get more dope. Instead he just robbed the one he was in and got high right there off the stolen proceeds. He then nodded off in the same house he just robbed. No one in the house would dare do anything to him. If he was in the dope house and his hair needed to be braided. He would have one of the girls there getting high braid it for him, while he was getting high. Although he is addicted to heroin, he didn't shoot heroin. He sniffed it. Among heroin users there are "classes" of users. The lowest kind of user is the main liner, the addict that shoots up. The smokers and sniffers are considered to be better than shooters. Antonio's sister Tina was a shooter. She had been released from prison while he was gone. Although I'd seen her in the neighborhood, we had yet to meet. The things I'd heard about her didn't draw me to her.

When we first got together, Antonio told me about his family. He grew up the youngest of seven; four girls and three boys. His mother was single. His father died right before Antonio's sixteenth birthday. He had eight children of his own. Antonio was somewhere in the middle of them. He basically told me that Tina was a manipulative, angry, raging junkie who got their other sister strung out. (That's me paraphrasing)

When Antonio and I met, he was on the wagon and had been for a few months. He was very open and honest about his addiction from the beginning; I never felt the desire to hold it against him. The person I met and fell in love with was sober. When he fell off the wagon I was already in deep. I had given up my apartment in Atlanta and moved to Baltimore to be with him. I learned a whole different side of him. It was agonizing sometimes. It was confusing and hurtful too. I didn't know anything else to do but, to stick with him. My pride wouldn't let me go back to Atlanta with nothing. Even though, I would be looking at this guy who was strung out on dope. I could still see the person I met, just below the surface. He loved dope, plain and simple. If I gave him the ultimatum of it or me, I knew I would lose. So, I never gave it to him. It was because of the person he was, while he was on the wagon that I stuck with him through his addiction.

Antonio had been clean for over nine months but, it wasn't by his choice. It was due to his circumstances. While he was locked up, he went through withdrawals cold turkey. He told me it felt like having his intestines contorted. He assured me he was done with it for good. I hoped he was telling the truth.

Antonio

After a few days of business meetings and family reunions, Antonio was ready to head down to Pigtown. Everyone knew he was out but, they hadn't seen him yet. He arranged for some of his business meetings to happen at the local barbershop on Washington Blvd, his stomping grounds. Big Dope Boys from all over Baltimore would be dropping by the barbershop to meet with Antonio. I went with him.

We arrived, parking the car in front of Stan's. By the time we walked up the block, the news traveled quickly that he was on the Blvd. People from all over the neighborhood started showing up to see him and welcome him home. It was like a mini parade of people. Antonio had been in this neighborhood all his life and he knew everyone here. These people were his family and no matter if he were clean or sober they treated him like the golden child. He was feared and loved at the same time. It's a strange dynamic to describe but it's an accurate one. When we first got together, I thought damn near everyone in the neighborhood was related to him because they all called him "Uncle Tonio". It wasn't until a man who was old enough to be his grandfather called him "Uncle Tonio" that I asked him about it. He explained to me that it was a term of respect.

As different people came by to say hello to him they would also greet me. Since Antonio had been gone, I'd gotten to know damn near everyone in the neighborhood and had developed my own relationships with them. He noticed it after the third or fourth junkie walked up to me smiled and asked how I was doing. I thought it was funny. He was very selective as to who talked to me prior to him leaving and everyone respected that. During the time he was gone I became my own person in the neighborhood and people seemed to like me. I got to know them as they did me. It was quite evident during Antonio's first hour back on the block. Once he noticed that a large part of the neighborhood and I were on friendly terms he looked at me and said,

"You became quite popular since I been gone." He has a thick Baltimore accent. Think of The Wire.

"This is my neighborhood now." I said laughing.

"Oh, yeah?" That's his way of asking if I want to stick with that answer.

Sure enough as the day went on more and more people saw him home and spoke to both of us. I could see that was getting on his last nerve and I enjoyed it.

Antonio is the type of man that doesn't talk much, he's very reserved. If he considers himself close to you, then he will talk your ear off. If he doesn't feel he knows you, he won't say a fucking word, while staring you right in your face. He's approachable but not really. What I mean by that is, you can approach him but, the minute you do, he's sizing you up as prey. Antonio's major flaw is this, if he loves you he will do pretty much anything for you, including be a sucker. The problem with that is this, I don't want a sucker. I'm really not that type of girl. I appreciate Antonio's loyalty. I cherish it. So much so, I'm fiercely protective over it. I allow no one the benefit of attempting to take advantage of him, without me pointing it out to him the first moment we're alone. It has always been the biggest thing we argue about. When I see someone trying to take advantage, I pull his coat to it immediately. I'm the one in his corner that doesn't give a fuck about anybody around him because I know HIM. Whoever I meet through him is just that, through HIM. He is the alpha and omega of my relationship with anyone I meet through HIM. This became my reputation when people spoke about me in Baltimore.

He brings major weight into our relationship. He is FEARED. He made his name on both the Baltimore streets and in the Maryland prison system, where he spent the last of his teen years and most of his twenties doing a dime. (Ten Years)

Let me tell you who Antonio is in Pigtown, he's PROTECTION. He's one of the biggest predators in a city full of them. The deeper into his addiction he was, the more dangerous he became to those he considered prey. He doesn't rob the broke. He robs money boys. No one will come into Pigtown and rob you. Young hoppers coming up trying to make a name for themselves rarely wander into Pigtown for a robbery. If they do, they only make that mistake once. Pigtown is seldom robbed. For this luxury, the dope boys in the neighborhood pay a tax. While they're paying him a tax, he's dipping off into other neighborhoods and robbing dope traps. No one ever came looking for him to retaliate. I mean not once. Friends of his would come in from all over the city to tell him how they heard he just robbed this one or that one. It was so well known that if Antonio robbed you nothing would be done that workers wanting to steal their pack would just say Antonio robbed them. One night, before he got locked up, he came to me with a story his friend Tracy from Park Heights came to tell him.

"Bay, you'll neva guess what Tracy just told me."

"What?"

"He said nigga's taw'in' 'bout I robbed a spot up Park Heights. He said they got a retarded girl working up in the spot. She said, 'Tuh-Tuh-Tonio did it."

"You robbed a retarded girl?"

"Fuh' naw I ain't rob her ass. Them niggas jus' sayin' that so they can keep the fuh'in money. C'mon now, Bay?" I got complete side eye.

"If people keep saying you're robbing them, then won't people come looking for you?" I'm concerned.

"Do people ever come looking for me?" He looked me right in my eyes.

Antonio's been gone for nine months and no one was robbed the entire time he was gone. It's time to pay the Piper.

People genuinely like Antonio. No one wants to be on his bad side. If he has a disagreement with you, he's not going to argue with you. He will discuss it but, that discussion will consist of him telling you exactly where he stands. You can either accept it or not. He's very reasonable, when he's in the mood. If he's not in the mood then you're shit out of luck. He's not budging. He's very charismatic, with a nice smile and a quick wit. He's a major predator. A gun looks as natural in his hand as a basketball looks in Kobe Bryant's. I must admit I found that very sexy about him. His loyalty is known and sought out by heavy nigga's in the game. People bend over backwards to be on his good side. It's my job to make sure no one tries to play him.

All of these people want to give Antonio work. They want to load him up with coke and dope so he can blow South Baltimore up. There's a lot of money to be made and Antonio being sober means he's on top of his game. They all know it and they want to be the one he makes money with. Whoever he chooses to work with gets the benefit of having a killer on their team. Antonio's reputation is so well known from the streets to the cell blocks, just the mention of him on your team puts everyone on high alert that you don't want to fuck around.

He's emotional. I have never met a man who will cry at the drop of a hat. If you tell Antonio a personal story that caused you pain, he'll cry. He won't make a sound or a face but, tears will roll down his cheeks.

Since coming home Antonio has met with at least 15 different people from all over Baltimore. Before each meeting he briefs me on who we're about to meet and how he knows them. Today at the barbershop, he's meeting 4 more people. The first person we meet is his cousin, Dome. Dome just came home from doing time with the Feds. (Federal Prison System) He did ten years but, apparently he came home with a major connect and he wants Antonio working with him. I met Dome a few days earlier at Mondawmin Mall in W. Baltimore, where we live. He was a good looking, chocolate brown, unsuspecting guy. He had a gold tooth in the front, wore glasses and always had on baggy clothes. Being a woman, I picked up on certain energy from Dome when we first met. That led me to take a closer look at him. In doing so, I looked passed the gold tooth, glasses and baggy clothes. I realized that Dome was actually fine as hell. The clothes were hiding one of those prison bodies. His hair was always lined up and behind the glasses he was really nice looking. Seeing as this was our second time meeting and he was Antonio's cousin, essentially making him my cousin and no threat to Antonio. I decided to greet him in a way I saw fit.

As he approached us he gave Antonio dap and a one armed hug. He then turned to me and put his arms out to give me a hug. I lifted my arms up too but, instead of giving him a hug I started feeling him up. Groping his ass, back, arms land legs, even squeezing his pecs. I didn't rush doing it either. I did it just fast enough to make it last less than a minute. Everyone on the corner in front of the barbershop was yelling, "Daaaamn!!!" while Antonio stands there watching me shaking his head. I enjoyed it and I didn't hide it. I enjoyed it so much that after I had touched every part of his body and squeezed his pecs. I patted him on his ass and said, "You alright." I then looked at Tonio looking at me and I asked him, "He's my cousin, right?" To which Antonio just nodded his head. After being thoroughly molested Dome and Antonio stepped away from the crowd to talk, with me trailing behind in earshot.

While Antonio was deciding whose offer he was going to accept we went about the business of getting the neighborhood ready. We had to decide where we would set up shop. Seeing as I had already set up Stan's, we knew that was the first place. Antonio's roots in addiction meant that we will have a team of dope fiends working for us. He will manage them, with me being the one who sets the plan and watches the money. I make sure everyone is paid, especially us and that every one's pay is right.

The plan is to grab a little bit of work, as I had planned

originally. That will get the flow going. When he decides who we'll work with, we'll just merge it in with ours, fading ours out. Once we stack our money off their investment and we're ready to branch out. We'll renegotiate a new deal. Whatever we buy outright, the Connect will match at a better price.

Poopie's been living in Stan's, getting high and keeping an eye out on what's going on in the house. The light skinned guy's name is Shorty. According to Poopie he's pretty cool but, the other one is an asshole, just as I had suspected.

The day after the meetings on the Blvd, Antonio and I went to see Stan. It was early afternoon when we arrived. I walked in the house ahead of Antonio. As soon as I walked in, I saw Shorty's partner sitting on a stool to the right, just inside the door. He didn't see Antonio behind me and said,

"What's Up Baby?"

I looked at him in both disgust and fear for him. Antonio stepped in the door quicker once he heard him.

"Who the fuh' you callin' Baby?" His accent stung. His voice was deep and it scared me. The guy jumped up clearly taken by surprise, knocking his stool over.

"Who the fuh' is you?" He snapped trying to hide his surprise.

"Nigga, I asked you who the fuh' you calling Baby? Don't worry about who the fuh' I am!" We stepped further into the cramped living room. Stan must've heard Antonio because he was down the stairs in a hurry with his lisp and chipped tooth smile. He tried to distract Antonio but that wasn't going to happen. Antonio had his sights on dude. He wasn't going to take his eyes off him until he felt the guy was neutralized in some way. Dudes' best bet was to lie on the nasty floor and show Antonio his naked belly.

"Yo, Stan who the fuh' is this nigga?" The guy asked Stan with a shaky voice. He was clearly trying to figure out how to get out of his predicament. Before Stan could respond, Antonio snapped again.

"Bitch Nigga don't you ever disrespect my woman again. Keep

your fuh'in' comments to your fuh'in' 'self. Don't you ever let me hear you talk to her like that again! Don't ever let me hear you even spoke to her. Do you fuh'in' understand me?"

The group of highed up hoe's, john's and chili pimps lying about, were all getting up and moving toward the back of the house. They stood there for a second before the guy put one foot forward. Antonio took one step back and made a move toward his waist.

"Hold up Nigga, what are you moving for?" Tonio snapped. The guy froze and put his hands up.

"Let's go Bay." He said to me as he walked out the door. I walked behind him not saying a word. The guy got scared and came out of the door calling for Antonio.

"Hold up Man. I'm sorry. I didn't mean no disrespect to your wife. I'm sorry." He followed Antonio to the car. Antonio was at the highest level of pissed-tivity. He whipped around and looked the guy dead in the eye and said,

"You got 20 minutes to pack up and be out or get it how I give it. I give it all kinda ways Nigga, how ya want it?" I was shocked. I couldn't believe he just gave this guy heads up on what he was in store for. In my mind this guy could now go and get a gun and catch Antonio slipping. I yelled at him,

"Why the fuck would you say that?" The guy then killed all fear I had of him with his next statement.

"Yeah, why you wanna say that? It ain't even that serious. I said I was sorry. You didn't even give me a chance to say I was sorry."

"You heard me Nigga." With that Antonio got in the driver's seat and I in the passenger's seat. We drove off. He dropped me off around the corner at the bar. I didn't ask where he was going. He didn't offer to tell me. As the woman of this type of man, I have to know when not to ask questions, for my own safety.

We went back over Stan's later that afternoon to conclude our business with him. When we got there the guy was gone. We went up to Stan's room and told him we wanted to open up shop. He was all for it and made it known he was happy Antonio was home. Antonio thanked him for looking out for him while he was locked up. We negotiated a fee that we would pay Stan for using his house. Antonio handled that because he knew the going rate. Antonio and I decided that we would wait a couple of days before we started. That would give the house a chance to be quiet before we got it crunk. We figured three days would be good. Sunday night we would open up.

We went to Stan's everyday leading up to Sunday just to make sure that no one was in there selling and to make our presence known the hangers on. One day while we were there Shorty came in. He saw Antonio and approached him very respectfully. He asked if he could speak with us for a moment. We walked away from everyone and went to speak in Stan's room. Shorty started the conversation.

"I want to start by apologizing to you both about how my partner acted the other day." He was looking at me. Antonio just stared at him. Neither of us said a word as he continued, turning his focus completely to Antonio.

"I need to talk to you, to see if there is a way we could both work together in here?" Shorty was a humble dude.

"No" Antonio responded. (See what I mean?)

"I know you're running a night shop." He said.

He gets a blank stare from Antonio.

"Well, I run a day shop." Antonio just stared at him. I interjected.

"So what you're asking is if you can run the day shop while we run the night shop?" I asked as I looked at Antonio from the corner of my eye. He just stared and listened.

"Yeah, that's what I'm asking." He meekly smiled at me.

I looked at Antonio knowing I wouldn't get a response. I told Shorty we'd talk about it and let him know. I got his number and locked it into my phone. Tonio never said another word to him. After I got Shorty's number he left. Antonio and I left shortly after.

Saturday we went and bought the coke and dope. We spent Sunday day mixing and packaging the heroin at home. Sunday night we were in business.

I was upstairs in Stan's room while Tonio and Poopie ran the front door and the back window. The window faced the alley. It was dark and not visible from the street. The cops don't drive back there. The ladies and their john's could use the front door. I mixed the dope so it was mixed right. I mix like they mixed back in the 70's so my mix was good. Leonard taught me back in the late 80's. He was king if the city back then and brought me to Baltimore to live when my mother went to prison and my older brother Kenny was in the Navy. He had just been released from prison back then and knew my mother was just sentenced to 22 years. They had dated back in the 70's when I was a little kid and remained close friends throughout the years. When Leonard went to prison in the early 80's, The Carmen always made sure he was taken care of. When he got out and took over the city he sought me out to make sure I was okay. I was a teenager living on my own in a city with no family. He didn't think it was safe for me to be there alone. He brought me to Baltimore and gave me the house we were living in. Atlanta is my home but, I know I always have a safe place to go whenever I need it so, it makes Baltimore my home too.

Antonio mixed the quick way, which meant we used more dope. His was prettier but mine was right. The spot took off from the first night. Fiends in the neighborhood appreciated how I mixed my dope and followed it. We had crack and heroin so we were a one stop shop. By morning everything was gone and we made a profit. Branching out would be no problem.

We made Poopie a partner seeing as he was going to be living there and working just as much as we were. He was a dope fiend living in a dope house. He couldn't keep money on him in there so he asked me to hold it for him. Every morning when I got home I'd count the money up and divide it into four stacks, the startup, mine, Antonio's and Poopie's, in that order. At the end of each week I would let Poopie know how much I had of his money. Things were going so good that Antonio didn't give anyone his decision for several weeks. Ballers kept courting him like they were trying to sign him to their team. They'd give him money and invite him out to bars and clubs. He didn't really go into bars in other neighborhoods so we would meet them in restaurants in the "white" parts of town. On the other side of the Harbor where nothing crazy would happen and you wouldn't be likely to run into other people you did business with. Sometimes we'd meet people out in White Marsh, which is about twenty minutes away from South Baltimore. This was my idea. Antonio seemed to like it.

There were times when I wouldn't be in the trap with them. Everything was working smoothly. I started focusing my energy on other ventures while Antonio and Poopie ran Stan's. I wouldn't be gone long periods of time, maybe a night here and there. I would always count the money in the mornings though. I started noticing that when I wasn't there the money was off. I asked Antonio about it. He told me Poopie was running downstairs while he was upstairs. I asked Poopie about it. He really didn't have an answer. I made mental note of it and moved on. Money continued to come in and each of our piles was growing. I made an entire budget for us. We had $25 a night to spend on food and cigarettes.

Antonio and I talked about the conversation we had with Shorty. We agreed we'd talk to him again. Antonio asked around the house about him. Everyone seemed to like him. They all said he was a stand up dude. We didn't care about the day shop but, we had to make sure the house didn't get too hot and fuck us up. That was the priority. Shorty came through and the three of us sat down and talked.

"I appreciate y'all giving me a call." He said when we met at the Mom's bar.

"I asked around about you and everybody in the house said you was cool." Antonio said taking a sip from a Heineken.

"I try not to be disrespectful. It's not good for business." Antonio nodded in agreement.

"You know you don't have a partner no more." Antonio told him.

"Excuse me?" Shorty asked confused.

"I said you don't have a partner no more." Antonio repeated looking him square in the eye. "I mean you can roh' it in the day, but your man can't come. He's not your partner no more. If I think his money is involved, I'll take all of it. If you don't have the money to start a day shop, then I'll go in with you and you'll pay me out of it. Can you live with that?" Shorty thought about what he was just told and answered accordingly.

"I understand what you're saying." He paused before continuing. "I guess I have to go hurt his feelin's."

"You do that. Let me know if you need me on that. Call my Baby. She'll get you straight if you need it." With that Shorty left the bar.

I had a hard fast rule, NO FRONTING. I did not play that shit. It fucks the count up. I'm too busy watching for the police. Preparing to run out the window I'm perched by. In case the police come in and I have to jump across a couple roofs get to the fuck out of there. I don't have time to remember who owes what. Poopie and Antonio always laughed at me about that.

Shorty got back with us, he got rid of ole dude and he was ready to start work. He said he was good on the coke but, wanted to know if he could hit him with some dope. After talking it over, we decided that we didn't want to take the chance of the house getting hot while we were gone. "Ready" (crack) didn't attract the attention or traffic that dope did. If there was only crack during the day then the traffic would be at a minimum while we were at home resting.

One night I was upstairs when a couple of the working girls bought a couple of John's in with them. One was a nondescript black guy and the other was a very well dressed older Middle Eastern guy. He flashed a wad of money, roughly $5000. I saw the money and was hoping they were going to sit in the house all night and rock out. The girls came, copped and they all left. Shorty was with me that night. He'd become a part of our crew in the weeks he'd been running the day shop. Antonio had to take care of some business outside of the house. He asked Shorty to watch my back while he was gone. After the group left Shorty and I talked about the guys wad. We hoped they'd come back. Poopie wasn't working. He was enjoying the fruits of his labor and was getting fucked up. It was cool. Things were running smoothly that night.

About 4am the Middle Easterner came back. He said he'd been robbed by the guy who was with him earlier. I asked him why his friend would rob him. He told me he had never met the guy before that night. We talked for awhile. He told me he would go to the ATM and get some money to spend with me. I looked at the way he was dressed in Italian leather shoes, cashmere sport jacket over a turtleneck and determined he could afford to get high. I was hoping he'd spend a small fortune.

"Do you think I could get something before I go? Just one and then I'll go get money and sit here with you." He asked. I agreed and gave him a rock. Shorty left after I asking me if I was cool being alone with ole dude. He smoked and kept talking. By 3pm he owed me $900. He asked if I was going to send someone with him to the ATM. I yelled for Poopie who was in Stan's room behind the closed door from where we were sitting. Poopie didn't respond when I yelled for him so I had the man open up the door. Poopie was in the bed with two white girls fucking and smoking crack. He looked up at me and said,

"Come on Sis? I don't feel like going."

I looked at the guy and told him, "Let's go." We jumped in his

1990's burgundy Volvo. He tells me his bank has an ATM just down the Blvd going toward the expressway. When we get to where he says it is, he says it's not there. He drives to one he knows on the other side of town. To make a long story short, this motherfucker drives me from South Baltimore to Columbia Maryland over 19 miles away if you're on I-95. He's using the streets. I realized when we didn't find the second ATM. I had a problem. I'm in a car with a perfect stranger. To make matters worse, I forgot my phone in the chair I was sitting in back at Stan's. As we're driving toward Columbia he starts talking crazy trying to scare me. It was working. I wished I had a gun. Then I thought, if I had a gun and showed it to him, all he would have to do is ride up to a cop. It would all be over with, so I was glad I didn't have a gun. I was preparing myself for anything, having to jump out of a moving car, having to fight him, being put out in the middle of nowhere, and not having a phone. He kept asking me questions in a 50's horror movie manner.

"I could just put you out of my car, right? I could just say fuck you."

"Yes, you could but then where would you go?" I said very calmly. He flinched hearing it. He drove me around for three hours talking to me crazy. I calmed down a little when I realized we were headed back toward Baltimore. I listened to him and the radio keeping my cool. It was just getting dark when he pulled back up in front of Stan's. Still trying to intimidate me he gave me a crazy look and put the car in park. He told me to get the fuck out of his car. I grabbed the keys, turned the car off while snatching them out of the ignition, at the same time with my right hand. By the time he realized it, I was opening the car door with the same hand. I swung at him with my left hand. Keeping him from grabbing the keys, I slipped out of the car and walked to Stan's house. I knew Antonio wouldn't be there until 11pm. I was hoping Shorty was there. Actually, I was praying Shorty was in there. I had to walk past three houses to get to Stan's. The guy was hot on my tail. He knew not to touch me. He just followed behind me yelling for me to give him his keys. I ignored him and walked into Stan's house screaming for Shorty. I didn't see him when I walked in so I asked the Darryl Hannah looking prostitute where he was.

"He left." She said, wanting to know what the fuck was going on. I was about to panic because there was a very strong chance I was going to have to fight this man. Once I knew Shorty wasn't there I turned to face the man as he entered the door. I saw someone coming up the steps behind him but, couldn't make out who it was. I could tell by the way he was dressed, it wasn't a junkie. I kept looking past the Middle Eastern dude to see who it was, still praying it was Shorty. He had on a Crimson and Smoke Gray thick cotton hoodie Shooters {A local designer) sweat suit on with the hood over his head. He was looking down as he slowly walked up the steps. I knew it was Shorty. I breathed a sigh of relief. As he reached the top step and walked in the house he looked up. I saw Antonio's freshly lined up five o'clock shadowed face look up from under the hoodie. I thought I heard trumpets playing. He saw the stress on my face. He walked right past the Middle Eastern guy and gave me a kiss while asking me what was wrong. I told him everything still holding the keys in my hand. The Middle Eastern guy was scared now. Poopie had come in with Antonio. After hearing what I had to say, Antonio immediately turned to Poopie and said,

"How the fuh' you let her walh' out here with this Nigga?" His accent was thick and deep. Poopie froze for a second and then responded.

"Bruh, I didn't know she was goin'. She didn't tell me anything about it." I didn't have the heart to tell Antonio that Poopie refused to go. I was just happy to have gotten back in one piece. I was elated to see Antonio. I knew I was safe and he would handle it. I figured we lost the money but at least I was back safely. Antonio responded to Poopie.

"How the fuh' did you let her leave this house and not know

where she was goin'?" Poopie had no answer so Antonio turned his attention to the Middle Eastern guy.

"So where's my money?"

"I don't have it."

"What happened to you going to the ATM?"

"Sir, I'm sorry. I don't have your money."

"So, you was lyin' the whole time, gettin' over?" Antonio asked him.

"Sir, I don't have your money. I'm sorry."

"What were you thinkin' letting' his ass get that far in without seein' any money?" Antonio asked me.

"He had a huge wad of money when he came in. You can ask Shorty. He came back and said he got robbed but he could go to the ATM and get some more." I handed him the keys while giving a lame effort at defending myself. I was just happy to be back. I knew I had no defense. I was just giving the man the respect of answering him. Poopie, said, "Fuh' that, keep that Nigga don't give him back his car keys." Antonio responded to Poopie.

"How you gonna keep a whole Nigga, Yo? That's kidnappin'. We can't keep him forever." That's it, we lost the money, I thought. Then Tonio placed the keys on the coffee table in the living room where everyone could see them and said.

"I can't keep your keys from you but, you're not leaving here until I get my money." He then took a seat right next to the keys. He took a lollipop out of the pocket of the hoodie and slowly un-wrapped it, before placing it in his cheek.

"Sir, I don't have your money. I'm sorry." The man pleaded again. He gestured toward me in an exacerbated manner and began talking to Antonio about me. All he could get out was,

"Sir, this woman, this woman" before Antonio pulled the sucker from his mouth. He wagged it from left to right a couple of time. The man shut up instantly.

"Here's what you're gonna do. You're gonna get on the phone

and you're gonna call somebody to bring you my money." Antonio said placing the sucker back in his cheek.

"But, Sir I don't have the money." Antonio pulled the sucker from his mouth and pointed at the man as he began to talk.

"Pick up the phone and call somebody to bring you my money. Call your wife. Call your mothuh. Call your husband." One of the girls sitting in what would be a dining room walked over and placed the phone on the coffee table away from the keys without being asked. She returned to the would be dining room that had a love seat in it and a group of people sitting all over the floor watching what was going on intently. Without taking his eyes off the man, Antonio pointed the lollipop at the phone.

"Sir, I don't have any family here." The man pleaded.

"Call ya neighbor. You're not leaving here without payin' me my money." As calmly as he was speaking it was clear Antonio was not playing, with this guy or that lollipop. The man understood and made a call to who he said was his boss. When the phone was answered he began to speak in Arabic. Antonio put an immediate stop to that.

"Whoa, tell him to hold on. (The man did as he was told.) Don't speak in Arabic. Do *not* speak in Arabic. Speak in English so I can completely understand you. Do you hear me?" Antonio then said something to the man in Arabic. It took all of us by surprise. The man continued the rest of the conversation speaking English. Antonio placed the lollipop back in his cheek, leaned back in the chair and just listened and watched the man. He told the person on the phone that he owed some people money. The people wanted their money before he left. He told them how much he owed. They agreed to bring the money. We agreed to meet them at a gas station on Washington Blvd right by the expressway in 2 hours. Antonio didn't trust going with him to the gas station. We enlisted Sara to get in the car with the guy and go with him to get the money. We had her john follow them up there in his truck. We rode with him.

Another girl went for the ride so Sara wasn't alone with the guy in the car. As we pulled in, we see an SUV with at least 5 people in the car waiting for him. At first we thought we'd been set up but, quickly realized this was a family. Sara and he parked the car and they both walked over to the SUV. They approached the passenger's side. All the people were obviously asking a bunch of questions. Sara seemed to politely bring the focus back to the money and they handed it to her. While they kept talking she and the other girl walked away and got in the truck with us. We went back to Stan's house. I didn't hear the end of that for a couple of days. I didn't care. I deserved it.

Here We Go Again

Antonio and I made the agreement that we wouldn't visit Stan's during the day. The reason being, if the police raided the house during the day and Antonio was in there they would undoubtedly charge him with whatever was in there. It made no sense to take a charge for Shorty. After work we'd go home, count money and sleep. Antonio isn't really a sleeper so half the time I woke up he was already up and out. He'd come pick me up when I was ready to get out.

Antonio had been home a little over a month. My phone was ringing continuously one late Saturday morning. When I finally woke up to answer it I saw it was Antonio's sister, Tina.

"J.O., you've got to wake up now Sis." She said, and her voice had urgency in it.

"What's up Tina?" I was groggy and my voice was deep.

"I need you to wake up. They just ran up in Stan's house." I'm wide awake.

"So?" I asked. I figuring she was letting me know I didn't need to show up for work tonight.

"J.O., Antonio was in there." She sounded scared to tell me.

"WHAT?! What the fuck was he doing in there?" I yelled.

"He was in there with Shorty and Wayne. (A junkie from the house we used to work) Yo and them ran up in there and took all three of them down to central bookin'." She explained. I was pissed.

"What was he charged with?"

"I don't know."

"How long ago did they leave?" I asked

"About 20 minutes ago."

"All right, thank you for letting me know Tina. I've got it from here."

"I know you do J.O. that's why I called you." We hung up the phone.

To say I was pissed would be putting it mildly. I knew with him having been taken out of Stan's within the half hour I still had a few hours before he was processed. I wouldn't be able to get the amount of his bond until then. I called Stan to see if the car was parked in front of his house. The police never arrested Stan, don't ask me why. He confirmed the car was there. I got up, took a shower and grabbed a hack for South Baltimore. I had my own key so getting in the car wasn't a problem. I went into Stan's house when I got down there. He took me into the bathroom to show me the toilet. It was in half. The cops broke it with a sledge hammer looking for drugs they thought were flushed. I told Stan I'd have someone bring in a new toilet. I called Renee from the bathroom and filled her in on what was going on. She was shocked and told me to keep her informed. I headed back home to make the call to the jail, find a bondsman and count the money to bond him out.

He was charged with possession of drug paraphernalia and his bond was $250,000. I called a bondman who told me it would cost 10% to get him out, I was about to cough up $25,000. SMFH. Then the bondsman said,

"Look I'm going to tell you something. You don't want to pay that bond."

"Yes, I do."

"I know you do but, if you pay $25k then the IRS gets involved. My suggestion for you is to pay a lawyer to get a bond reduction. Then come and see me." I thanked him and hung up the phone.

I called Renee back and let her know I needed her to get his bond reduced.

"I'll bring you the money on Monday morning after I get off of work."

"Good, I'll see you then." We hung up the phone.

Sunday morning I got up early and headed to Pigtown. I woke Stan and everyone in the house up to let them know I was about to go find someone to fix the toilet. Poopie walked with me to the other side of the neighborhood to find the Handyman. The whole neighborhood was still asleep. The only thing moving in the street was all the trash being blown around by the warm spring breeze. It was like this every Sunday. No one came out until after 1pm. So, we didn't find a Handyman. While walking down the Blvd back to Stan's Poopie and I talked about the raid.

"So tell me what happened yesterday?" I asked Poopie.

"Sis, I had just left the house. Not even five minutes before they ran up in there. I went around the corner and when I came back around they were haulin' Tonio, Shorty and Wayne outta there. I heard they ain't even find anything on 'em though."

"Who told you that?

"Shit, ask the people in the house. They all said Yo and 'em ain't find nuh'in''." His eyes were wide.

"So what the fuck did they charge them with?"

"I don't know but, they said he had a new cop with him. I think it's his partner."

"Fuck this shit. I'm gonna lean on Yo's ass when I get a chance." Poopie laughed when I said this. As we approached the stoop I used to pitch from I saw a patrol car coming toward us. I walked to the curb and started to flag it down as if it were a cab.

"What the fuh' are you doin'?" Poopie asked me wild eyed.

"I'm getting ready to lean on Yo." The cop car pulled up to me and stopped. Poopie told me I was "fuhin' crazy" and kept walking to Stan's.

The officer that pulled over was a chocolate brown nice looking guy. He rolled down the passenger window and I leaned into it.

"Where's Yo?"

"He doesn't work with us anymore. He's with the narcotics unit now."

"I know that, but where is he?"

"Oh, he's off today." The cop seemed nervous talking to me.

"So, you know him right? You have his number right? Call him. I need to talk to him." He reached for his cop radio, caught himself and looked to see if I noticed it. Before he could say anything I said,

"No not on that. Call him on his phone." I pointed to the cops Nextel fastened on his shoulder. He unhooked it and called Yo.

When Yo picked up I could hear him talking from across the car.

"Hey Man sorry to bother you on your day off but, somebody here wants to talk to you." The patrolman explained. I could hear Yo say,

"Who is it?" The officer looked at me.

"Tell him J.O." I said in an irritated voice. As soon as the officer said my name I heard Yo say, "J.O.?" and I reached my hand out and said,

"Give me the phone." He looked at me like I was crazy.

"What? You think I'm gonna steal your phone? Really?" He handed me his phone.

"Yo?"

"Yes, J.O, what's up?" he was faking annoyance.

"Yo, what the fuck is going on?"

"What do you mean J.O.?"

"You know what the fuck I mean. Why did you lock him up again?"

"J.O. it wasn't me. It was my partner Ramirez." He pleaded his case.

"No it wasn't Yo. It was you. Who the fuck is Ramirez? He doesn't know Tonio. You know Tonio. It was you Yo."

"J.O., I'm off 'til Tuesday, when I get back to work I'll talk to my partner and maybe I can get him to do something."

"Really Yo, you expect me to believe that? Yo he has a $250,000 bond, Yo. This is what I want you to understand Yo (I was almost yelling at this point) you're digging in my pocket. This shit comes out of my pocket. You're not fucking with him Yo. You're fucking with me. What the fuck makes you think I have $25,000?"

"It wasn't me J.O. Call me Tuesday and I'll see what I can do."

"I don't have your number. Why would I have that?"

"Get it from Donna." I heard what he just said but I was too heated to give him the satisfaction of responding to it. I hung up on him, gave the cop back his phone and headed to Stan's house.

Monday morning after work I went to Renee's office. Court was at 9:30am so I had to be there by 8 to pay her. I gave her the $750 she charged for a bond hearing. It was the first time I'd seen her since the trial. I enjoyed seeing her. She had an energy that I trusted. I told her what happened making sure she knew I was told he didn't have anything. She said she'd make sure to check the paperwork for that.

"Have you been working all night?" She asked me noticing I looked tired.

"Yeah, I should be asleep by now."

"Well, go home and go to sleep. I'm taking care of him. I'll have someone call you as soon as I leave court to tell you what his bond is." As always I felt relief from her. I headed home and fell asleep with the phone, so I wouldn't miss the call.

I woke up at three in the afternoon. I grabbed the phone to see how many times Renee's office tried to call me. They hadn't. I called the office confused and asked for Renee.

"This is Renee." She answered after I was put on a short hold.

"Renee, its J.O. What happened in court?" I was concerned and ready for bad news.

"Wait, no one called you?"

"No. I just woke up. What happened in court?"

"I'm sorry about that. My assistant was supposed to call you."

"That's okay. What happened in court?"

"Who's your favorite lawyer?" She asked. I got excited.

"You are." I was scared to smile but did without control.

"He's getting out on his own recognizance."

"WHAT?!" I yelled into the phone sitting straight up in the bed.

"Yes, he's signing his own bond. He should be out about 5:30 tonight. You better get down there and pick him up. I'll take care of the rest. I'm pretty sure I can get this thrown out."

"How did you get it dropped down to a signature bond?"

"He didn't have anything."

"What do you mean he didn't have anything?"

"I mean he didn't have anything. They arrested him for possession of paraphernalia but, in the report they said he didn't have anything. They actually wrote "none" in the quantity box. So I argued that and the judge let him out on his signature," I couldn't believe it. That fucking Yo is all I could think.

I got showered, dressed and headed down to the jail and waited for Antonio to be released. I was there before 5:30 in case he got out early. He didn't walk out until after 7pm. When he got in the car he told me all about court.

"Bay, you should'uh been there. It was crazy. They bring e'erybody in whose going to a bond hearing, right? We're all talking to each other, telling each other what our bonds are. You know how nigga's are when they locked up, they all lawyer's. They telling me my bond'll probably get lowered to about $50K. I know the judge ain't letting me go. Not me. So when she gets through pleading my case I tune out so I don't have to hear the bad news. The next thing I know, I got all these guys hitting me asking me did I hear what the judge just said. They're all excited after hearing the judge said and I still didn't know what he said. They had to tell me and I didn't believe 'em when they did. Renee came over and I asked her just to be sure. Then all the dudes waiting for their turn, start asking her for her card and shit. I was just sitting there stuh'. Happy as shit but, stuh'."

"I told you she was a bad motherfucker."

"Yeah, you did." I pulled off and headed home so he could get showered and changed.

Antonio decided the shop was hot and needed to cool down for a few days. So instead of going to work we just went to hang out in the neighborhood. He knew that once Yo found out he'd been release Yo would be back. It wasn't worth the risk so we were on vacation.

Tuesday we got up and out by early afternoon. We went and ate lunch at Lexington Market and then headed over to Pigtown. Once we were there Antonio went about the business of getting the toilet fixed. He had someone go into an abandominium, which is a dilapidated house junkies occupy, to take a toilet. It was already at Stan's waiting to be installed. He then found someone to install it. Antonio had cleared out Stan's house. No johns or pimps were allowed in the house. The girls were allowed to stay but they couldn't bring any men in. Stan and Poopie were the only ones. Shorty had an open warrant when he got arrested, so he was gone for the foreseeable future. Antonio, Stan and I were upstairs watching the guy install the toilet when we heard the door get kicked in again. The cops didn't run in this time they walked in. We could hear them yelling for Stan from the living room. It was Yo doing the yelling. Stan, Antonio and I all calmly looked at each other as if to make sure the other was ready to head downstairs to hear what Yo had to say.

"I guess he knows I'm out." Antonio said to us.

"I guess he does." Stan lisped. While we were still standing there Yo appeared in the doorway. The Handyman kept working after he was reassured by Antonio he would be okay.

"What are you doing in here?" Yo asked Antonio. Tonio NEVER talks to Yo, so I respond to him.

"We're getting the toilet fixed."

"Everybody get downstairs!" Yo instructed us.

"Uh, he needs to finish the toilet. I'm not paying him for whatever you're in here for." I told Yo. He looked at the Handyman and said,

"Yeah you can stay right where you are." The rest of us went down to the living room followed by Yo.

When we walked into the living room we saw the new cop I'd been hearing about. He was a little short Latin guy who could pass for white. He had light brown hair and almond eyes. Once we were all gathered in the living room, Yo began a public service announcement. Antonio took a seat in the dining room on a footstool by the window and leaned against the wall. In a loud voice Yo started talking to the junkie's in the house.

"I'm telling all of you right here, right now, I am going to keep banging this door down as long as you let this scumbag keep shoveling shit out of here." I looked at Antonio and he didn't even flinch at the insult. He slowly put his hand in the pocket of the light jacket he was wearing and pulled out a lollipop. While he took his time unwrapping it Yo kept talking.

"I can't for the life of me get it through my head why any of you would let this fucking guy around you." I wondered if Yo realized he was talking to a group of drug addicts about their dealer.

"If I have to shut this entire house down and confiscate it as a nuisance house I'll do it." He looked at Stan when he said this. Stan didn't say anything.

"Am I understood?" he asked the whole room. No one said a word. He stood there in the middle of the living room staring at Antonio wanting him to say something. Antonio pulled the sucker from his mouth and yelled,

"Ay Herb, you about finished up there with that toilet?"

"Give me about 10 minutes, I'll be done." Herb yelled back. The whole time Antonio and Yo just looked at each other. Yo and his partner left without saying another word. Once he was gone everyone resumed doing nothing. We went back upstairs. It was clear that Yo wasn't about to let up on Antonio. Antonio didn't seem to let it faze him. I on the other was very concerned. I didn't talk to Antonio about it I just made a mental note.

Friday came and we went back to work. I was upstairs handling the money while Poopie was handling downstairs. Antonio was in and out of the house handling other business. Poopie had started getting lazy over the last few weeks and the vacation seemed to have made him worse. He was irritating me because he was more concerned with getting high and fucked than paying attention to the money. I had spoken to Antonio about him. Tonio just kept asking me to "Stall him out." Meaning, give him a break. So I did. That entire weekend I gave him a break. I didn't say a word. On Sunday morning when I was counting the money I informed Antonio that the money had been coming up short. The only time it seemed to come up short is when Poopie was downstairs working without Antonio. Antonio said he'd talk to Poopie about it. I was unhappy. I didn't grow up with Poopie so my attitude was different toward him than Antonio's. I wanted to get rid of him. There were plenty of people that could pitch and not get a partner's cut. I wanted him gone but, I yielded to Antonio.

A few more days went by and I asked Antonio if he'd talked to Poopie and he hadn't. A few more days and he still hadn't. I decided I'd waited long enough. I went to work that night and told Poopie before I left for the night the three of us would have a talk. Antonio knew I was stepping around him to deal with this. He didn't put up a fight about it. He didn't even say anything about it but, I knew he didn't like it. When I noticed around 4am that we didn't have enough work to make it to 6am I decided to talk with Poopie a little early.

"Okay, so I've asked you this before and didn't get a satisfactory answer either time so, I'm going to ask you again. Why is it that the money comes up short when you're down there on your own?"

"I don't know Sis. You doin' the cou'in'." I looked at Antonio out of frustration, he said nothing.

"So once again, I'm asking you why the money keeps coming up short when you're in charge and again you can't give me an answer. I'm sick of this shit. You play with my money I play with yours. I'm keeping your money and you're out of the house." Antonio still hadn't said a word but, I knew he didn't like what I just said. Poopie didn't either and protested like a motherfucker.

"How the fuh' you gonna put that on me?"

"The only time the money comes up short is when you're down there by yourself. You don't even have a reason why that happens. You're getting higher and higher as the weeks go by. So, I don't have to put much thought into why the money is the way it is. You take from me, I take from you. I'm just taking more from you. Be out by tomorrow when we open up."

"Where the fuh' am I gonna go?" He shouted.

"There are a lot of places you can shack up around the neighborhood. Just not here."

Antonio didn't say a word during the conversation. That meant I just took that shit. When we got home, I was doing the usual counting and separating of the money I took Poopie's stacks and divided them equally between Antonio and me. He still didn't say anything. He didn't have to. He conveyed all he wanted to say within the energy in the room. He didn't like it but, make sure he gets his half of the money.

When we arrived at the house that night Poopie was gone. He'd moved into a house on W. Cross St. that he could get high in and stay for free. The owner was a crack addict named Brenda. We put a guy named Billy on the door at Stan's. Antonio and Billy went to middle school together. He was a raging junkie and we could pay him like one. He worked just to get high. As a business woman I couldn't ask for a more profitable situation. Once again I left that up to Antonio. He knew how much an addict's labor was worth. I just knew how much the dope was worth. With the money only being split between Antonio and me, I was happy with the arrangement. I still kept a nightly budget of $25 so Billy ate when we ate. If he liked it, I loved it. That week went pretty smoothly.

Antonio had been giving Poopie dope to sell from out of the house he was living in. He didn't discuss it with me. Like most things that Antonio did I found out after the fact. I didn't care as long as the money was right.

The Thursday after I kicked Poopie out of business was unusually slow .So slow, we didn't even bring all of our work in from the secret compartment in the car. On regular nights either Antonio or I would take turns running to the "store". When we went to the car we would bring the money that was in the house to the car and put it in the compartment where we also kept the drugs. When we returned from the "store" we'd bring in more dope and coke. Nobody knew about the compartment but the two of us. It was about 4am when Antonio told me there was a rumor we were going to be raided that night. I asked him why this was the first I was hearing about it? He really didn't have an answer for me. I asked him who told him and he said "Poopie". I was puzzled as to why he hadn't told me and why we even opened for business. It all made perfect sense why we were so damn slow all night. I was the last person to know the house was being raided. Just as I stand up to leave, I hear car doors slam outside. I walk into Stan's room and look out the window. I see police cars in the middle of the street. Some with doors wide open. I see about eight cops coming toward the house. One of them looked up at me in the window and told me not to move as he charged up the steps to the house. The door was then kicked open and the yelling started. "Everybody Get On The Floor!!!!!! Now!!!!" I walked back in the room I was sitting in with Tonio and Stan. I sat on Antonio's lap. I felt safe there. A young black cop came charging up the steps with his gun drawn, yelling for us to get on the floor. It was the same cop that Puerto Rican Yo sent to get me when he "introduced" himself to me. Antonio tapped my hip twice indicating for me to get up. I took my time. He and Stan lay on the floor but I didn't. I took one look at that filthy fuckin' floor and sat down in Indian chief position with my palms up. The cop was young and full of adrenaline. He kept yelling for me to lay down with his gun pointed at me. I just shook my head and told him, "I'm not lyin' on that floor. It's nasty. I'm not doing it." He pushed my shoulder to make me lay down while still pointing the gun. When I felt the push I let my shoulder go completely limp with the force and remained seated.

"I'm not a threat to you but. I'm not lying on that floor, sorry." Before he could say anything else another cop downstairs asked if he was okay. He was still looking at me and I nodded my head continuously and slowly, giving him the answer. He yelled back that he had everything under control. The voice told him to bring us down. Once in the living room we saw everyone lined up on the walls sitting quietly. I went and sat on the couch. Antonio sat on the footstool again. The cop who was yelling upstairs was the Sergeant in command of the raid. He was a short, fat, older black man, with square black rimmed glasses. They went into the back yard to check for drugs and found nothing. They checked every part of the house. They found nothing. I was nervous because I knew we had work in the house. They searched for about thirty minutes before the Sergeant made a call. No less than five minute later Yo and Ramirez walk in the house with an attitude.

"I told you I'd be back!" Yo said as he walked in. He looked at everyone in the room as he walked through. The Sgt. was waiting for him in the back yard just at the bottom of the five or so steps. I could hear them talking but, I couldn't make out what they were saying. All of a sudden I hear Yo call my name. I walk to the back of the house and sit on the steps in front of him and the Sgt. I listen to what he had to say.

"What are you doing here?" He asked me.

"What do you mean?" I asked trying to buy myself the time I need to come up with a story.

"Why are you in this house?" He was trying to sound like he was irritated with me.

"Oh, I spoke to Stan earlier today. He said he had a problem with someone in the house. So, I told him I'd have Antonio deal with it when I got off of work.

"What?" He asked me giving me a look of disbelief. So, I repeated myself.

"What type of problem?"

"He said there was a guy in here selling drugs to the girls. He told the dude to stop and get out but the dude wouldn't leave." Mind you this is the hottest dope house in the neighborhood.

"What?" Yo said not only giving me a crazy look but coming just short of calling me an outright liar to my face. I continued.

"Yeah, see Stan's boyfriend Sam is coming home from prison in a month. Stan's trying to get everybody out and the house in order so Sam can parole here. (Yo is just stuck. He can't say a word.) He told me he doesn't want to take any chances with Sam coming home. He told me the guy was ignoring his rule and he wanted him out. I told him I'd have Antonio come put him out when I got off of work."

"Why would Antonio help Stan?" Yo asked not believing a word I was saying.

"Because when Antonio was locked up, you remember that. (I pointed at Yo) Stan put a separate line in his house for me to use so Antonio could always call me. I use to keep the line transferred to my cell phone. He could call right through anytime he wanted. That means a lot to him. He was gone for a minute you know." This shit was just slipping out of my mouth I don't know where I was getting it from. The Sgt. seemed to be buying it.

"You expect me to believe that Antonio was kicking people out of here because Stan doesn't want people selling drugs out of his house?" Yo had one foot on the bottom step and his arms crossed looking directly at me, his face balled up in disbelief that I was telling this bold faced lie.

"I don't expect anything. I'm just answering the question." He looked at the Sgt. for a moment without saying a word and then told me to go back inside.

The young cop was searching all the men. They called for a female officer to come search all the women while they ran everyone's name for warrants. The young officer turned his attention to me while he was frisking people. He started getting slick out of his mouth with me.

"I wonder how long it's gonna take before you start looking like one of them?" Even though he was looking at me, I didn't think he was talking to me. So I didn't respond. He noticed that and kept talking to me while Yo is calling other people to the back door to talk to him.

"You ever think about that? How you're going to look in a couple of months? That shits gonna eat you up." I was still just staring at him wondering who he was talking to. Then one of the junkies said,

"She don't get high." It wasn't until then that I realized the asshole was talking to me.

"She don't get high? Yeah, right she don't get high. She gets just as high as all of y'all asses do. She don't get high. Yeah, right." He said in disbelief.

"Watch your mouth." I said looking him right in his eyes.

"She don't get high." Another junkie said. The young cop never took his eyes off of me while he continued searching people. I started smiling at him. He didn't know me.

"What makes you think I get high?"

"Look where you at."

"What? I can't know an addict unless I'm an addict?" Before he could answer Yo walked in and over to Antonio. "Stand up." He searched Antonio and said,

"No, she doesn't get high. She could probably pass a drug test before you." I was shocked that Yo just defended me. I didn't let it show. He then handcuffed Antonio and took him out of the house. The female officer passed them on her way in. She got instructions to search us, starting with me. She patted me down, making me lift and shake my bra to make sure I wasn't hiding anything in it. Once it was known I didn't have anything on me, they informed Yo. He was outside sitting in his car just outside the door. He told them I could be released once they were done. They searched the house, all of us in it and came up with nothing. Antonio was the only person that was taken out and they didn't find anything on him.

The work that was brought in the house was stored in the frame of the door in the kitchen that led to the basement. There was a 380 pistol in there too. Antonio had taken a couple of nails out to loosen it and used one nail to keep it securely in place. I was afraid to take the dope out of the house when I left. I knew for sure that Yo would grab me before I made it to the car. I wasn't taking any chances; I left without the dope or the gun. During the drive home I called Renee to inform her I may be in need of her services again.

"What? (She yelled into the phone.) He has to get out of here. They are going to keep locking him up until they find something that sticks." I agreed with her even though I didn't say it. I told her I'd call her about the bond hearing and we got off the phone.

I went home and went to sleep. I knew he wouldn't be booked and ready for bond until tonight so there was no need in fretting about it. When I woke up I went back to Stan's and checked the doorframe and everything was gone, including the gun. I knew for a fact that the cops didn't get it. I knew it was someone in the house. Oh well, there goes that. I had bigger fish to fry.

I called the jail around 6pm and found out he was charged with possession. To my surprise he had a bond of $15,000. Antonio was home by midnight.

That night we decided we couldn't keep Stan's house working without us being in it. Billy could handle it without us. With Poopie's spot up and running we could hang out in Mom's bar, which was in between both houses. The weather was warming up. So being outside after the bar closed wouldn't be so bad. The bar didn't close until 3am and people hung out until dawn anyway around there. Once again we shut down Stan's house for a week. This time we steered our clientele to the back of Brenda's house in the alley and got it popping over there.

In the back of my mind I didn't trust Poopie. I didn't share my reasons with Antonio, it wasn't worth it. I decided to keep doing what I'd been doing, pulling his coat to the things that were going on in front of us. I knew it would only be a matter of time before Poopie would do something again. With Antonio paying Brenda for Poopie working out of there he essentially dictated what went on in there, which meant I had say so too.

Another childhood friend and fellow addict had been staying at Brenda's too. His name was Sean. He would've been a good looking man if he hadn't let drugs take over his life. He was a deep chocolate brown with red tones all through his skin. He had sharp cheekbones and big brown cat eyes. His hair was black and curly. I liked Sean because he was a realist. He knew he was fucked up and admitted it. He got high but, he knew how to count. He and I had a bond. He understood how I felt about math. He watched Poopie for me.

Camden Yards and M&T Bank Stadiums are located in South Baltimore. Pigtown is separated by Martin Luther King Jr. Highway just off I-95. Antonio calls going over to that side of South Baltimore, "Over the bridge". He'd been going over the bridge a lot recently. He finally told me we were setting up shops over there. He had a couple of cousin's over there he wanted to put to work. We increased our volume and our profit. I never dealt with the people over the bridge that was all Antonio. With Antonio over the bridge, Stan's working with Billy running the show. Brenda's running smoothly under Sean's watchful eye, I didn't hang out as much. When I chose not to go out, Antonio would bring the money in the morning. I'd count it when I woke up. There were mornings I would wake up and Antonio hadn't been there. I'd call him and couldn't reach him.

One afternoon I took a hack down to Pigtown after he hadn't come home again. I jumped out of the cab in front of Stan's house to see if the car was parked out front and it was. I knew he was in the neighborhood. I found out he was in a house his sister Tina was renting a room in. Tina sold dope too, just not for us. I went to the house and the people who lived there let me in. I asked for Tina and a woman went upstairs to get her for me. Tina came to the top of the steps and leaned down to talk to me.

"Have you seen your brother?"

"No, J.O. I haven't."

"When you see him, tell him I'm looking for him."

"I will, Sweetheart."

I left Tina's and walked through the neighborhood to see if I saw him. People I ran into, who get high kept telling me he was in Tina's house. I gave up. I knew I'd see him eventually. I sat on Grace's stoop and enjoyed another of our good conversations. Surprisingly, I didn't have to wait long to find him. He came walking from the direction of Tina's house about 20 minutes later. I whistled to get his attention. He walked right over to Grace and me.

"Where have you been?" I asked.

"I been up working." He replied.

"No, where were you last night? Where have you been up 'til now?"

"I've been hugging the block. Like I always do. I spent the night down here and I'm just coming from Tina's house." He explained.

"I just left Tina's house. She said you weren't there." My voice was getting louder.

"I just left from over my sister's house. Leave it alone." I left it alone but, I made a mental note of it. He came home that night and the next few after that. With business picking up I spent less time in Pigtown. I just counted the money and mixed the dope. I started spending more time with my family, Leonard's children, who were like siblings to me. His two oldest daughters were older than me. Ever since I was a little kid, I would follow them around. Now that we were all adults, Niecey and Gwenie were my still my big sisters. Antonio had taken over both sides of the bridge and it wasn't even summer yet. The pressure of people wanting him to accept their work was still brewing. He hadn't made up his mind. He didn't have a reason to rush because things were going well without anyone's help. Antonio decided he wouldn't make a decision until summer. Until then we'd keep doing what we were doing. In about seven weeks we'd saved 28k each. We would've had more but we started going shopping, going out to restaurants and supporting Antonio's mother's bingo habit.

Antonio is a clothes horse. Whenever he goes shopping for himself, he shops for me. He never comes in the house without bringing me something. I don't care if it's a bottle of orange juice. He always has something for me. Even when he was strung out on drugs, he would come in with a rose if he didn't have any money. He essentially dressed me. I'd amassed a pretty good wardrobe in the short time he'd been home. Clothes were all over the place. He would even buy me shoes because he knew my shoe size even though I never told him.

One morning Leonard knocked on our door and woke us up. He came into to tell us that he was on his way to the store in the car. When he went outside the car was gone. It took a moment for it to set in. I went outside and sure enough the car was gone. DAMN IT!!! I reported it stolen and went back to sleep. When we woke up I called my god-sister Gwenie and asked her to take me to pick up a rental car. I refused to go back to hacks. Antonio didn't come home that night.

I had the rental car so the next morning, I drove down to Pigtown once again looking for Antonio. When I got down there I was told he was over in Tina's house. I went over there and again Tina told me he wasn't there. Even though the people who answered the door told me he was upstairs. I knew what I was dealing with. I didn't have the time to deal with it at that moment. I had business to take care of now that the secret compartment was gone. I had to find a safe place to stash the dope and the money. I decided to go talk to Grace.

Grace answered the door with her usual smile and good energy. I stepped in the house and asked her if we could talk for a minute. As always she was welcoming.

"I want to talk to you and ask you a favor. I don't want to offend you in the slightest bit. That's not my intention."

"Alright, I know that. Let's talk." She said nodding.

"I want to know if you'll consider letting me put a safe in your house. I'd hold my money and dope in it. I'd pay you of course." I hoped I wasn't insulting her. She sat there thinking for a moment before answering.

"Hell yeah, you payin' too." I smiled at her.

"Cool, I thought you'd be offended but, I had to ask. I can't trust people around here. You're the only one I'd trust with my money."

"No, I'm not offended. I'm broke. Who all is gonna know it's here?" she asked.

"The two of us, Tonio, no one else can know." I was dead serious about that.

"That's what I'm talking about."

"I'll talk to him about it when he surfaces. He'll talk to you about money. He handles all that stuff."

"Good. Where is he, anyway?"

"He's in Tina's house hiding." The look she gave me let me know she knew what I knew. I left Grace's and went to Mom's bar.

Atlanta

I was still in contact with Cuzn. He kept asking when I was coming home. We were introduced by SK over the phone years ago while I was in Baltimore working. So he knew I worked in Baltimore when things were slow in Atlanta but, things were great in Atlanta. So, he didn't understand why I wasn't there. I didn't tell Cuzn anything about Antonio for two reasons. One: It was none of his business and Two: He still had feelings for me. I wasn't about to let the fact I had a boyfriend ruin the chance to make money.

Cuzn is an alpha male. If he feels like there's another man around, he can come on really strong. He'd try to buy me back or he could cut me off all together. I didn't want him back and he couldn't buy me. That could lead to me being cut off again. He made his feelings known to me several times while I was home. During one of his plea's, I told him repeating the same mistakes and expecting different results is crazy. He respected that. I treated Cuzn the way I treated him before we became intimate. Like my friend and teacher. The energy was noticeably different between us. I don't know if it was because he hurt me the way he did or because he still had feelings for me after hurting me the way he did. Nonetheless, he always asked when I was coming home. My answer was always the same.

"I have some things I need to finish here and then I'm on my way back." Week after week I gave the same answer. I knew I could go home and make money. I knew I could go home and get back together with Cuzn. I knew I'd be taken care of if I chose to. That knowledge and the $28k I had in my closet at home, was my foundation.

Antonio surfaced and the neighborhood told him I was in Mom's. He came looking for me. Instead of a purse I carried a knapsack. Antonio took the knapsack and walked out of the bar. He came back ten minutes later and placed it in my lap as I sat at the poker machine. It was noticeably heavier. I knew the money from last night and first part of the days take were in there. I knew I had to take it home immediately. I asked him to ride with me but, he had to go over the bridge so he couldn't.

The guys who were trying to get Antonio to work with him were aware of his progress in South Baltimore. Instead of getting work fronted from them he took turns buying from them. He said it was to see who had the best products. It was working, we could tell by the client reaction whose coke and dope was worth working with. My original investment was $1,500. We were now buying $15,000 worth of coke and dope twice a week. The big boys were paying attention and wanted the consistent business from Antonio. If he wasn't going to let them give him work, then the least he could do was spend that $30k with a single person. He was too busy to give it a thought. He was single minded right now and wasn't letting anyone distract him. The big boys waited patiently.

That night Antonio took a hack home. I was still counting the money when he walked in our room. I told him about my conversation with Grace. He thought it was a good idea. I asked him why he wasn't at work. He said things were running well and he just wanted to see what I was doing. He left about an hour later and didn't come home.

His use was starting to become visible to me. He wasn't on heroin. I could tell because he wasn't getting ill. He wasn't waking up with a backache. He hadn't started disappearing for days yet. Nonetheless I could see it in his skin. I figured, if it wasn't dope then it was coke. Antonio was smoking crack. WTF?

I went directly over to Tina's house, as soon as I hit Pigtown. I didn't need anyone to tell me where he was. She was a raging junky and I knew she was getting high. Her place was where he could get high and no one in the neighborhood would find out. Once it came out he was getting high our stock would fall. It could affect the price of dope and coke. Big boys would look at him like a junkie with money and raised the price because they wouldn't respect him as much. This was not good on so many levels. So he hid in Tina's house where no one from outside would know. He didn't talk to the other people in the house so they only knew him by reputation. They wouldn't dare let what they thought was going on in the room be reported outside. They wouldn't want him holding them responsible for that. I knocked on the door and asked for Antonio. The person who opened the door told me he was upstairs. I told her not to bother calling up there. I walked to the bottom of the stairs and saw Antonio and Poopie's sneakers at the top of the steps. I called Tina's name. As soon as he heard my voice he walked back down the hall past my viewpoint toward Tina's room. Poopie followed behind him. Tina appeared at the top of the steps once again not coming down but, leaning to see me. I asked her if Antonio was there and once again she lied.

"If he's not here then why did I just see him and Poopie's sneakers at the top of the steps?"

"You didn't see their feet Honey that was somebody else's."

"Really? Tell whoever was wearing a pair of Ivan Lendl Adidas to come down here. So I can congratulate them on their taste in sneakers."

"They're not visiting me J.O. They're here for someone else."

"I don't care who they're here to see. I want to congratulate them on their sense of style. That should be welcomed seeing as they cost $150 and the person lives in a crack house. Tell 'em to come down."

I'm looking at her bent over and I see Antonio step behind her and head down the steps. She looked busted. I watched him descend the staircase. I asked Tina to come into the kitchen and talk to me. She only came down the steps when Antonio beckoned her to do so. She was a tall thick woman. She stood about 5'10" and weighed about 190 lbs. She took a seat in the kitchen after pulling a chair from under the table and turning it facing Antonio and me. We both stood by the sink. She looked at me as if she really didn't want to talk to me. She was tolerating me for the sake of her brother. I ignored the look and began to speak to her.

"Your brother just got off trail where he was facing 25 to life. He's got a chance to do things the right way. Not getting high. Why wouldn't you as his big sister help him stay on the right path? Why wouldn't you see him wanting to get high and try to talk him out of it? Why would you, even if you're getting high, not want better for him or yourself?" Antonio stood silent leaning against the sink with his arms folded looking at the floor. I waited for her response as I looked at him.

"Because he's a grown ass man an' he can do what the fuh' he wants to do." She replied.

"That's your answer? He's a grown ass man?" I asked questioning her intelligence.

"Yeah, he's a grown ass man and he don't need no bitch telling him what to do!" She yelled at me.

"So, you're calling yourself a Bitch?" I asked knowing better.

"No Bitch! I'm calling you a bitch, Bitch!" Her neck was rolling as the spit built in the corners of her mouth. I looked at Antonio to see if he was going to check her for calling me a bitch. He stood there arms crossed not saying anything but, he did look up when he heard her call me a bitch. I continued.

"What kind of sister are you? He just got home. Let the man have a chance to be sober without you helping him be fucked up? Just 'cause you're fucked up, you want him to be too?"

"You're not his mother and if you keep thinking you are he's gonna leave yo' ass." I looked at Antonio and said,

"This is what you want for your life? This is the type of relationship you want to have with your sister, who was locked up for two years? The two of you bonding over a crack pipe. Crammed up in a room smoking crack and reminiscing over your childhood?

That's what you fought to get out of jail for? This is what all of that time was for? So you could start smoking crack again?" I asked Antonio directly.

Tina yelled at me. "Who the fuh' are you to come in here and tell him anything? Who the fuh' let you in here anyway?" She started looking around to see who let me in but, there was only us. I kept looking to Antonio for an answer to my question. He finally answered.

"No." he said sheepishly.

"Then what are you doing?" I asked quietly. Tina was yelling something but, I'd tuned her out when she said the last stupid thing. Still looking at Antonio I said,

"I'm leaving, are you coming or staying?" I turned to walk out of the door and he followed me. Tina continued yelling, following us out the door. When we got outside and started walking up the sidewalk toward W. Cross St. Tina brought the argument outside. She stood on the steps and continued yelling at me. We stopped and turned around to listen to what she was saying.

"You ain't his fuh'in' mother Bitch!!! You ain't shit!!! You think you run his ass. You don't run shit!!! He's gonna leave yo. You fuh'in' Bitch!!!"

"Go back in the house and shoot up. You fuckin' junkie!" I yelled back at her laughing at her.

"Fuh' you! You fuh'in' Bitch! You ain't his mother. That's you're fuh'in' problem, you think you own him!!! You think you his fuh'in' mother. He's gonna leave you Bitch!!!! He's not gonna take that shit!!! Quit trying to be his fuh'in' mother Bitch!!"

Tonio just stood there looking at her in disbelief. I watched him watch her continue to call me "Bitch" and not say anything. I made a mental not of it. I looked at him looking at her and I said to him,

"This is what I broke my ass getting you out of jail for? To have your sister call me a bunch of Bitches and find out you're getting high again? This is what I fought so hard for?" We both turned away from Tina while she remained on the steps yelling like an idiot. We didn't say anything to each other as we walked to Mom's bar. I was pissed about being called a bunch of bitches and him getting high. I sat down at my usual poker machine in Mom's and started winning money. I forgot all about Tina for the time being but I knew it wasn't the last time I'd find him in there.

Things were getting better by the week and Cuzn was calling for me to come home. He said business was great at home and he needed me back. I couldn't tell him what was going on we didn't talk like that over the phone. I could only tell him the usual. I wanted to go home though. I was growing tired of Baltimore. I started talking to Antonio about it. Bye this time, he knew all about Cuzn. He knew Cuzn used to be my man. He was as comfortable as he could be about it. He knew I loved him and had a good idea I would be faithful to him wherever we were. He said he wanted to go but, I could tell by how our business there was growing it wasn't a priority for him. It was becoming one for me.

He had never been to Atlanta, so it was a distant thought to him. It was a vivid one to me. Although we didn't argue about him getting high, there was definitely a tension between us over it. I was constantly worried he'd disappear or the money would get fucked up before I had a chance to get down there and collect. I didn't know the cousin's from the other side of the bridge that well and worried I'd have to call my "cousin" Bodie from West Baltimore to handle any problems I may run into with Antonio on hiatus. All these thoughts were going through my mind but I never talked to Antonio about it. I knew that he would take it as me not having faith in him. I just planned and stressed not saying a word.

The day after the argument with Tina, Tonio and I got up early and drove to a Lowe's and bought a safe. It was the size of a stereo about 3x3 so we bought a stereo and TV too. We gave the stereo and TV to Leonard. We put the safe in the stereo box and brought it down to Grace's house where we stored it in the basement. Antonio had to use a dolly to move it around because it was so heavy. It needed a digital code and a key. Tonio and I shared the code and I kept the key. The key worked if the wrong code had been entered incorrectly two consecutive times. There was also an addition code we had to set that would be used to reset the code if the key was needed. I was the only one who knew that code.

Antonio and I continued to talk about going to Atlanta. He continued to open up new shops all over South Baltimore. He had now spread the business on the other end of the neighborhood that I didn't even go to. It was the block next to the gas station we met the Middle Eastern people to get the money. I had to meet him over there a couple of times. Soon after, I met the guys that were working. He was running out of trustworthy junkies so he started giving out packs to the dope boys who weren't getting much business since we came back in town. He continued to get high. I continued to give him his space with that. It wasn't something I could control and I didn't bother to try. The only thing I could do was be a support for him and try to keep him focused on the benefits of not getting high. In other words, I resumed my usual role.

Billy had gotten completely out of control over Stan's house. He was getting so high that he wasn't properly performing his duties. The working girls were telling me he was being aggressive with them. A few arguments had broken out between him and them. That meant the police could potentially be called to the house for domestic violence. I hadn't been going in the houses since the raid so I hadn't seen Billy. There was no need for him to leave the house since Antonio would send Sean over there to re-up and collect money. There was a girl named Kim who sold crack in the neighborhood. I used her connect when I first opened up Stan's. We had grown so big that Kim couldn't really make any money. We hired her to run Stan's for us. She would work all night and kept her 3 year old son with her too. At least now he wouldn't be in a car all night. I don't know if that was better or worse seeing as it was

Stan's house we were talking about. She looked like Queen Latifah, dressed in baggy jeans; white tees and kept her hair in a short ponytail. The best part about Kim working was, she didn't get high. She drank a lot of beer but, she didn't even smoke weed. I had quit smoking when Antonio came home. With all the tension between us I was starting to miss it. The thought of weed only made me think of Atlanta.

After Antonio evicted Billy I got a chance to see him on the street. He looked shot out. He was already ugly and now he was worse. He was a dark skinned, black man, with a nappy, short afro. Now that he was strung the fuck out his afro looked dirty as did his skin. His beard had grown in. It looked like it needed to be picked with an afro pick. He looked terrible. His clothes were filthy. I didn't even want him around me because he looked so dirty. I was disgusted by his appearance. I think Antonio took special notice of Billy's decline. I hoped he noticed just how quickly it happened. Billy had gone from smoking crack and sniffing dope to shooting crack and dope. It was a sign that sniffing wasn't getting him a good enough rush. People who start out sniffing usually remain sniffers. It's a bad indication of someone's addiction if they go from bad to worse. He seemed to dive in head first.

I was growing tired of constantly being around addicts in a city that was filled with them. I longed for the clean streets of Atlanta. I longed to be around my friends and family. Who no matter what they did for a living, carried themselves in a certain way and maintained a certain lifestyle. Antonio was in his element. The tension was getting thicker.

One night I was hanging out in Pigtown and everyone was in a good mood. Kim, Poopie, Sean and a couple of others that worked for us were going to hang out at Kim's after work. I had been feeling a pain on my right side all night. It was a nagging pain but, I didn't say anything to Antonio about it. As the night came to a close the day shift was soon to take over the neighborhood. I was ready to leave. I told Antonio I wanted to go home. I wasn't feeling well. He wanted to go hang out over Kim's. I told him to drop me off first. He kept asking me why I didn't want to go in a suspicious manner. The answer I was giving didn't seem to resonate with him. He kept asking me, as I sat in the passenger's seat leaned back holding my side while we were parked in front of Brenda's.

"C'mon Bay? We can go over there for a little while. Then we'll go home."

"Tonio, I don't feel good. I've been in pain all night and it's getting worse. Just take me home and you can go." I pleaded.

"I don't wanna go without you. I wanna go together. C'mon Bay, just for a little while. You'll be okay."

The pain was getting intense. I stepped out of the car and circled it thinking that would make me feel better. Tonio got out and asked me if I felt alright. He was concerned.

"I'm okay. I just want to go home. I really don't want to go over Kim's house. Just take me home please?" He seemed to get upset with me as we got back in the car. He agreed to take me home but, wanted to go eat breakfast first. I was getting upset because I couldn't understand why he just wouldn't take me straight home. We ended up at a breakfast restaurant on Edmondson (pronounced Emmison) Ave in W. Baltimore not too far from Leonard's. Antonio ordered a huge breakfast for both him and Leonard to go, after I pleaded with him not to make me stay there while he ate. He drove the long way back to the house. Grilling me as to why I didn't want to go to Kim's. We were driving down Bentalou (pronounced Bentlow) He was grilling me while the pain in my side is becoming unbearable. In my pain and frustration I wanted him to shut up. We were approaching the street to our house. Without thinking, just done with the inquisition, I picked up the bag with his and Leonard's breakfast in it and threw it right in his face. The car came to a screeching halt. I winced in pain that slamming on the breaks caused me. When the car stopped and I was finished wincing. I looked at him. He had grits all over his face and the window. Food was everywhere in the rental. I was in agony holding my side. He looked at me with grits hanging off his eyelashes and asked,

"Bay, why you throw grits at me?"

I opened the door and rolled out of the car groaning in pain. I was determined to go get in my bed. I walked toward the house holding my side doubled over while Antonio drove beside me continuing to ask me the same two questions.

"Why don't you want to go to Kim's? Bay, why did you throw grits on me?" When I refused to answer he sped off and drove to the house. I finally made the walk from the corner to the house in the middle of the block. Antonio was waiting for me. He was sitting on the car in the front of the house. I reached the house but, couldn't make it up the steps. I had to rest first before trying. I sat on the bottom step doubled over in pain unable to talk. Antonio got off the car and came to stand over me. He put his hand on my shoulder gently and asked me,

"Bay, why did you throw grits at me?"

I groaned, shook my head and wiggled his hand off my shoulder before he could ask me another stupid question or the same one. Our next door neighbor Diane, who was on her patio watching, came down the steps next to me and asked if I was okay. I just shook my head no. She looked at Antonio standing over me. "You need to stop asking all those stupid ass questions and get her to a hospital." It was the first time it registered to Antonio that I was in trouble. He looked down at me and said, "Bay, let me help you into the car?" I shook his help off and told him, "I just want to go upstairs and get in my bed." Diane tried to persuade me to get in the car and go to the hospital. I just wanted enough strength to make it up the steps to get in bed. In my mind, my bed was my salvation. It was the only place I could think of to go. I mustered the strength to stand up and headed up the steps. When I walked in the house Leonard was in the kitchen. He instantly knew something was wrong and asked if I was okay. I waved at him nodding my head and walked up the steps to my room. Antonio and Diane were right behind me. Antonio followed me upstairs. Diane went to Leonard in the kitchen to tell him what she just witnessed. I heard her urging him to get me to the hospital. I finally reached the top of the steps and got a burst of energy out of nowhere that took me to my room. I walked in and collapsed on the bed. Antonio sat down beside me, put his hand on my head softly, looked me in the eyes and asked,

"Bay, why did you throw grits on me?" I looked at him.

"Leave me alone."

I guess I passed out because the next thing I knew, I woke up to Antonio sitting next to me crying. I looked at him and said,

"What are you crying for nooow?" the pain was slightly less but, I was still in fetal position. I was facing Antonio on the bed.

"Cuz Bay, first you don't want to go to Kim's and then you throw grits on me and now you're balled up in pain. I don't know what's going on with you."

'Oh my God, (I grunted through a surge of pain) leave me alone!" I rolled over and tried to go back to sleep. Antonio picked up the phone and called his mother who lived around the corner from us. When she picked up the phone and heard his voice she knew something was wrong.

"What's wrong Bay?" I could hear Ronnie through the phone. She sounded alarmed.

"Mah Mah, something's wrong with my baby," He sounded worried and scared.

"What do you mean something is wrong with her? Speak up Man!" She demanded.

"I don't know Ma. She said she was in pain and then she threw some grits on me. I don't know what's wrong with her, Ma."

"She's in pain? (Ronnie's voice was getting louder) What kind of pain? Where's the pain coming from?" I could hear her clearly.

"I don't know Mah Mah, I'll ask her. Hold on?" He touched me delicately not knowing I was listening and asked me where my pain was coming from.

"On my right side." I answered. Ronnie heard me and immediately responded before Antonio could tell her.

"Tonio, she's having a miscarriage. You need to get her to the hospital immediately!"

"Okay, Ma I'm taking her right now. I'll call you from the hospital. Come on Bay; let me take you to the hospital?" He touched my shoulder gently while hanging up the phone. I couldn't move. I just needed a minute to get myself together. Leonard came upstairs and asked me to let him help me get out of bed. I could see he was worried about me. I let him help me out of bed and all the way to the car. Antonio finally started taking things seriously.

Once we got to the hospital I had to be helped out of the car and brought in by wheelchair. They immediately took Antonio and me to the back and put me in a room. A nurse came in and informed me that I would be getting a sonogram. It was quickly determined that I was 6 weeks pregnant with an ectopic pregnancy. They gave me a shot of morphine through my IV to ease the pain. Antonio was excited that I was pregnant not understanding that the baby was in my right tube. He started talking about it being a boy. I was really just over him for the day. I let him go on about us having a boy. I didn't have the energy to tell him I wouldn't be having his baby. The Doctor came in to tell me they would be performing emergency surgery on me to remove the fetus from my tube. Antonio thought once they removed it from my tube they would put it in my uterus for it to finish growing. After the doctor left and the morphine starting to kick in, I explained it to him. He was sad and upset. He lay on the bed next to me rubbing my hair. The nurse came in and kicked him off the bed, telling him the beds were only for patients.

Sheree just happened to call me. With the morphine having kicked in I wasn't in pain. I answered the phone. I filled her in on what was going on. I knew she would tell Cuzn. She was worried and wanted me or Antonio to call her once I was out of surgery. The nurse walked back in the room to check my I.V. and threw Antonio off the bed again. They were waiting for an operating room to open up so they could take me to surgery.

Antonio got back on the bed with me. He asked me to explain everything again. We laid there together, with him on his right side and me on my back talking. I explained everything to him, while he played in my hair and looked at me attentively. The more I talked to him I could see the worry in his eyes.

"Could you die?" he asked me after he had a full understanding of the situation.

"If they don't operate then the fetus will keep growing. At some point it will be too big and the tube will rupture. That could kill me. That's why they're taking it out now." Tears filled his eyes and rolled out until they landed on the pillow. I knew he was genuinely worried and scared. I knew he felt helpless. It was the most loved I've ever felt in my life. I rolled over, putting my back to his stomach and drifted off into a morphine sleep.

While I was asleep I barely heard a couple of nurses come into the room. One said to the other,

"Should we wake him up and tell him to get off the bed?" The other one responded.

"Don't bother. I've kicked him off a few times already. He's not going to stay off of it." I drifted back off to sleep.

The nurse woke us up to tell us the operating room was ready. They were going to be moving me in a few minutes. She looked at Antonio when he woke up and said,

"You know you can't be in the bed with her while they're operating, right?" He looked at her and said.

"That's okay. You can just come and get in this one with me." She looked at me and I said,

"I'll be too busy to care." She shook her head and laughed.

Antonio got up and stretched. I started getting a little anxious. I gave him a list of things to do in case I didn't come out alive.

"Take my money and make sure you give it to Buttah." He looked at me like I was crazy.

"What?"

"Make sure if anything happens that my daughter gets my money. Call The Carmen and get the address. Just send it over night by Federal Express."

"You are fuh'in' trippin." He walked towards the door still stretching.

"I'm dead ass for real. You can pay for my funeral. You've got enough."

He looked at me and I was smiling at him. I could see the relief wash over his face.

"I'll be right here when you get out. I wonder how long it's gonna take?" He walked back to me and kissed me. The nurse came in and they wheeled me out. I heard Antonio tell the nurse,

"We should change the sheets before you come lay down. It would be tah'y if we didn't." The nurse laughed at his joke and I was too far away to hear if she replied. I was rolled into an operating room. Everyone introduced themselves to me. They lifted me from the bed I was rolled in on onto the operating table. A doctor appeared over my head and asked me to count backwards from 100.

"99, 98, 9………"

I'm gagging. I'm gagging. It's dark and I'm gagging. Something's down my throat. I'm asleep and I'm gagging. I'm trying to wake up but, I'm gagging. Someone's rubbing their knuckles on my breast bone. It hurts like a motherfucker. I can't wake up to tell them to stop. I'm gagging. What the fuck is this in my throat? I can't close my mouth. My tongue is being weighed down by this thing in my mouth. It's a tube. What the fuck? I can't get this thing out of my mouth. It's going down my throat. I'm gagging. Who is that rubbing their knuckles up and down my chest? I'm sleepy.

"Joy, can you hear me?" I thought I heard someone say. The tube wasn't in my throat.

"Joy, can you wake up for me?" There it is again. Who the fuck is that?

"Joy, if you can hear me squeeze my hand." Huh?

"That's good Joy. Can you open your eyes and look at me?" I feel my eyes fluttering; I want to see who the fuck is calling me Joy. No one calls me that. I could barely see a woman leaning over me, holding my hand and looking directly into my eyes. I fall back to sleep.

"Joy, I need you to wake up for me. Can you do that for me? Wake up, Joy. Can you wake up for me?" I realize I need to fight to wake up. It's hard but I'm determined. I had to get her to stop calling me that. My eyes start fluttering fast. She's rooting me on.

"That's right Joy, wake up for me." I continue to fight the sleep and start moving around while fighting my eyes to open. It was then that I remembered I was in the hospital. I tried to wake up. I knew I needed to wake up. The surgery was over. I finally got my eyes to stay open and everything started to come into focus. I was in post op. I was a little scared. She must've seen it in my face because she responded accordingly.

"It's alright. You're alright. I just need you to wake up. Your surgery went well. The sooner we get you wide awake the sooner you can go home. So let's get you up and moving around. Okay?" I nodded and tried to sit up. My body was like cement.

"Don't try to sit up yet, Sweetheart. I just need you to wake up first. I'll let you know when I need you to sit up. Okay?" I was relieved I didn't have to sit up yet. I knew that was impossible. The next thing I remember I was in a wheelchair being rolled through some double doors. When they opened Antonio, Poopie, Kim and Kim's son were standing there waiting on me with big smiles. I was too tired to say anything but I was thinking, "Great, I had to hang out with them after all." I don't remember being driven home or getting home for that matter. I just remember waking up the next day seeing Antonio asleep beside me.

"I told you, you were pregnant." He said smiling after his eyes opened and he saw me watching him sleep. The week Antonio got home, after we were done making love one night, he stood up and said,

"Yeah, I think that one made a baby." That's what he was talking about.

"I guess you were right. Next time don't shoot it in my tube." He just laid there laughing at me.

"It's always my fault. Everything's always my fault." He said.

"What if I would've had the baby?" I asked.

"What do you mean? It would've been a little boy."

"I mean what would it have looked like?" I asked enjoying the possibility.

"He would've looked like me with your hair." He said as if he had seen the baby.

"I bet our baby would've been so pale it would've been clear. Like a jellyfish with long black curly hair." He laughed at me. I continued.

"What if our baby would've come out black as hell?" I asked him.

"If, our baby would've come out black as hell, that wasn't OUR baby." He had a point.

I stayed home for the next couple of days while Antonio worked. He came in throughout the day to check on me and bring me money. I cut dope in the bedroom so I didn't have to go downstairs. Leonard was there too. He made sure I had everything I needed.

I was up and running again back in Pigtown within the week. The word got out that I suffered a miscarriage. People from all over the neighborhood were offering their condolences. I was kind of perturbed by everyone knowing my business but, they seemed to genuinely care so, I got over it quickly. The weather was warming up. All I could think about was going home. I wanted out of there. I knew once the summer started things would only get busier. Then I'd have no chance of convincing Antonio that we should leave. I was home sick. I wanted out of Maryland, period. Sheree could tell by my voice when we talked on the phone. It didn't help she was always having fun while we talked. I had to get out of there. I didn't know how I would get him to budge.

I called my mother to check in with her. She told me she was on her way to Myrtle Beach, S.C. My step father Wayne's job was having him move there. They just bought a condo not too far from the beach. She was excited to live next to the beach and couldn't wait to go. It only made me want to go home worse. We talked about summer approaching and my daughter coming to Atlanta from Houston for summer vacation.

"What are you going to do? You missed last summer with her because Antonio was locked up. Don't do that again." She was mothering me.

"I'm not. I'll send her to you in Myrtle Beach. I'll come get her from there and take her home."

"Home, where's home? Here or Baltimore?" She asked.

"Atlanta. I'll bring her back to Atlanta for the summer. I'm wrapping things up here and headed back there as soon as I'm finished." There that lie was again. I knew once I told my mother it wasn't a lie anymore. I had to get myself ready to leave Baltimore. Antonio was going to have to make a decision.

"Fly her here. I'll be going back and forth between here and the beach moving things. Fly her into Atlanta. I'll make sure I'm here to get her from the airport. She can drive back with me to the beach. I'll have Erica too. So she won't be the only kid." Erica is my Brother Kenny's, youngest daughter and Buttah's best friend. They were two years apart in age.

I was prepared to talk to him about it that night when he got home. He dropped me off earlier in the evening and told me he'd be back. He didn't come back that night. I woke up the next morning and instead of going to look for Antonio I called my daughter in Texas. We discussed the plans we had for the summer. She was excited because we hadn't seen each other since Christmas when I flew her to Atlanta. Last summer, was the first summer, I didn't spend with her and I wasn't locked up. I wasn't going to make a habit out of ditching my kid. Antonio was home. There was no reason I couldn't or shouldn't spend the summer with my daughter. He was officially on the back burner.

I had my daughter when I was 22. It was an abusive relationship. He was in the Navy. We spent a lot of time apart. He always put me down and said mean hateful shit to me. When I got locked up for the very first time she was in Texas visiting his mother. Kenneth was stationed in Florida. He went into a courthouse there and sued me for custody telling the judge she lived with him. He told the courts I was in prison for 5 years. I was locked up for 6 months. He won custody and had been raising Buttah since she was 6 years old. I spoke to her on the phone almost every day. She didn't know why I was in Baltimore. She was only 12 years old. Her birthday was coming in June. She was excited to be spending it on the beach. She told me the date she got out of school. I discussed her travel dates with Kenneth's wife Crystal. Kenneth and I didn't get along after the custody hearing. While he was stationed all over the world, Buttah lived with Crystal. She and I together talked about what Buttah needed. She would relay our conversations to Kenneth. Now that I had made the arrangements and set the dates, I was obligated to get back to Atlanta. I hung up from Buttah and Crystal, called my mother to book the flight on the dates I gave her. I took a hack to a bank in South Baltimore to put the money in my mother's account to pay for Buttah's plane ticket.

Bye now the arguing had started between Antonio and I. Tensions had started to build. We bickered about little things. Both of us knowing it was the really big thing but, not mentioning it. I made it a habit not to tell Antonio about his addiction. There was nothing I could tell him he didn't already know. ME telling him to stop getting high wasn't going to change anything. I'd just get frustrated repeating myself. Telling an addict to not get high is the best way to waste your breath.

I remember when he first fell off the wagon, after we got together. It was the first time I'd seen anyone in the throes of addiction. He's a Sunni Muslim, converted while he was in prison doing time for murder. I don't care how high Antonio got, he NEVER ate pork. He is serious about being a Muslim and not eating pork. He is so serious about his diet that he only lets his mother and I fix his food. He didn't even trust his sisters to cook for him. When we ate out he'd order fish. "Can't put pork in fish" he once told me. So one day I asked him, "How is it that you won't eat pork under any circumstances but, you'll sniff dope?" He just looked at me, Then I said, "It's pork to you. You need to think of it as pork." From that point on we called heroin pork. He didn't quit sniffing it but, I could see he was feeling differently about it. Antonio loved dope but, used crack to keep him from nodding out. Since he's been home, he's been smoking crack. It doesn't have the physical withdrawals that heroin does. He stays awake to do business all night. He smokes in two day sessions. He'll stay in Tina's house, buy her coke, which makes her money, doesn't dip into our inventory and keeps everyone out of his business. He'll stop smoking long enough to go collect money and maintain the traps. The weight he put on while locked up is starting to shed away. The only ones who knew he was getting high was Tina, Poopie, Sean and me. None of us would tell anyone.

One late night, I went down to Pigtown to check my traps. With Antonio holed up in Tina's room, he could be missing things. I stayed away from over the bridge because I had nothing to do with starting those 3 traps. I benefited by sharing in the profit but, I was a silent partner. They knew who I was but, I didn't speak to them. I wasn't particularly friendly with them while being cordial at the same time. My reputation grew into a legend of sorts the way I held Antonio down, got him a lawyer, beat his trial, got him back on the street sober and making A LOT of money. People who I didn't even know, knew my name and would approach me all the time. When I met people with Antonio they always said they'd heard about me. I didn't pay it any mind. It wasn't putting food in my mouth even if they were paying for dinner.

I went to Stan's house, got with Kim to give me a rundown on how business was for the night. She gave me the count. The money matched up. I took the cash she had on her, $4800 and bounced. She let me know, Tonio had been through earlier and picked up $12,000. I was upset that he let the money get that high before he picked it up. The police could've raided the house and got all that. I went to Brenda's to check on Sean and Poopie. I talked to Sean and grabbed $3,800 from him. He told me Tonio had grabbed $16000 from him too. I didn't let Sean see that I felt a kind of way about that.

"Where's he at?" I asked.

"Over Tina's I guess." He responded.

I put all the money the safe at Grace's and saw that Tonio had been there too. The money he picked up earlier was in the safe. He'd even been over the bridge. Each house had a different color rubber band they wrapped their money in. I could count how much each house had in the safe. Each rubber band held a thousand dollars. While I was glad he collected the money and put it in the safe. I was still upset that he was waiting so long to do it. Like I said, anything could happen in that long period of time. I hung out with some of the girls in the neighborhood on a stoop, waiting to see if Tonio would come outside. I was out there for a couple of hours and never saw him. At about 3am I pulled the money out of the safe and drove home.

The next night I still hadn't seen him. I went to Pigtown a little earlier. About 11pm. I check Stan's, picked up money. Again he waited to pick up the money, same at Brenda's. I look in the safe and everything is there. I head out to Mom's Bar to play the poker machine. It was a warm Friday night so everyone was in there. The jukebox was playing and I was winning. Time seemed to slip by and before I knew it 2:30am had arrived. I left the bar with the $200 I won on the machine. I checked my traps and collected money. Tonio had been there while I was in the bar and restocked them. Sean said he'd been there too. I was irritated by this. Not because he was doing what he was supposed to but because he didn't look for me. He knew I was in the neighborhood and didn't even come find me. Now I'm feeling like a girl. How dare he? I didn't bother him. I just emptied the safe and drove home.

Now this is the 3rd day and he hasn't been home. This is getting out of hand. I didn't wait for night to go down there. I got down there about 2pm. I went straight to Tina's house. I knocked on the door. The lady who answered just stepped aside when she saw me. I didn't ask if they were there as I usually did. I just walked in and went upstairs. I walked down the hallway and heard Tina's big mouth from behind the closed door at the end of the hall. I walked passed two other bedrooms and a bathroom to get there. As I walk, I hear Tina talking and Antonio laughing. When I knocked on the door everything got quiet. I could've heard a pin drop in the room from the hallway, that's how quiet it got. I knocked again.

"Who is it?" Tina's voice came barreling from the other side of the door.

"It's J.O." I said. The room got quiet again. Then I heard mumbling. I knew she was asking him what she should do. Should she lie and say he wasn't there? Then quiet again.

"Hold on a minute." She yelled not as loudly. I could hear things being moved around. They were hiding things I guessed. I heard someone walk to the door across the hardwood floors. The locks on the door were being unlocked. The door opened and Tina's was standing in it. Antonio was sitting across the room by a window on a stool next to the full size bed. I walked in and Tina sat at a desk next to the door. I left the door open because the room was already small and cramped. I stood a step or two in the door and looked at Antonio sitting there. The fact that he didn't get up to greet me,told me this was a conversation he needed to be sitting down for.

"Is this what I spent all my time and money to get you out of jail for?" He looked at me and dropped his head. I waited for him to look at me again before I continued to speak.

"I'm asking you a question. Did I spend all that time and money to get you home so you could get high again?" He didn't answer but he didn't look away either so I kept talking.

"You need to tell me something. If this is what I busted my ass to get you out for, you at least need to be a man and tell me yes." He still had no answer.

"I'm confused here, Tonio, help me out, why dontcha? You get locked up for something you didn't do. Face 20 to life, get out of that and come home to smoke crack? Do I have this right or am I missing something here? Feel free to fill me in if I'm missing something. Feel free to set me straight on any facts I might have missed."

"You need to stop trying to be his mother." Tina chimed in. Without breaking my gaze on Tonio I responded to Tina.

"Stay out of this Tina. I'm not talking to you and this is none of your business." Antonio still hasn't spoken a word.

"He's my brother. That makes it my business." Her voice was loud and challenging. I looked at Antonio to see if he was going to interject and tell his sister this wasn't her business. I got nothing. I looked at Tina and said, "Anything that has to do with me is none of your business. I don't even know why we're arguing. I'm not here talking to you or anything about you. Mind your business." I turn back to Antonio.

"Lil Bruh, why is she here anyway? You don't fuh'in' need

her." Tina said while she got her needle ready to shoot up. I looked at her in disgust and turned back to him.

"This is what you want for your life? Sitting in shooting galleries, smoking crack? Is this really what you want?"

"No." He finally answered.

"Then make up your mind Tonio because I'm not going through this again."

"You don't need her Lil Bruh. Let her ass go. Fuh' her!" Tina yelled.

"Stay out of this Tina. Don't say 'Fuh' her' either. Don't talk to her like that" He said looking me dead in my eyes, finally sticking up for me.

"I'm just telling you, you don't need her. Tell her get the fuh' on." She was thumping her syringe. I cringed and looked at him and asked,

"You'd rather sit around smoking crack and watching your sister shoot up? What happened to living and not existing?"

"No." He replied.

"Fuh' her Tonio. She ain't no bad mother fuh'er."

"Tina, watch your mouth. You really don't want any part of her. I'm telling you. You don't. Cool out." He said.

"Fuh' her," She repeated looking right at me.

"Why don't you fuck me Tina? Why don't you put that needle down and show me what a bad motherfucker is?" I said smiling at her, welcoming her to get up. She stayed seated and ignored the challenge.

"I'm not sticking around for this again." I said to him.

"You ain't going anywhere." He told me. I mean it, he TOLD ME. He looked at me as if I had just been ordered. As if there would be consequences. I looked at him like he was nuts and walked out of the room. Tina shut the door behind me and locked it. As I walked down the hallway I heard her say, "Fuh' that Bitch Tonio!" I immediately turned around, walked back to the door and kicked it open. Tina screamed and Antonio jumped up from the stool. When he saw it was me he relaxed a bit. I looked at Tina and with my left hand grabbed her by the throat as she sat in the chair. I started squeezing her larynx, lifting her out of the chair. She was choking and I was talking to her as I moved her to the floor on her knees.

"I'm sick of your junky ass calling me a bitch. You bitch!" Just as I was about to punch her with my right hand and send her to the floor Antonio grabbed my arm and pushed me to the wall. He held me there as Tina got up coughing from her knees. He was yelling for me to calm down.

"Let me go!" I yelled. I was watching Tina get on her feet. I was worried she'd hit me while he had me pinned to the wall.

"As soon as you calm down I'll let you go!" he yelled at me. Tina was on her feet bent over coughing and holding her throat. She looked at me and I could see the plan formulating in her face. I yelled for Antonio to let me go. He was back facing her and couldn't see her if she was coming. He saw the look on my face and turned around to look at Tina. He let me go and lunged at her to stop her before she got started in my direction.

"Stop it both of you! (He yelled standing in between us.) Bay, calm down, Tina, let it go! I'm telling you. You don't want to take this any further with her! She will fuh' you up! I'm telling you."

"I'm calling Mah Mah!" She yelled as she crossed the room to pick up the phone.

"Call her and tell her everything! Call her and tell her y'all are sitting up in here getting high." I yelled back at her.

"She knows!" Tina yelled back. It hit me hard. I looked at him and shook my head.

"Everybody knows I was an idiot." I said as I walked out the door. I left the house and drove home.

I was in my room for over an hour when he came in. He didn't say anything at first. I was watching TV and sitting on my side of the bed (the left side) and he took a seat on his side. When the show was over he started talking.

"You didn't waste your time and money. You saved my life. How could that be a waste?" He was looking at the bed.

"You're back to your old tricks, Tonio. How was it not a waste?"

"I'm not sniffing dope." He looked at me.

"You will be soon." We sat quiet for a while.

"I know."

"I can't do it anymore. I won't do it anymore."

"You're not goin' anywhere." He said it again.

"What the fuck does that mean?" I snapped.

"You're my wife."

"I'm not your wife."

"You are my wife. We're soul mates. You're not going anywhere. You can't be without me and I can't be without you. You're not going anywhere." He was explaining this to me.

"I'm not going through this again."

"You're my soul mate." With that he got up and left the house. At 530am, I drove to Pigtown. The neighborhood was quiet, only a few of the junkies copping. I checked Stan's and picked up the money. $1200, it was a slow night.

I went to Brenda's. Poopie came outside to talk to me in the car. He told me Antonio had come by earlier and picked up some money. He couldn't tell me how much though. I figured Sean gave it to Tonio. I asked him where Sean was. He was in the house asleep. It was a slow night all over the neighborhood. That just let me know to have little inventory on stock and get out of there as soon as possible. After leaving Poopie I went into Grace's house using my key so as not to wake her. When I reached the basement, I found Antonio there sitting in a chair watching TV. I was shocked to find him there. I wasn't expecting it at all.

"Hey, what are you doing here?" I asked him with a smile.

"Not getting high." We both laughed.

"I just left Stan's and Poopie. We don't need to have anything big in either of them tonight. It's slow as fuck. They don't need it. How's it going over the bridge?" I asked

"The same, it's that time of the month. Right before the first, you know how it is." I forgot that we were approaching the end of the month when government checks were depleted and business was slow. Memorial Day was next weekend.

"How much are they holding?" I asked

"Everybody's got four packs of hard *(crack)* and soft *(heroine)* each. I been feedin' them like that since this afternoon. They don't need more than that at one time. They really don't need that much. I'm just doing that so I don't have to keep running baah' and forth forreal. Bye the way, I decided we're gonna rock with Goo." Goo is another cousin of Tonio's who recently came home from federal prison. He's got dope. He's one of the people I don't really talk to.

"So, who are we getting the coke from?"

"I hadn't decided that yet. Maybe Dome. I'm still thinkin' about that." His Baltimore accent was thick, deep and slow. He was tired. I convinced him to go home and get some sleep. We emptied the safe and went home.

We woke up around 11am. I took my shower first and got dressed while Antonio took his shower. I was counting the money from last night's take when he came in wearing a towel and started getting himself dressed to go to work. All the money was right except for Brenda's house. I called Antonio's attention to it.

"Sean and them are off on the count." I said

"Oh, yeah by how much?" He asked

"$1,200 and change." His eyes got big as he looked at the pile of money on the bed with all the yellow rubber bands that identified Brenda's house as the source of the money.

"He told me last night that it was off but, he didn't know how much it was off by." I said

"He didn't tell me it was off when I got it from him." Antonio said.

"I thought seeing as he didn't know it meant you got it from Sean. He told me Sean was asleep when I asked where he was."

"There's no way it should be off let alone over a stack. Let's finish up so we can go down there and find out what's up."

He got dressed and we headed down to Pigtown. I was pissed because I knew Poopie didn't have $1200 lying around. I knew I had taken another lose. My attitude is starting to show on the drive down there. I'm irritated at having to go through this again. I'm sick of all the fiends. I'm sick of this dirty ass city. I'm sick of not seeing the places that are familiar to me.

"You alright?" Antonio asked me.

"I'm pissed."

"Bay it's only $1,200. Cool out. Don't get yourself worked up about it."

"It's only $1,200 dollars? Okay then, give me the $1,200, if it's not that much."

"Look, don't start. Let's just go down here and taw' to him and find out what's going on?"

"What are we going to find out? That he left it in another pair of pants? He's a fuckin' fiend and he fucked it off. So what are we really going down here for, to hear him make up a bunch of excuses that won't make any sense?"

"Just hold off until we get down there. That's all I'm saying. Hold off on blowin' your stack, do that for me, please?" I sat quietly for the rest of the ride to Pigtown.

I never went into Brenda's house. When Antonio went in to get Poopie I stayed outside leaning on the car. When they came out of the house Poopie looked like Antonio woke him up. He was holding his jeans up with his hand because he didn't have on a belt and he wasn't wearing a shirt. I was grossed out by the hair on his chest, it looked like tumbleweed. His hair wasn't combed and he had a look on his face like he knew what this was about. Ever since I put

Poopie out of Stan's house I didn't really deal with him. Antonio made it very clear without saying a word that he was going to work with Poopie no matter what I said. So I said nothing and collected the money. This was the first time it was off in the weeks since so, I didn't really have a reason to talk to him. I dealt with Sean, even though he was an addict he made sure the money was right, all that's changed now.

"Sean isn't in there. Brenda said he left about twenty minutes ago." Antonio told me as they walked up to me.

"So, why is the money short?" I asked Poopie.

"I don' know Sis." He replied.

"How is it that you don't know when you had the money and the work?" I asked him. Tonio just listened.

"I wasn't the only one who had the money and the work Sis." He said while exposing his palms.

"So where's Sean?" I asked.

"I don't know. He left out while I was asleep. Bruh, just woke me up."

"Did you get any money from him when you woke him up?" I asked Antonio.

"Yeah, I got a few dollars from him."

"Does the money match up with the work?"

"Nah, it's off again." Antonio replied giving Poopie a 'why are you making my life hell right now' look.

"So, why's it off now, Poopie?" I asked.

"I don' know Sis. I'm tellin' you, I don' know." I looked at Antonio and shook my head. There was nothing we could do until Sean got back to get to the bottom of this. I went into the bar to play the poker machine until he got back. I wasn't playing long before Tonio came in with Sean. Poopie wasn't with them.

"Sean, why's the money short?" I asked

"J.O., Poopie worked all day yesterday on his own. I wasn't feeling good so I slept most of the day. You can ask Tonio. He came in and woke me up a couple of times to see if I needed anything." I looked at Antonio as if to ask him why didn't he tell me that in the beginning. Why were we waiting on Sean when he knew Sean was sick? I was really irritated after hearing this. Once again I find some shit out he knew that pertained to the situation at hand and just didn't say shit.

"So what the fuck was he doing to the tune of 1200 dollars Sean?"

"$1,200; he fuh'ed off 1,200 dollars? I don't know what the fuh' he was doing to fuh' that off J.O. I mean I know but, you know what I mean. Shit you know too, forreal." He just looked down and shook his head. I looked at Antonio to see if he had something to say. He didn't. I walked out of the bar and headed over to Brenda's with the two of them following. Once the four of us were standing outside Brenda's Poopie looked like he wished he was anyplace but there.

"Now, Poopie explain to me how the money came up short?" I asked him again.

"Sis----"I cut him off.

"Don't give me 'Sis' nothing. Let's talk math and not relation. It was a slow night last night, right?" I asked getting heated.

"Yeah." He answered

"Okay, so seeing at it's been slow tell me where the pills went?"

"Sis, I don' know what you want me to tell you. I don' know where the pills went."

"You're kidding me right? You have got to be fucking kidding me right? You don't know what I want you to tell me? I want you to tell me where my money went. How hard is that? You were the only one who was handling things yesterday. So you should be able to give me a blow by blow of everything that happened. Did you get stuck up?"

"Come on, Sis? You know better than that." He pleaded.

"So we can mark that off as a possibility of what happened to the money. Did you lose it? Where'd you go yesterday toting twelve-hundred?"

"I didn't go nowhere Sis?"

"Another possibility scratched off the list." I made a checking motion.

"So, is it safe to say you just took my shit?" I asked

"Nah, I ain't do that, Sis." He was shaking his head and looking at the ground. Antonio just leaned against the car with his arms folded and remained quiet.

"Then go in the house and get my money then, Poopie."

"Sis, I can't go in the house and get your money. I don' have it." He was pleading for me to let up on him but I wouldn't.

"So you can tell me you don't have my money but, you can't tell me where my money disappeared to? Do I have that right Poopie? Tell me if I have all the facts?"

I'm sorry Sis. I don' have the money." I look at Antonio and ask him how much the money he just got from Poopie was off?

"$300" Antonio replied.

"$300!" I yelled. Antonio just nodded his head and looked at Poopie. Poopie was looking at Antonio pleading for help with his eyes.

"So now the total is $1,500. That's just fucking great. I don't suppose you can go in the house and bring me $300? Or am I to assume it's in the Bermuda Triangle with the rest of the money?" Before he could answer I turned to Antonio and began talking.

"So, am I to take this as we're cutting Poopie off or are you going to keep throwing money down this hole?" I pointed at Poopie.

"I say give him another shot and if he fuh's up then we'll deal with him." He gave Poopie a glance and Poopie's eyes opened wide. He was surprised that Antonio was mentioning hurting him.

"So, you think giving him a third chance to fuck up some more money is the right thing to do? Let me ask that another way. You think giving him more work for a third time is going to make him stop stealing from us?"

"I think we should give him another shot. If he fuh's up again then he's gotta go." Antonio said.

"Just let him go? Fuck up again and you'll be fired? That's what you're saying?"

"Yeah." He nodded when he said this.

"You do realize that I didn't grow up with you three and I don't give a fuck about Poopie, don't you?" I asked

"Come on Bay, that's fuh'ed up." Antonio pleaded with me.

"No, I'm for real. I don't give a fuck about Poopie. You do. He's your friend. You grew up with him. Not me. To me he's a fiend who keeps fucking up my money and getting away with it. That's what I see. That's who I'm looking at. I don't see Poopie from back in the day. When I met him he was grown ass hairy fiend and look at how much he's changed since then?" We all looked at Poopie standing there all skinny and hairy with no shirt on and his bottom lip drooping. I continued after we all took him in, Sean stood there shaking his head.

"So, you can continue to give him all the coke you want. That's your project anyway but, the dope is my project and he's not getting one fucking pill. You want to keep throwing your money away on this bum, feel free but, he's not getting another opportunity to fuck my shit up anymore. Do I make myself clear Sean?" I started the conversation looking at Antonio and shifted to Sean when I asked him if he understood me.

"Yeah, you giving me the dope and Poopie can't touch it or the money, I gotchu, J.O. No problem." Sean replied. I liked Sean.

"That's exactly what I mean. If he touches one pill of my shit he better have handed you ALL of the money for it or you're paying for it. Feel me?"

"You got that J.O., say no more." Sean replied. I turned my focus back to Antonio.

"Let's step to the side for a minute." I said as I walked away from Sean and Poopie. Antonio lifted himself from leaning on the car and followed me. We walked down W. Cross St and began talking.

"So what are you going to do?" I asked.

"I'm gonna give him another shot."

"Why are you going to keep fucking with this dude? He is only going to cost us more money. This isn't about your friendship. This is about of business. Do you really think it's good business to keep fucking with this nigga?"

"I'm giving him another shot J.O., that's my decision. You made your decision when you said what you said. That was fuh'ed up too by the way. You didn't have to go all out on him like that. That was just fuh'ed up." Antonio seemed to be a little upset.

"Do you really think I give a fuck what you or him thinks of how I spoke to him? Do you really? You couldn't. Fuck him. He can give me my fuckin' money if he don't want me talking like that to or about him. If he don't like the way I talk to him. He needs to stay out of my fuckin' pockets. So long as he's in my pocket I'll talk to him the way I feel like. Fuck him."

"That's fuh'ed up Bay. You know that's fuh'ed up."

"You're more of a friend to him then he is to you. You stick up for him and give him chance after chance and he repays it by stealing from you. At least when I say 'fuck you' I look a person in the eye and say it. He says fuck you and sneaks around to do it. You don't even do that but, you accept it from him. That's your friend not mine." Before he could respond I said,

"You know what? I don't give a fuck anymore. I'm talking to myself here. He is your friend. This is your town. I'm the one who isn't from here. I'm the outsider around here. I'm not from here. I'm going home. Fuck this shit!" I turned and walked back to the car. As I was walking Antonio yelled to me,

"What do you mean you're going home? Where the fuh' are

you talking about?"

"Home Nigga, Atlanta. I'm out. I'm going HOME, my HOME. I'm out of here, TODAY. You can have it. I'm not from here. I'm going back to where I'm from."

I got in the car and as I was starting it, I saw Kim drive up to Brenda's and pull up behind me. I pulled off and headed toward Wal-Mart over the bridge. As I got out of the car after parking, I saw Antonio pull into a parking spot next to me. He was driving Kim's car. I didn't say a word to him. Didn't wait for him to get out of the car. I just walked into Wal-Mart and found the suitcase section. He was right behind me every step of the way. I grabbed a five piece suitcase set and headed to the register. Antonio grabbed his own five piece suitcase set and followed right behind me. I paid for the suitcase and headed for the door. By the time I was in the parking lot he was walking out the door. When I was almost to the car he yelled from behind me,

"If you're going, I'm going. You're not leavin' wit'out me." I didn't respond. I wasn't in the mood for games. I just loaded the suitcases on the trunk and headed to West Baltimore. I lost Antonio somewhere along the way.

I was at that place where you're more calm than mad. I was relieved having made the decision but, kind of mad with myself for not making it sooner. I was happy. I felt a warm relief wash over me. Before I started packing my clothes I had to take care of the most important thing, MY MONEY. I got a cardboard box from the store on the corner before I came in the house. I put clothes in the bottom of it padding it. I took all of the stacks of money I had in the closet, 70 stacks in all. I put 60 neatly in the box and put clothes on top of them filling the box and taping it shut. I addressed it to my mother in Myrtle Beach South Carolina with the return address to her Atlanta loft. I then called my mother and told her to look out for it without telling her what it was. If I had, she would cut it open and I'd have a whole new wardrobe before I saw her. I asked her to look up a flight for this evening and buy it for me. I needed enough time to get the box mailed and put the money in her account. I put the box at the top of the steps so I could just scoop it up when I left. I wasn't going to rush. I was going home. I could feel Atlanta as I packed my bags. I was getting excited.

Antonio came in while I was packing and dropped his suitcases on the bed. He took the smaller suitcases out of the largest one and put them on the floor. He started packing his clothes. I didn't say anything to him. I was too busy.

"So what time is our flight?" He asked putting folded clothes neatly in his suitcase.

"The flight leaves at 8:15." I replied.

"It's 2:30. We've got plenty of time. Did you buy my ticket?"

"No."

"Why not?"

"I'm leaving. I bought my ticket." I replied zipping up my large suitcase and placing on the floor. I walked out of the room and he yelled after me,

"Where are you going?"

"I'm going to mail this box and to the bank." I yelled back as I picked up the box and headed down the steps. I could hear him yelling something but couldn't make it out.

I mailed the box and made it to the bank. I was feeling like my old self again. I didn't feel the suppression I'd been feeling since I'd been back. At home I didn't have to watch everyone. I didn't have to worry about being shot sitting on a stoop. I didn't have to worry about being robbed. I knew the city. I had my family and friends there. Like Mel said, 'There's safety in numbers and my numbers were in The A'.

Before I went back to the house to get ready for the flight, I went and got a shrimp salad sub from Lexington Market. When I got back to the house no one was there. I straightened up the room and put things back in their place. I knew I wasn't going to take five suitcases with me on this trip. I took three of the bags and placed them neatly in the closet. I'd have to come back to close things out. I'd take them back with me then. I took the two largest bags with me. One was filled with clothes and the other shoes and sneakers. I took a shower and put on the clothes I'd laid out for the flight. I was putting on the final touches in the mirror when Tonio came in and asked if I was ready to go?

"Where are we going?" I asked.

"Kim's outside. She's gonna take us to return the ren'al car and then drop us off at the airport. You ready? We need to get goin'?" He went in our room and started bringing the luggage out to the car. I didn't say anything about him going. I didn't ask if he had a ticket. I just sat back and watched.

I finished up in the bathroom and straightened up before returning to the bedroom to grab my purse. It was a brown leather bag that was long like a duffle bag but, not as long. It was made to be worn across your back like you would a duffle bag. I picked up the six of the stacks I had laying on the bed and put them in the bag. I gave the other four to Leonard when I went downstairs to leave.

Antonio and Kim were in the car waiting to follow me to the rental car office. I knew that Antonio riding with her meant he was handling business with her. More than likely he was leaving Kim in charge of things while we were gone. I got in the car and headed toward the airport.

After returning the car I jumped in the car with Tonio and Kim. As soon as we pulled off, Antonio handed me a wad of money and told me to put in my bag. I just threw it in there without thinking about it. Kim dropped us off at the terminal. We got our tickets and checked our bags. We had plenty of time. I was getting really excited. We walked through the security checkpoint, all I could think about was what magazines I would buy for the flight. I was on my way home.

As we were putting on our shoes and belts after going through the metal detector, my bag was on the table in front of the TSA agent. She was going through the bag. She was a light skinned plump girl with an orange jheri curl. She looked deep into the bag all the way to the bottom. When she saw the money she looked at both of us. She looked deep into the bag again moving the money with one of her hands. She looked at the two of us and asked us,

"How much money is this?"

What we should've done was stopped everything and count the money but, that's not what we did. I didn't know how much he handed me and he didn't know how much I had in there already. We both just said a number. I said, "$9,000". Antonio, said "$8,000". With that, the TSA agent asked for our I.D.'s. Walked over to the police officers stationed in the center of the security area. Once she walked over there, she said a few words, handed them our I.D.'s and pointed us out. While we're watching her do all of this, the other TSA agents come over to us. One of them tells us, "Man, I don't know why she even did that? We don't even bother with money anymore. She knows that." The other TSA agents agreed with him. There were three officers. One took the I.D.'s and went to run our names. The other two came and separated us. One officer stayed with me and the other took Tonio across the room and had him sit in a chair. The officer that was with me asked,

"Where'd you get the money?"

"I'm a bartender. He's a landlord. We deal with a lot of cash. It's not from anything crazy." I replied.

"I understand. We just have to ask when we see money wrapped in rubber bands. We're not concerned with it though. We have to run your names since we came in contact with you. My partners doing that right now and we'll have you guys on your way in just a moment." He was very polite and I was glad we weren't being harassed. We had plenty of time to make our flight so it was no big deal. I watched the officer who had our I.D.'s come from around a corner and walk over to Antonio, say a few words and hand him back his I.D. I was happy to see that and was ready to go. I could feel the excitement welling up inside of me. I'd be home in two hours. The other officer headed over to me. Before he handed me my I.D. back he looked at me and said,

"How are you doing today? I'm Officer Marl and I have your license here. I ran your name for warrants and I found a warrant for your arrest. At this time we're going to have to take you into custody. Please place your hands behind your back?"

The officer that had been waiting with me was now behind me and placing me in handcuffs. They had a few officers stand in front of Antonio so he couldn't make his way to me. He didn't know what was going on any more than I did. The difference was he was losing his cool and I wasn't. They placed me under arrest. I was escorted through the security checkpoint, through a back door and placed me in a jail cell under the terminal. I'm locked up and that's all I know. WTF?

Made in the USA
Middletown, DE
27 August 2020

17148087R00156